CHAINED
TOGETHER

CHAINED
TOGETHER

MANDELA, DE KLERK, AND
THE STRUGGLE TO REMAKE SOUTH AFRICA

DAVID OTTAWAY

TIMES BOOKS

RANDOM HOUSE

Library of Congress Cataloging-in-Publication Data

Ottaway, David.
    Chained together : Mandela, de Klerk, and the struggle to remake
South Africa / David B. Ottaway. — 1st ed.
        p.   cm.
    Includes index.
    ISBN 0-8129-2014-7
    1. De Klerk, F. W. (Frederik Willem) 2. Mandela, Nelson, 1918–   .
3. South Africa—Politics and government—1989– I. Title.
DT1970.087 1993
968.06′4—dc20   93-27970

Designed by MM Design 2000, Inc.

Manufactured in the United States of America

9 8 7 6 5 4 3 2

First Edition

To my loving parents

ACKNOWLEDGMENTS

In nearly three years of living in South Africa as a reporter, I was privileged to meet scores of blacks and whites of all political persuasions and social rank. Through their personal stories and insights, all of them helped me in one way or another to understand the historical and racial complexities of the gripping and never-ending drama of the Old and New South Africa. It is impossible, of course, to acknowledge my debt to each of them by name. But there were some of special importance whom I wish to mention, even while freeing them immediately of any responsibility for the views expressed and conclusions drawn in these pages. I think immediately of five South Africans I would like to thank particularly: Allister Sparks, who for many years wrote for the *Washington Post* and initiated me into the mysteries of South African politics; Phillip van Niekerk of the *Weekly Mail*; John Matisonn, the U.S. National Public Radio correspondent in 1990 and 1991; John Battersby of the *Christian Science Monitor*; and Patrick Laurence of the *Star* in Johannesburg. Among foreign correspondents, John Carlin of the *Independent* of London gave me invaluable insights into the workings of the de Klerk government, while Chris Wren of the *New York Times* provided me on many occasions with his equally invaluable company as we traveled together to cover one massacre or another.

In my search for an understanding of the Afrikaner people, I am particularly grateful to Wim Boyce, an independent risk analyst based in Pretoria, and Hermann Gilomee of the University of Cape Town. For help in coming to terms with the mysteries of white politics, I turned often to Peter Soal of the Democratic Party and David Welsh, also of the University of Cape Town. I feel particularly indebted to Robert Schrire of the same university for helping me to fathom the character of President F. W. de Klerk.

In the arena of black politics, I remain extremely grateful for the warm friendship and continual instruction extended to me by Rich Mkondo of Reuters and Eugene Nyati, the latter a very independent-minded analyst. Nor can I forget the frequent help and insights of Mpho Mashinini, Mono Badela, Ismail Legardien, and Moeletsi Mbeki. Zbu Mngandi, an investigative reporter for the weekly *City Press*, was also extremely generous in sharing his extensive knowledge of Natal politics, for which I am very grateful. Many African National Congress officials and members generously shared their knowledge of historical and contemporary events pertaining to that organization. But one of its spokespeople, the tireless Gill Marcus, was of special help in getting me to see not only her colleagues but also the downtrodden victims of the political violence in the townships.

This book was made possible by a combination of the time extended to me by my editors at the *Washington Post*, who arranged for me to take a six-month leave of absence, and the encouragement of Peter Osnos, my longtime colleague turned publisher, whose faith in me and in this project never wavered. I also owe a debt of gratitude for the thoughtful editing of Paul Golob and Sarah Flynn. Together, the latter two people helped to shape the book with breathtaking speed—and mostly at long distance—as I traveled around the former Yugoslavia on my new assignment. I thank them most appreciatively for their commitment and endurance during my peripatetic travels.

Finally, the person with whom I most discussed the unfolding drama of change in South Africa was my wife, Marina, whose more detached perceptions and scholarly approach were often of tremendous value to my own understanding of day-to-day events. While she was collecting material for her own separate book on South Africa, together we constantly traveled the length and breadth of South Africa in what turned out to be an unending adventure in search of the ever-elusive South African truth.

CONTENTS

CHAINED
TOGETHER

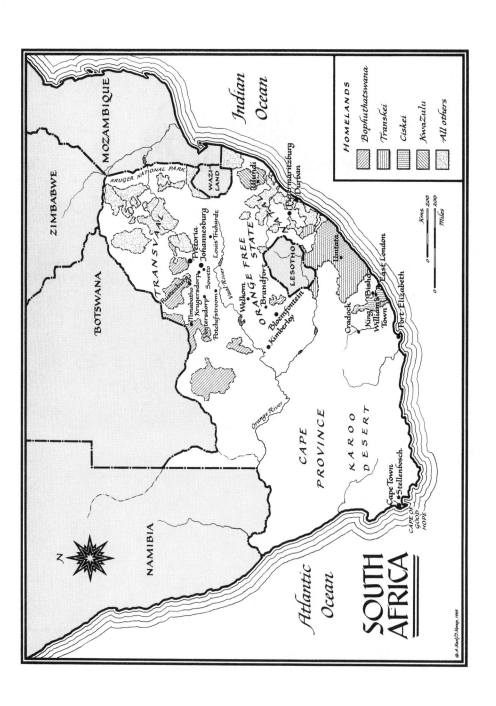

INTRODUCTION

February 11, 1990, when Nelson Mandela was released from prison, was a momentous day. Who will ever forget the incredibly engaging, radiant smile of a man come back to life as he walked hand in hand with his wife through the gates of Victor Verster Prison outside Cape Town? There was great hope, in South Africa and around the world, that at last the world's worst racial conflict was about to be resolved through peaceful negotiations. Mandela was committed to compromise and racial cooperation and so, too, was his white liberator, State President F. W. de Klerk. South Africa's salvation was finally at hand, or so it seemed on that extraordinary day to the tens of millions of people around the world who watched Mandela's walk to freedom on television.

Mandela and de Klerk quickly won worldwide acclaim and admiration as they set about their search for an historic compromise. Two such peace partners South Africa—indeed, the entire world—had never seen. Mandela, the symbol of enduring black resistance to apartheid, apparently bore no hatred or grudges toward whites even after twenty-seven years in jail. De Klerk quickly became compared to Mikhail Gorbachev, the great reformer of the Soviet Union, because of his political courage and initial cascade of reforms. Thus did Mandela and de Klerk set out together to lead their respective peoples into the "New South Africa."

But more than three years later, there was still no peace in South Africa—a reality dramatically highlighted by the April 1993 assassination of Chris Hani, a top Communist Party and African National Congress leader. In fact, there was scarcely any sign of racial cooperation and only limited movement toward a possibly peaceful settlement to the conflict. Real change remained elusive. Violence

3

of all kinds consumed the country on a daily basis. Blacks were hacking other blacks to death, whites were shooting blacks, and blacks were retaliating by burning or stabbing whites. Mandela and de Klerk were barely on speaking terms, reduced to talking to each other only to avoid total disaster in the painful search for a negotiated settlement. What had happened to the dream of February 11, 1990? How had a country so full of hope become one of seemingly constant death and destruction? Why had despair replaced great expectations? What had happened to the two great peacemakers who had been so full of noble purpose and mission that glorious day of Mandela's liberation?

South Africa, a complex jigsaw puzzle of contending ethnic and racial groups, has found no easy solution for its own moral and political redemption. The country's 4.5 million whites have not yielded willingly or gracefully to the loss of power after more than three centuries of domination. Its 33 million blacks, divided by either political allegiance or ethnic affinity, have turned inward to fight each other as much as their common white overlords. Mandela and de Klerk were repeatedly sidetracked in their peace endeavors by one or another explosion of violence. The peace process was derailed, or delayed, a year or more by recriminations over who was responsible. Starting in 1990, South Africa became engulfed in the worst political violence and crime wave it had ever experienced. The white security forces committed massacres against black protestors, but the ANC and Chief Mangosuthu Buthelezi's Inkatha Freedom Party also escalated their struggle for power and their slaughter of each other. White extremists, not to be outdone, showed with Hani's killing that they too were a force to be reckoned with.

The violence in South Africa has had many fathers and worn many faces. It is not a compressed, large-scale convulsion, as the world is currently witnessing in Yugoslavia's ethnic warfare. The death toll in Bosnia after six months of fighting was higher than all the deaths from violence in South Africa since 1984. Instead, the killing in South Africa, although on a relatively small scale, was insidiously persistent, averaging six to ten deaths daily either in township clashes or from some kind of terrorist incident. The main "killing fields" were in the beautiful rolling green hills of Natal

Province along the Indian Ocean, where Chief Buthelezi's KwaZulu homeland is located, and in twenty or so drab, garbage-strewn rabbit-warren townships around Johannesburg. The violence was punctuated by what were generally described as "massacres" but which were sometimes just running battles of several days' duration. There were constant raids with machetes, knives, and guns on commuters riding the trains into Johannesburg from the surrounding townships.

Each group had its own style of terror. Inkatha's preferred tactic was ambushes and indiscriminate killing, usually in the form of hit-and-run attacks on groups of unarmed civilians in trains, taxis, or funerals. ANC supporters, on the other hand, seemed to be more focused on going after their enemies individually. They would target people they knew, or suspected, to be Inkatha members, policemen, or police informers. They did not shy away from burning down homes or "necklacing" their victims with gasoline-soaked tires that were then set afire. Cyril Dorkin, one ANC street fighter I met in the black township of Soweto, near Johannesburg, was quite frank about it: "I prefer necklacing, myself," he said. "It's better than being hacked to death the way they do to us." White supremacists often attacked blacks for no reason at all. In 1991 a group of whites in the city of Louis Trichardt beat up a group of black schoolchildren just for daring to picnic on the lawn of the town hall. White extremists in the mining center of Welkom formed vigilante groups and for a time chased out all "suspicious-looking" blacks from the white suburbs at nightfall. There were even two or three cases in Johannesburg in which whites simply went out to get themselves a *kaffir*, a black, and either beat up or killed an innocent pedestrian. And the police took part as well in this violence, sometimes by opening fire on mass demonstrations, but more often by looking the other way as one group slaughtered another.

While whites could arm themselves more or less legally and in the open, for its instruments of death Inkatha relied on the so-called traditional or cultural Zulu weapons. These included machetes (known in South Africa as *pangas*), spears, and wooden-knobbed clubs called knobkerries. But the weapon of choice for both Inkatha and the ANC soon became the Soviet-made AK-47 automatic rifles smuggled into the country by the thousands from neighboring Mozambique. Police recovered 1,800 of these automatic rifles in 1991 alone. Even bank robbers and carjackers took to using them.

The Western media persistently focused on the horrendous political violence tearing at the fabric of South African society after Mandela's release. But perhaps a better barometer of the social trauma brought on by the profound changes under way was the rise in criminal violence, far worse than in the 1980s as white authority crumbled and criminal elements took advantage of the chaos. Carjackers, frequently armed with AK-47 rifles, were everywhere, often killing their victims—both white and black. Between 1989 and 1993, the murder rate doubled, and on a per capita basis it was ten times that of the United States. Cape Town's murder rate was the highest of any city in the world with a comparable population. Of the 15,100 murders officially recorded nationwide in 1990, somewhere between 11,000 and 12,500 were the result of criminal rather than political violence. In 1992, the total number of murders in this nation of 40 million people rose to 19,400, of which, according to police calculations, fewer than 2,500 were politically motivated.

Most crime and violence occurred in the black community, where police patrolling became almost nonexistent, partly because of the climate of political violence in which policemen, too, became targets as servants of the dying apartheid order. In 1992 a record number of policemen, 226, were killed, twelve times the number killed in the United States during the same period. But of the total number of murder victims from political and criminal violence in 1990 and 1991, 96 percent were black. The townships became jungles where middle-class blacks were preyed upon by thugs, car racketeers, and carjackers. Blacks living in Soweto returning home at night from the white northern suburbs of Johannesburg lived in constant fear of highway robbers and car thieves.

Though they had less to fear from political violence, whites lived in perpetual fear of criminal violence. In the northern Johannesburg suburbs, homes were turned into armed camps with ever-higher walls. The residents of one community, Dunkel West, even proposed at one point to build a wall around the entire district to keep out thieves. Homeowners bought vicious dogs, the favorites being rottweilers and pit bulls, and many installed barbed wire on outside walls or fancy electronic devices to detect intruders. Private security firms flourished, providing homeowners with an "instant armed response" if the house alarm sounded. Whites became increasingly reluctant to venture out at night. The fear of attack was so great that neighbors drove their cars to each other's homes for dinners rather than walk even a short distance. "We are living in a country, alas, where nobody feels safe anymore," commented the white-oriented conservative newspaper *The Citizen* in January 1992, imploring the government to curb the soaring crime rate lest the country "descend . . . into anarchy."

Few appreciated in early 1990 the enormity of the obstacles that lay ahead for Mandela and de Klerk. Despite the dawning of a new world order, the international setting was strangely inauspicious to the success of their quest for a peaceful settlement. All the currents coursing through black nationalist politics in South Africa seemed to be running against the tide of contemporary history. While most South African black leaders yearned to remold their apartheid-divided country into a unitary state, the forces of ethnic separatism were splitting asunder the Soviet Union, Yugoslavia, and Czechoslovakia. While they hoped to meld the country's diverse ethnic and racial groups into a unified nonracial nation, nationalists in Eastern Europe encouraged South Africa's white leaders to persist in their own narrow ethnic nationalism (heavily tinged with racism), making it that much more difficult to create a nonracial nation.

South Africa was out of sync in another way as well: a lot of "old thinking" still prevailed in the minds of many South African black nationalists. For them, communism and socialism were just as valid components of "liberation theology" in 1990 as they had been in 1960. The unbanned South African Communist Party flourished, while its counterparts elsewhere in the world were struggling to survive. There was a Rip van Winkle quality to the New South Africa, as if the nation were waking up from a thirty-year sleep. Its black nationalist leaders were only now coming into power, thirty years after their contemporaries in most other African countries. They had no experience in government, nor had they had the occasion to learn any of the hard lessons of independence. Typical of the 1960 generation of African leaders, they were mesmerized by the vision of power and office. Their attitude was the same as that of Kwame Nkrumah, the leader of Ghana's independence movement in 1957, whose motto had been "Seek ye first the political kingdom. Everything else shall be added unto you."

On the African continent itself, conditions were scarcely favorable to Mandela and de Klerk finding a peaceful solution to their nation's conflict. Civil wars among rival black nationalist groups had turned Angola and Mozambique into wastelands after fifteen years of independence; clan fighting had reduced Somalia to total anarchy; and general mismanagement had reduced the majority of African countries to pauperism. Even Zimbabwe, once held up as a shining example of racial reconciliation, was sliding toward economic disaster.

Between the violence at home and the ethnic warfare under way elsewhere in Africa and in Eastern Europe, it was little wonder that de Klerk and Mandela found it tough going to convince whites and blacks that racial reconciliation was possible, and the building of a new nonracial order in South Africa feasible. Making matters even worse, their own personal relationship—so vital to the whole peace endeavor—fell victim to the violence. They became increasingly disillusioned with each other, each questioning the ability of the other to deliver his constituency and discovering that they held strikingly different visions of how the New South Africa should be governed. At times, the two keystone peacemakers seemed bent on a course of mutual destruction, clashing vehemently in public and denouncing each other's "double agendas" and perfidy. De Klerk seemed unable to decide whether Mandela was his chief partner or chief adversary. Mandela seemed equally uncertain about de Klerk. Each accused the other of "talking peace while making war."

The peace process was only made more difficult by the failure of both leaders to respect either the letter or the spirit of the first series of preliminary accords they reached. Time and again, de Klerk and Mandela would lead their followers into agreements that immediately became disagreements and the subject of unending misunderstandings and arguments. Their problems were compounded by the fact that they often faced challenges to their leadership. They spent as much time negotiating with their allies as they did with each other. Small wonder, then, that not a single accord struck between May 1990 and September 1992—whether over the release of political prisoners, the return of exiles, the ANC's hidden arms caches, or the curbing of violence—was carried out on time or according to the letter.

As peacemakers, de Klerk and Mandela at times exhibited remarkable shortcomings. De Klerk did some things, and failed to do others that he must have known would undermine the whole peace process. Mandela launched vicious personal verbal attacks against de Klerk that left one wondering why he was still talking to the state president at all. He also sometimes lacked political courage, shrinking from chastising his own followers for the same excesses of violence he accused his ANC opponents of indulging in. And both occasionally had to be reminded that they were not behaving like good peacemakers, or even good leaders. Mandela, the increasingly frustrated spokesman for the powerless and downtrodden black masses, perhaps could be excused for his lapses into rage. But there was less reason for excusing de Klerk, who had the power of the state and its security apparatus to make things happen if he so willed. It took a third party, Judge Richard Goldstone (who headed a commission investigating state security's role in the political violence), to point out that both Mandela and de Klerk were partly responsible for the political violence, and that both had duties to uphold as the country's two leading statesmen. It would not do, Goldstone said, for them to see themselves only as defenders of narrow partisan and nationalist interests.

Even so, de Klerk and Mandela have played—and continue to play—crucial roles in South Africa's belated search for racial reconciliation and nonracial democracy. It was Mandela, after all, who while still in prison single-handedly stretched out the black nationalist hand of peace to the beleaguered Afrikaners hunkered down behind the crumbling wall of apartheid. Single-handedly, too, he opened a dialogue with the Afrikaner elite and convinced them that negotiation with the ANC was a viable alternative to eternal oppression of the black population. De Klerk proved equally indispensable, leading the fearful white community on the irreversible leap into the unknown of peace talks, and then dismantling the legislative scaffolding holding together the rotting apartheid edifice. Whether acting separately or together, each of these men pulled the country back from the brink of anarchy and civil war, maneuvering behind the scenes to get the shaky peace process back on track. Despite their disillusionment and later a deep personal animosity, they discovered they were chained irrevocably together by their common mission of saving South Africa from the abyss of eternal racial conflict.

1

"MY PEOPLE ARE WAITING FOR ME"

W as he a latter-day black Moses? Or a modern Jesus Christ rising from the catacombs of South African prisons? Nelson Mandela, the world's most famous political prisoner, was regularly compared to both Biblical figures as he was about to be released from prison in 1990. Certainly Mandela loomed on the horizon as some kind of Messiah to his people—his freedom symbolizing theirs in the making—but could he part South Africa's turbulent racial waters and lead his people to the Promised Land? Or would he, like Moses, never see a land of racial reconciliation in his lifetime? Was too much being asked of a mortal man starting life again at seventy-one?

Already, Mandela had been turned into a living legend, the symbol of the suffering of an entire black nation that had been uprooted from its homes, extorted of 87 percent of its land, and reduced to slave labor under the odious system of racial exploitation known as apartheid. Mandela had been locked up by the white government for so long, close to twenty-eight years, that nobody knew for sure anymore what he even looked like. The few pictures available, those used to rally the faithful on posters, showed him in his fighting youth with a toughness in the lines of his face that made it easy to believe the celebrated activist had once been an amateur

11

boxer. The first glimpse of his physical metamorphosis came the morning of February 11, when President F. W. de Klerk released to the local media a color photograph of Mandela standing next to him in his Cape Town office. The two had met the night before to finalize the details of Mandela's release. Though I was well aware of his age, I was still shocked by how old Mandela looked in the picture. The boxer had gone out of him. He appeared almost frail, yet the aristocratic bearing of the tall, gaunt figure dressed impeccably in a light gray suit was unmistakable. He was clearly de Klerk's equal in dignity, poise, and stature.

As a human being and personality, however, Mandela remained a total mystery to his own people, a disembodied spirit of black resistance whose poster picture was filled with political symbolism but lacked blood and life. Who was this man called upon to lead the last black African people from white bondage into freedom? Did he have the wisdom, wile, and physical stamina to deal with the Afrikaners, who constituted 60 percent of the country's white population and considered themselves the longest-surviving "tribe" of whites? It would take months to come to know and understand this legend of a man as he really was in flesh and blood after decades of being a political myth. For me, an American correspondent witnessing the dawning of the New South Africa, the discovery of the real Nelson Mandela began with that riveting front-page picture in the *Johannesburg Star* the morning of his release.

Mandela's release, broadcast live around the world, was so powerful an event that it left white and black South Africans alike bewildered. Life for South Africa's 4.5 million whites was turned upside down as they came face to face with the real prospect of being ruled by 33 million blacks. Whites suddenly had to regard blacks as human beings of equal value, even compatriots, instead of just hewers of wood at the beck and call of the white "Baas" and "Madame." They even had to view blacks as their potential future bosses, who would soon be giving the orders. The shock for white South Africans was total; for some it was the ultimate nightmare about to come true. The notion that the political hierarchy established 340 years earlier was about to be inverted blew the collective white mind. For three decades, the African National Congress had been vilified as the source of all evil and the mastermind of the "total onslaught" campaign aimed at wiping out white civilization in South Africa. Local newspapers were forbidden even to print the words *African National Congress* or to quote any of its leaders by name. Then, suddenly, whites were witnessing Mandela's emergence from the Victor Verster Prison courtesy of the state-run South African Broadcasting Corporation (SABC), the once-authoritative voice of the Afrikaner propaganda machine. The person whites had grown up learning to hate and fear as the incarnation of the Black Power Devil had been miraculously transformed overnight into a world-renowned leader they were now supposed to revere and look upon as their country's possible next president.

For blacks, most of whom had never seen the man, Nelson Mandela was the long-lost father of the nation finally coming home to lead his people out of the wilderness. His release boosted their spirits like nothing else that had happened to them before. It marked the triumph of their long anti-apartheid struggle, the hard-won fruit of unending township rebellions that had relied on stones, burning tires, and crude street barricades to defy the police with their deadly bullets, barrages of tear gas, and snarling dogs. Blacks of all ages would celebrate his release by the hundreds of thousands all across the land, dancing the ANC *toyi-toyi* (a kind of stand-in-place war dance) in the streets and chanting repeatedly, "Power to the People." His return was feted with particular jubilation in his adopted home city, Soweto, the sprawling black township of two million people southwest of Johannesburg, with his old matchbox-sized residence, number 8115 Vilakazi Street, the focus of the celebration.

I had just arrived in South Africa to take up my assignment for the *Washington Post* as its Southern Africa correspondent, based in Johannesburg. Two weeks after my arrival, on February 2, President de Klerk announced at the annual ceremony marking the opening of Parliament his sweeping reform program that would usher in the New South Africa. All the anti-apartheid groups branded for decades as agents of world communism, including the Communist Party itself, were to be unbanned and henceforth allowed to operate freely. As soon as possible, he would begin negotiations with the African National Congress, talks aimed at ending white minority rule. Other reform measures included the immediate suspension of the death penalty; a pledge to release all political prisoners held in South African jails and to allow the 40,000 exiles to return home; a review of all security legislation to restore normal civil rights to blacks and permit free political activity; and finally, the lifting, as soon as possible, of the state of emergency that had been in effect since 1986. But the centerpiece of his revolutionary speech was the news that Nelson Mandela would go free within days. As if directing a masterpiece of suspense theater, de Klerk left the nation and the world in the dark about the exact timing of Mandela's release.

With these announcements, de Klerk effectively set out to reverse more than three hundred years of South African history and bring to an end his own National Party's forty-two-year struggle to force blacks into the straitjacket of cradle-to-grave apartheid. He spoke a language of radical reform that had never been heard before from the mouth of an Afrikaner president or prime minister. This time, he offered concrete plans, not just pious hopes for national reconciliation and negotiations with blacks.

The international press corps suddenly mushroomed into the thousands, many of whom went berserk not knowing how to prepare for the Great Prison Release, since the authorities would not say where or when it would take place. Would the government fly Mandela to Soweto overnight and free him there, as it had done in releasing eight almost as famous black political prisoners in October 1989? Would he be brought to Cape Town instead? Or would Mandela just walk out on his own from his pastoral prison? A special National Reception Committee set up by the African National Congress was also in a tizzy. ANC officials felt certain that de Klerk was trying to sabotage their own preparations for Mandela's release by deliberately creating an enormous confusion that would later be cited as an illustration of ANC incompetence. Making matters worse, reporters who had been assured by government officials that the release would not occur the following weekend (and that everybody would be given sufficient advance notice) were caught off guard on Saturday afternoon, February 10, when de Klerk unexpectedly announced that Mandela would walk out of Victor Verster Prison the very next day. The ANC's Reception

Committee and a horde of television, radio, and print reporters now had less than twenty-four hours to get in place. The problem, we later learned, was that the government, Mandela, and the Reception Committee couldn't agree on how, when, or where to release him. Mandela wanted to give the committee a full week to make preparations, but the government, after holding him for so long, wanted to free him as soon as possible. Strangely, the tables were turned: Mandela was ready to stay in jail another week while the government wanted him out immediately.

The matter wasn't decided until President de Klerk met personally with Mandela on Friday in his office at Tuynhuys, the official presidential office building in Cape Town. De Klerk proposed taking Mandela from prison that very night and flying him to Johannesburg, where he would be handed over to the National Reception Committee at precisely 3 P.M. on Sunday. Mandela rejected this option out of hand, and there ensued six hours of negotiations over the precise time, place, and manner of his release. Mandela remembers the experience as "a conflict between my blood and my brains." He wanted to go, he told the *Argus* newspaper a year later, but he wanted to give his reception committee seven days to make the necessary preparations. In the end, a compromise of sorts was struck after a round of whiskey was poured for the two leaders and their aides. Mandela would be freed on Sunday at precisely 3 P.M. and would walk out of Victor Verster on his own. De Klerk called reporters together Saturday afternoon to relay the news.

It wasn't quite general pandemonium that weekend, but it came pretty close. The plan was for Mandela to be driven from the prison to the steps of Cape Town's Old City Hall, where he would deliver his first speech to the nation as a free man. The Reception Committee decided to make his City Hall appearance the main event. But there was no way his historic walk to freedom at the prison gates could go uncovered. So reporters had to choose between the prison and the City Hall for a prime spot to cover the event.

Or so they thought at first. As the day unfolded, however, it didn't make any difference where the reporters were positioned, so numerous were the delays and so total was the confusion. The private jet that brought Mandela's wife, Winnie, from Johannesburg arrived ninety minutes late. By the time she reached Cape Town, it was past two o'clock, less than an hour before her husband's scheduled release. And it was almost three by the time she arrived at the prison, accompanied by daughter Zindzi and her two children, as well as other close friends of the family like ANC leader Walter Sisulu, who had been released from prison only four months earlier, and his wife, Albertina, herself a long-time anti-apartheid activist. Mandela, faced with the biggest moment of his life, strangely was in no hurry to leave. He had grown fond of his jailers, some of whom, like Warrant Officer James Gregory, had been with him for twenty years or more, and he had come to think of himself and his jailers as "a closely knit family." So the whole Mandela party had a final meal inside the prison before saying their farewells. Then Nelson gave the word: "We must get ready to leave because my people are waiting for me." Indeed they were—and getting ever more impatient. It was more than an hour after he was legally a free man that he finally began making his way to the gates of freedom.

Mandela was driven by car through the prison grounds until he was within view of the outer gates. He then alighted and triumphantly walked hand in hand with Winnie the last few yards to be greeted by a voracious international press corps. At first he seemed stunned, or he may just have been disoriented, like a blind man suddenly getting his sight back. He told us later that he had been overwhelmed by the size of the crowd of reporters and cameramen awaiting him. Winnie reacted first, throwing her left arm straight up to give the defiant clenched-fist salute for which she had become famous. Nelson quickly followed suit with his right hand, and the two burst into those radiant ear-to-ear smiles that the watching world would never forget.

My own first impressions upon watching Mandela's release on television not far from the impatient crowd in downtown Cape Town confirmed much of what I had gleaned from his picture in the *Star*. He was taller than I had imagined and more gaunt than I had expected. His cautious gait bore the mark of old-age physical frailty. There was not much time, however, to study him. Within seconds, what little discipline remained at the prison gates broke down completely as everyone rushed to get nearer to the Mandelas.

Nelson and Winnie hustled back into the car and drove through the crushing mass of reporters, ANC marshals, and supporters. "Only when I saw the crowd did I realize that I had not thought carefully enough about the events of the day," he would later reflect.

The prison departure was over in a matter of minutes, and the Mandela party wound its way to Cape Town, thirty-five miles to the southwest, through the neatly tended vineyards of some of South Africa's richest and oldest Afrikaner farms, as surrealistic a setting for a prison as one could imagine. Mandela later remarked that he was amazed by the number of whites who had turned out along the highway to greet him. Their number wasn't that great, but just the fact that some had come obviously left a lasting impression. He was to remark on it again and again over the next few days.

I am not sure whether the unexpected tragedy that followed on the Parade Grounds in front of the Old City Hall, where 50,000 people had assembled to see their messiah, was ever fully conveyed by the media. It was perhaps lost in the general celebration that surrounded Mandela's release elsewhere in the country and abroad. What happened that afternoon in Cape Town was a monumental disgrace to everyone involved—the ANC, the local authorities, and Mandela's youthful supporters.

The crowd had begun to assemble early that morning, and by the time Mandela finally arrived some had been standing there for as long as seven hours. The waiting began in an orderly fashion, but by noon there was hardly a trace of organization left. Young people had invaded the restricted press area in front under the City Hall balcony, and had taken over the steps leading into the building. They had climbed every tree, light pole, and building in sight; some were literally clinging to the sides of the City Hall's walls to get a better view. I was in the middle of that crowd for about four hours. At one point I saw NBC anchorman Tom Brokaw standing a few yards away, looking totally bewildered by the scene around us.

By midafternoon, some of the youths became exceedingly restless and began breaking into and looting the shops around the square. The police, undermanned and accustomed to relying on firepower, began shooting, first with shotguns loaded with small pellets and then with pistols. Volley after volley of shots rang out along the edge of the crowd and young people began falling. The great welcome for Mandela became a surrealistic fantasy: a big crowd of detached well-wishers and admirers looking back to watch waves of youths running into their midst seeking protection from police bullets. The arrival of each new wave set off a ripple effect of movement that passed right into the center of the assembled crowd. But the police-youth confrontation never triggered a general dispersement of people away from the Parade Grounds; it was as if the looting, shootings, and running youths were a distant sideshow taking place miles from the main event. At one point, there must have been twenty to thirty bodies stretched out in front of the emergency aid center set up on one side of the Parade Grounds. We were never able to determine exactly how many people died, but several were killed and scores were wounded.

Finally, the mood of the whole crowd turned distinctly sour, and not only because of the periodic police shootings. Inside the crowd, nimble-fingered thieves were fast at work stealing whatever they could. This included my tape recorder, the passports of several other American reporters, and nearly the portable laptop computer of *New York Times* correspondent Christopher Wren. In the end, Wren won the struggle and kept his computer. I will never forget one ruse the thieves used. I noticed a blind man wandering through the crowd bumping into people. He took advantage of these "chance" encounters to stick his hands into any available pocket. He then slipped his loot to a colleague carrying a large bag filled with stolen items. The shootings, shouting, and thievery went on for four hours, until the crowd dwindled steadily in size and interest. In the end, there were no more than 10,000 people on hand to salute Mandela when he showed up at nightfall.

As the hours wore on, the only comic relief—which nearly turned into tragedy—was the performance of Reverend Jesse Jackson. The irrepressible American civil rights leader and former presidential candidate was determined to have himself photographed alongside Mandela at whatever cost, possibly as Jackson was addressing the crowd, which he hoped to do. The "cost," as it turned out, was a government Mercedes-Benz put at his disposal and nearly his own life. Jackson insisted on pushing his motorcade of two cars and two vans through the densely packed gathering right up to the steps of the City Hall. The motorcade appeared about an hour after Mandela had been freed, and the crowd assumed that Mandela himself was arriving. Some tried to break into Jackson's car to greet the ANC leader. Within minutes, car windows began shattering and the roofs of several vans gave in under the weight of bodies crawling over the tops. Jackson, his wife, Jackie, and others with him were finally pulled from the cars by ANC marshals and hauled over the balustrade to the relative safety of the City Hall steps. "No one could convince the crowd that it was not the Mandela motorcade," Jackson told me the next day. "It was a very, very scary situation. You know, we were almost loved to death." Ironically, Jackson never achieved what he had risked life and limb to get—a picture of himself speaking to the crowd with Mandela at his side—but he did get to greet the Mandelas as they arrived at City Hall. "We met downstairs at the door and we embraced," he recalled with delight.

By the time Mandela finally made it to the podium it was almost dark, making it difficult for those who still remained on the Parade Grounds to see him. But they had no difficulty in hearing him. The voice coming across the powerful loudspeakers was unforgettable—strong, authoritative, and dead sure of itself. Mandela spoke slowly and distinctly, bellowing out his words in a steady cadence. It was right there and then, at his first public appearance in more than twenty-seven years, that I came to think of a Mandela address as something akin to Moses handing down the Ten Commandments. A hush fell over the crowd as every man, woman, and child gazed in rapt attention at this man of mythical stature they had been hearing about but had not seen for a quarter of a century.

I noted with interest that the mixed-race Coloureds, who made up the bulk of the crowd (they are the largest ethnic group in Cape Town), were visibly restrained in their applause for the black leader. It was the first indication of what would later become a real problem for the ANC: South Africa's three million brown-skinned Coloureds—a minority almost as fearful of black power as were the whites—evidenced little enthusiasm for the changes under way. Their enthusiasm was noticeably muted that day, even when blacks in the crowd roared out, "Amandla, Awethu": Power to the People.

Mandela's first speech to an expectant nation didn't live up to the momentous occasion, ostentatiously militant one moment and awkwardly conciliatory the next. He did not offer a vision of a future nonracial South Africa (à la Martin Luther King) or make an inspirational call for national reconciliation; rather, the speech contained a hodgepodge of themes, as if it had been written by a deeply divided committee. As was expected, Mandela was brimming with thanks for those who had helped him in his long struggle to gain freedom, and he went out of his way to affirm his undying loyalty to the African National Congress. Although he saluted all those he regarded as his loyal friends, the only person he chose to single out by name for special praise was Joe Slovo, the white general secretary of the South African Communist Party, whom he described as "one of our finest patriots." Such a choice of friends was certain to raise eyebrows among fearful whites brought up on the government's anti-communist propaganda.

Mandela portrayed himself as a tried and true militant. The armed struggle would continue until apartheid was dead and buried forever, he said, adding, "Now is the time to intensify the struggle on all fronts." In almost the same breath, however, he offered an olive branch to the government, saying that he hoped negotiations for a peaceful end to white minority rule would be possible and that there would be no further need for armed struggle.

At times, surprisingly, he was downright defensive. He apparently felt he owed his supporters an immediate explanation for his decision to engage in secret talks with the "enemy," the oppressive white government, while he was still in prison. It was all aimed at "normalizing the political situation in the country" and nothing more, he said. "I wish to stress that I myself have at no time entered negotiations about the future of our country except to insist on a meeting between the ANC and the government." But talks there would have to be, he said, and he felt de Klerk was the right man to deal with. He had found the state president to be "a man of integrity," four words that would come back to haunt him and that he would eventually retract. But at the time, just nine days after the president had unbanned all anti-apartheid organizations and had kept his word about releasing Mandela, the description seemed totally appropriate. Finally, almost as an afterthought, Mandela made a brief appeal to his "white compatriots" to join the ANC in building the New South Africa.

To both blacks and whites, his speech sent out confusing signals about his intentions. If he seemed needlessly militant to whites, he came across as totally ambiguous to blacks as to whether the way forward lay with guns on the battlefield or compromise at the negotiating table. To many whites he seemed locked in a time warp, still living back in the 1960s when he had gone to jail. He had used all the hackneyed buzzwords of the movement—"mass action," "armed struggle," and "mass mobilization"—and his effusive praise for Slovo seemed part of yesterday's alliances. At no point, however, had Mandela answered the question uppermost in every-one's mind that day: how it felt to be a free man after spending a third of his lifetime in prison. Many reporters, including myself, felt let down and more puzzled than ever about the true character of this mythical man. Had he lost touch with the realities of the late twentieth century, the death of Communism and the collapse of Communist regimes across Eastern Europe? Would he inspire his people to make peace and achieve national reconciliation, or would he only stir up a renewed black militancy against whites? He seemed to be calling blacks anew to the barricades, while de Klerk, by releasing him, had for the first time in white South African history opened wide the door to peaceful negotiations.

Only later did we learn that Mandela's speech had indeed been written by committee and reflected the conflicting concerns and interests within the ANC. Many ANC officials were worried about Mandela's image after months of rumors about his secret talks with the government, and felt it important that he signal that he was still a loyal "organization man," hewing to the party line. His words of militancy were there for the same reason, to demonstrate to his followers that neither he nor the ANC had "sold out" to the oppressor. It seemed sad nonetheless that Mandela had felt obliged to use his first speech to the nation to respond to parochial ANC concerns rather than to the crying need for a nonracial national vision. He was, after all, most likely the next president of whites and blacks alike. We didn't realize it then, but we had witnessed the opening shot in what was to become a protracted battle between Mandela and the various factions within the ANC over control of the movement's leadership and policies.

The next day, however, the international press corps saw another, far more appealing side of Mandela's multifaceted personality. The occasion was a press conference held outdoors on the tree-shaded backyard lawn of Nobel Peace Prize laureate Archbishop Desmond Tutu. The Anglican archbishop had put his home, one of the most luxurious in the virtually all-white suburb of Bishops Court, at Mandela's disposal. In this more intimate setting, Mandela seemed a different person, and the incredible warmth and humanity of the man came forth. He welcomed old reporter friends, even recognizing the names of some whose fathers he had known before going to prison. He seemed genuinely eager to greet every member of the sizable press corps personally. At the same time, there was a touch of aloofness about him. It was at that first press conference that I was reminded of how much Nelson Mandela belonged to an older generation of African leaders, but with one notable difference—his old-fashioned, almost British aristocratic air. In his extreme politeness, graciousness, and carefully constructed English, he seemed to have more in common with a European aristocrat than a traditional African tribal chief.

For someone who had not held a press conference for thirty years, Mandela gave a stunning performance that day. In fifty minutes, I revised all my impressions of his character gleaned from his appearance at the Old City Hall the day before. Instead of straining to show he was still a tried and true ANC militant, he projected a personality full of compassion, compromise, and great hope. His qualities as a statesman and diplomat came through immediately as he began answering our questions. Speaking in a soft, slightly raspy voice, he fielded an enormous variety of questions about his long life in prison and his first impressions of freedom. There was an ease and quickness in his answers that astounded his questioners. Mandela exuded an inner calm, a quietness and certainty about himself that was unexpected and overpowering. Most remarkable to many of us was the absence of any trace of bitterness about having spent the best years of his life behind bars, many of them while condemned to hard labor and living in horrible conditions on Robben Island Prison off the coast of Cape Town.

Though Mandela was extremely reticent on personal matters, he did let it be known that there was one issue that weighed heavily on his conscience. He had been denied during his years in prison the opportunity to be either a husband or a father. He felt particularly guilty that he had been unable to do anything to protect his wife and their two daughters, Zeni and Zindzi, from constant persecution by the police. "It is not a nice feeling for a man to see his family struggling, without security, without the dignity of the head of the family around," he remarked at that first press conference in Cape Town. Later, he would amplify on those feelings, making it clear he felt he owed Winnie a huge debt for her years of suffering on his behalf. It was a debt he intended to pay off now that he was free, he said. Only as the months unfolded would it become clear that Winnie Mandela would exploit her husband's massive guilt complex for her own personal political gain.

As for his first feelings about life beyond prison walls, Mandela said he had great difficulty putting them into words because he was so completely overwhelmed with emotion. "It was breathtaking," he remarked. "That's all I can say." Describing South Africa as "a totally different" place from the one he had known before his incarceration, Mandela again cited the fact that so many whites had lined the route from Victor Verster Prison to Cape Town the previous afternoon. He then made an emotional appeal to whites as "fellow South Africans," saying he wanted them to feel safe and to work hand in hand with blacks in building a New South Africa. "We appreciate the contribution they made towards the development of this country"—these were the kind of conciliatory words whites had hoped to hear from him the day before and that he had apparently been kept from uttering by his ANC handlers. Whites finally had cause to breathe a sigh of relief; Mandela was someone they could negotiate and cooperate with after all.

One lasting impression I had of that first press conference with Mandela was everyone's concern about the state of his health. He had walked down the stone stairs of the garden with the stiffness of an aging gentleman. We had already heard that after the turmoil of the City Hall reception a doctor had been called in to check him over. While in prison Mandela had suffered from high blood pressure, tuberculosis, and back trouble. He had eaten a salt-free diet for years. Nobody knew for sure what his physical condition really was or whether he could endure the certain stress of the ANC leadership that awaited him. A few days later, we asked him about his health during an inteview with a small group of American reporters at his old, three-room home in the Orlando West district of Soweto. He just shrugged off the question, saying his health was "reasonably good" and that he was continuing with the same set of exercises he had done for years in prison. "Of course, I'm not as young as you, and there are signs of old age, wear and tear which we must expect," he remarked jokingly.

Concern about Mandela's health remained a central topic of conversation among reporters, diplomats, and his own close associates during the first few months after his release as he kept up a nonstop schedule of rallies, meetings, press conferences, and long trips abroad. In early May, while on his second extended tour of African countries, he suddenly had to cut back on his schedule of appearances in Dar es Salaam, Tanzania, because of general exhaustion. In late May, just before he took off on a six-week trip to Western Europe and the United States, he underwent an operation to remove a cyst from his bladder amid a flurry of reports (unfounded, as it turned out) that he was suffering from cancer. Such speculation was indicative of the rumors circulating about his health at the time. Still, when he arrived in Geneva, Mandela had to cut short a speech before the World Council of Churches because he wasn't feeling well. His friends began to feel the ANC was pushing him too hard and had drawn up a schedule that might literally kill him. Eventually, his aides would learn how to pace him through his unending meetings and appearances, but not before his grueling ten-day visit to the United States that June. There, Mandela made the mistake of trying to meet everybody's wishes and demands to see him until he was near collapse. During those first few months of his freedom, ANC officials seemed oblivious to the fact that they were dealing with a seventy-one-year-old man who was undergoing enormous physical and mental strain after twenty-seven years of dull, routine prison life.

◆ ◆ ◆

The history of Mandela's release will make fascinating reading when the government records finally become available. They are certain to show a lot of agonizing among South Africa's proud Afrikaner rulers over whether they should take their chances and free him. As early as January 1985, President P. W. Botha gave the first public indication that he was mulling over Mandela's possible release. Speaking at the opening of Parliament, he made an offer to let the ANC leader go provided he "unconditionally rejects violence as a political weapon." Botha's offer was the sixth time since 1973 that the government had proposed to release him, always conditionally. Through these earlier offers, the authorities had sought to entrap him into implicit recognition of the apartheid system by agreeing to live "outside South Africa" in his native Transkei, a nominally independent "homeland" that the South African government had forced upon the Xhosa people in 1976 as part of its grand scheme to drive all blacks into separate reserves.

Mandela had always refused these conditions, and rejected Botha's offer of conditional release in 1985 as well. This time he delivered his response in a rather dramatic way. He had his daughter Zindzi read it aloud publicly at a gathering of ANC supporters in Jabulani Stadium in Soweto on February 10. "I cannot and will not give any undertaking at a time when I and you, the people, are not free," Mandela said. Freedom was indivisible and his release would have to be part of a package deal that included the unbanning of the ANC and freedom for "all who have been imprisoned, banished, or exiled for their opposition to apartheid." Mandela had, in fact, laid down to the white authorities the terms they would have to meet in order for him to agree to walk out of their prison. It would take exactly five years to the day before the South African government would meet his unchanging demands.

Mandela's high-level contacts with the government began in July 1984 when the minister of law and order, Hendrik "Kobie" Coetsee, came to see him in a Cape Town hospital where he was recovering from an illness. Nothing came of this visit, however, for two years. The next encounter came on May 16, 1986, when a Commonwealth delegation of so-called Eminent Persons was allowed to visit Mandela in jail. According to Joseph Lelyveld, the *New York*

Times correspondent in South Africa at that time, Foreign Minister Roelof "Pik" Botha asked the delegation if the government could send a minister along to hear what Mandela had to say. It agreed. But the minister, again Coetsee, arrived late at the meeting and might not have stayed had Mandela not seized upon the occasion to make an impassioned plea to Coetsee for the initiation of talks between the country's estranged white and black leaders. Within two months, such clandestine talks began, with Coetsee again the government's intermediary.

It was one of the many ironies of the long, drawn-out process that when Mandela's secret discussions finally began in July 1986, the country was in the midst of a major government crackdown on the anti-apartheid struggle. Under a nationwide state of emergency imposed the previous month, thousands of black activists had been rounded up and put in detention. And yet in the midst of the government's massive crackdown, the ruling Afrikaner elite was taking a small step forward in its reform of apartheid. Three years earlier, President Botha had brought the Afrikaner establishment around to opening up the all-white political system to the first nonwhites, creating a tricameral Parliament in which the Coloureds and Indians were given separate, but very unequal, houses alongside the main white one. Now, in the South African winter of 1986, Botha's reform process continued moving, albeit at glacial speed, toward the inevitable. In July, as Mandela held his first discussions with Coetsee, the ruling National Party approved its next reform, publishing with great fanfare a new plan for "power-sharing" between the white minority and the black majority. How this was to be implemented remained undecided, but the principle of black participation in political power at all levels of government was finally accepted. The next problem for the government was to find credible black partners with whom to negotiate such a plan.

After two years of resisting even the implicit recognition of the ANC as a legitimate negotiating partner, in May 1988 Botha established a special four-man committee to handle such talks with the ANC leadership. The committee's members were Niel Barnard, head of the National Intelligence Service (NIS); his assistant, Mike Louw; General Willie Willemse, the head of prisons; and Fanie van der Merwe, a senior government constitutional affairs expert.

These four men met repeatedly with Mandela in an attempt, as Barnard later put it, to "understand how Mr. Mandela's head works." Their goal, said Barnard, was to ascertain whether the ANC leader believed in a peaceful settlement, whether he was a communist, and what his view was of South Africa's political future. Mandela, in turn, used these encounters to press his demand for a direct meeting with President Botha. Barnard said he felt Botha "could not lose" by meeting Mandela but that the president had "struggled long over whether he should consent to the visit." Botha, however, made no promises and no commitments.

After these talks were under way, the government sought to expand them to make contact as well with the ANC's exiled leaders, but Mandela opposed this, fearing the government might exploit the two separate channels to its own advantage. The committee went ahead anyway and arranged a meeting with senior ANC leaders at a secret location in Europe. Barnard took great pride in the fact that the NIS and the ANC had succeeded in pulling off the meeting without any Western intelligence service finding out about it. In fact, the government's talks with ANC leaders went so well, according to Barnard, that Botha flirted with the idea of a public meeting with the exiled ANC leadership even before Mandela was released. Here was yet another irony of this period: while Botha and his ministers were publicly denouncing as "traitors" the scores of South African liberals, academics, and business magnates who had trekked to Dakar, Lusaka, and various European capitals to meet with the ANC, they were secretly doing the same thing. According to Barnard's account, the government had condemned these private initiatives because it wanted complete control over all contacts with the ANC. As head of the NIS, Barnard felt very strongly about not wanting outside intermediaries involved, because "as soon as there is a middleman, he wants something out of the thing."

Mandela's account of these early contacts conflicts with that of Barnard, who made it sound like he and the NIS had pioneered the peace process. Mandela told me that Coetsee was the government's senior negotiator throughout its intermittent secret talks with him in the late 1980s. He regarded these discussions as the most substantive and important he held with any government officials. Between 1988 and 1990, Coetsee had many meetings with Mandela, sometimes alone, sometimes with other ministers, like Gerrit Viljoen, the government's chief constitutional thinker and negotiator. Mandela said he saw Coetsee on "countless" occasions and Viljoen at least four times. They met secretly at Coetsee's Cape Town home and later at Mandela's "residence," a warder's home on the edge of the Victor Verster Prison. They talked mostly about the violence tearing apart the country and about the need to find a peacefully negotiated settlement before the nation was totally destroyed. Coetsee would later recall that he and Mandela broke the ice by talking history, and the minister was struck by the fact that "Mandela knows more about the Afrikaners' history than many Afrikaners themselves."

Mandela said he spent "hours and hours" explaining ANC policy to Coetsee and why the ANC had felt it necessary to resort to armed struggle in the first place, back in 1961. It was only after the government itself had spurned all peaceful means of settling the conflict, he reminded the minister, that the ANC had been forced into taking up arms. Coetsee, on the other hand, was still trying to convince Mandela to renounce the armed struggle. He told Mandela the government wanted to negotiate with the ANC, but not before it abandoned its commitment to violence, ended its alliance with the South African Communist Party, and gave up its demand for total black majority rule. Mandela never yielded on any of these issues.

On July 5, 1989, in one of the last significant acts of his presidency, Botha finally worked up the courage to call Mandela to his office at Tuynhuys. Less than six weeks later, the state president would be forced to resign by his own rebellious cabinet, fed up with his imperious ways and his refusal to step down gracefully. But no evidence has come to light that Mandela's visit to Tuynhuys was an issue between Botha and his colleagues. Indeed, de Klerk later pointed to it as proof of a consensus in National Party thinking on the need to open up negotiations with the ANC. The timing can most probably be explained by Botha's own determination that he was still very much in charge of the government and South Africa's destiny.

Barnard and General Willemse took charge of driving Mandela

by car and smuggling him into the Cape Dutch-style building next to Parliament without anyone discovering that the meeting was taking place. Their encounter was more than anything else a signal that the government was ready to take another step toward the inevitable and wanted to prepare whites for what was coming. Botha, the hardline anti-ANC warrior, shocked the nation by making public what he had just done, but afterward, everyone knew that Mandela's release, and the negotiations between the government and the ANC, were now just a matter of months, not years.

Mandela told me in March 1992 that he was surprised by how little actually happened at his historic meeting with Botha and how well it had gone. He had gone into the meeting "a bit frightened" and expecting "war" because of Botha's reputation as an irascible old ANC hater. To his surprise, he found Botha relaxed, open, and friendly. The only issue of substance they discussed, he said, was the release of Walter Sisulu and the other top ANC leaders with whom he had shared long years in prison. Mandela had refused to be freed before they were released; he also felt that, if all went well, such a gesture by the government would help to create a good atmosphere in the country for his own release.

In retrospect, there can be no doubt that Mandela's "prison diplomacy" did break the ice and served as indispensable prenegotiations both for his own release and for the later negotiations between the ANC and the white government. But what is most striking is that Mandela had begun these meetings without telling anyone else in the ANC leadership. In a ten-page document he wrote in preparation for his meeting with Botha, and discussed with President de Klerk on December 13, 1989, he explained that he had made this decision because it was "necessary in the national interest" for the ANC and government to "meet urgently to negotiate an effective political settlement." He conceived of his mission as "a very limited one," namely "to bring the country's two major political parties to the negotiating table." This document reveals the very clear sense Mandela had early on of his own special historic mission, and *mission* was the word he himself chose to use. It also reflected a tough personality, a lawyer rigorously defending the ANC's policies of armed struggle and alliance with the Communist Party. If the government was willing to deal and make agreements with "foreign Marxists" in Mozambique and Angola, Mandela asked, why was it so uncompromising in its refusal to talk to South African Marxists?

Yet one also sees in his words a man lost in time, still thinking in romantic terms about Marxism the way many African leaders of the early 1960s had done. Whites wanted to know whether Mandela himself was a Marxist, but his reply was simply to cite what he had said at his 1964 treason trial: he was indeed "attracted by the idea of a classless society" and this sentiment was derived partly from his readings of Marx, who he said had influenced him much as Marx's thinking had influenced Gandhi, Nehru, Nkrumah, and Nasser. "We all accept the need for some form of socialism to enable our people to catch up with the advanced countries of the world and to overcome their legacy of poverty," Mandela wrote in the 1989 paper. "My views are still the same."

There was a brash self-assuredness in his argument, almost a tinge of arrogance, but never of bitterness or revenge. He was all business, lecturing his white captors on what they should know about Western-style democracy and its implications for their future in South Africa. He wanted to know why, if democracy was so good for whites, it should be such a disaster for blacks. If whites wanted "internal peace," they would have to come to accept majority rule. Peace and democracy were "two sides of a single coin." The only way for the whites, indeed the entire country, to achieve this "internal peace" was through a negotiated settlement. This, in turn, could only be obtained by the government dealing with the ANC. Mandela then went on to outline the political conundrum that all sides would have to face and resolve: how to square the black demand for majority rule with the white insistence on "structural guarantees" to assure that majority rule did not lead to black domination. Reconciliation of these two seemingly opposite demands would be "the most crucial task" facing peacemakers, he predicted. "Such reconciliation will be achieved only if both parties are willing to compromise." Mandela then suggested how he thought the negotiating process should proceed. First, the government and the ANC should meet to work out the preconditions for "a proper climate for negotiations." Once this was created, the talks could then begin. He also spelled out the first compromises he felt the ANC would be prepared to make, provided the government showed a willingness to reciprocate with some of its own. The ANC would "suspend," though not formally end, its armed struggle if the government showed it was willing to negotiate directly with the country's "acknowledged black leaders." Mandela was effectively outlining, months in advance, the first compromises the two sides would eventually strike.

By the time he was released, and before the outside world had had a chance to take his measure, Nelson Mandela had already exercised extraordinary independent statesmanship. He had demonstrated sufficient self-assuredness to open talks on his own with the apartheid government. He had gained the confidence of his white interlocutors and impressed them by his political realism and conciliatory approach toward the problems at hand. He was clearly not going to be easy to deal with, but he recognized the need for compromise and "structural guarantees" for the whites. He seemed to be talking about some form of power-sharing, though, as time would prove, his and the government's notion of the term were miles apart. There was clearly a sense conveyed in that ten-page document that Mandela believed he and de Klerk were going to operate as co-peacemakers, the yin and yang, as it were, of the peace process. The two had apparently come to appreciate each other and had established a measure of confidence and trust. So the country's Afrikaner rulers had finally found their black negotiating partner, who, they hoped, would shepherd his community down the uncertain road to a new nonracial democratic society.

2

THE
REVOLUTIONARY CHIEF

I t was far easier to understand the mission Nelson Mandela had
set for himself than to fathom his character. The more I saw of
him in those first few months of his freedom, the more I was
confirmed in my initial impression that he belonged to a past
generation of African leaders who had run their countries with an
authoritarianism typical of traditional tribal chiefs. Mandela initially seemed out of step and ill at ease with the highly decentralized
grassroots protest movement that had evolved out of the long
struggle against apartheid, so different was it from the centrally
directed anti-apartheid movement Mandela had known in the mid-
1950s.

Nelson Mandela came from a tradition and method of struggle
that was just as radical in its time, but far more restricted in its
scope and social base. The black, Coloured, and Indian activists of
his generation were middle-class intellectuals, lawyers and teachers,
not the half-educated and angry teenagers who manned the township barricades in the 1970s and 1980s. Mandela had missed the
two great formative events for today's younger generation of black
leadership: the schoolchildren's revolt against Afrikaner education
in the mid-1970s and the township uprisings of the mid-1980s. In
many ways, he was a leader returning to a whole new world of black
political protest.

Nelson Rolihlahla Mandela grew up in a very traditional African tribal setting in the Transkei, a backwater reservoir of poverty in the southeastern part of the country best known for its export of labor for the back-breaking jobs in white-owned mines and industries. The Transkei is populated by the Xhosa people, the second-largest African ethnic group (after the Zulu) in South Africa. Mandela was groomed to become a future paramount chief of the Tembu tribe; he told the American playwright Arthur Miller in a BBC interview in early 1991 that he grew up with exactly the same ambitions as his father, "who had five wives and calculated his wealth in sheep and cattle." Indeed, Mandela maintained an air of a paramount chief in his post-prison years and I soon learned that it was important to keep in mind this side of his personality if I was to understand him.

Two and a half months after his release from prison, Mandela went back home to greet his extended family and his Madiba clan for the first time in thirty-four years. I went with him because I was curious to see the land and people of his childhood. The backwardness of his family even today was striking, and I couldn't help wondering how Africans like Mandela had ever gotten as far as they had given the unrelieved poverty from which they had come. The hamlet where he grew up is called Qunu, about eighteen miles south of Umtata, the capital of the Transkei homeland, one of South Africa's ten fictitiously described "independent" or "self-governing" black states set up by the apartheid authorities. *Hamlet* is probably too fancy a word to describe what is in fact a series of round-shaped mud and thatch huts, or rondavels, scattered across rolling hills along the main road leading south from Umtata. In one group of huts, right alongside the road, live Mandela's surviving distant relatives, many of whom had never set eyes on him before or only dimly remember him as a child. But they all shared one unmistakable family resemblance: the narrow, almost Asian facial features—slanting eyes and flat faces—of the Madiba clan.

Not much had changed since his last visit home, Mandela told the reporters accompanying him. "The poverty that was here when I last visited this place, that poverty is still there staring me in the face. As I travel to the countryside, my heart becomes sad indeed." Just as sad was the obvious sense of social distance that separated

Qunu's most famous native son from his relatives after so long an absence. The clan gave him a traditional homecoming feast, complete with roasted meat carved from a freshly slaughtered ox, and ordered its praise-singer to recount Mandela's many virtues. But before the feast, he visited the simple graves of his mother and father, marked only by upturned bricks and stones in an open field below a cornfield where his own family rondavel had once stood. Nattily dressed in a dark blue suit, creaseless blue shirt, and blue and yellow tie, Mandela seemed totally out of place standing next to his relatives, who wore threadbare crumpled Sunday suits, old-fashioned dresses, and battered, mud-caked shoes. The homecoming proved a very formal ceremony, lacking in warmth or real affection, and Mandela tried his best to get away early. Before he could go, however, he was dragged into one of the better-constructed huts to share lunch with a select group of family members.

Mandela told us he was not actually born in Qunu back on July 18, 1918, but in Mvezo, fifteen or so miles away on the banks of the Mbashe River. He had grown up in Qunu because the white authorities had deposed his father as chief of Mvezo "for insubordination." He didn't explain to us that day how or why his history took a different turn than that planned for him by his father, but according to various accounts of his early life, upon his father's death in 1930 he was sent to the "palace" of the Tembu paramount chief, Jongintaba Dalindyebo, his cousin and guardian, to be schooled in chiefly ways. Toward this end, the young Mandela was enrolled in a Methodist missionary school, and he then moved on to Fort Hare University College. Fort Hare was about the only institution open to blacks between the two world wars, and it had become a cauldron of black nationalist politics. Among its graduates were South African leaders like Mandela, Walter Sisulu, Oliver Tambo, and Chief Mangosuthu Buthelezi, as well as the Zimbabweans Joshua Nkomo and Robert Mugabe. Two events changed Mandela's life irrevocably in his early twenties when he revolted against both tribal and university authorities. First, he was suspended in his third year from Fort Hare for helping to organize a boycott of the Student Representative Council. Then, he fled the Transkei to avoid a traditional marriage with a local girl who had been handpicked by Chief Dalindyebo.

At age twenty-two, Mandela headed for Johannesburg and entered the world of black nationalist politics. Despite his revolt against tribal traditions, Mandela told a gathering of tribal chiefs in Umtata a few days after his Qunu visit that he might still have become a Tembu tribal chief had it not been for the friendship he formed in Johannesburg with Walter Sisulu. It was Sisulu who not only helped Mandela through law school (at the University of the Witwatersrand) but also introduced him to the African National Congress, which had been founded in 1912 to press with great moderation the first demands of black South Africans for better treatment. In the early 1940s ANC politics were consumed by a revolt of the young members against the stodgy and ineffectual national leadership. The youths were also extremely hostile to the traditional chiefs, whom they regarded as puppets of the white government. Mandela became swept up in this current of youthful rebellion, which in 1944 led to the establishment of the ANC Youth League and the birth of more militant nationalist politics. The Youth League, whose prime movers were Mandela, Sisulu, and Tambo, set as its task the rejuvenation of the ANC's thinking and tactics to promote the national liberation struggle. As one of the new generation's leaders, Mandela positioned himself as a firebrand and a rebel against all authorities—family, tribal, and governmental.

Mandela was never a great theorist of revolution. He was an activist, a doer rather than a thinker. He was a rebel with a very definite cause. Together with Sisulu and Tambo, Mandela set about changing the whole character and tactics of the ANC. To do so, the rebellious trio had to engineer a coup against the ANC's stodgy national leadership under Alfred Xuma, using the Youth League as their springboard. In 1949 the young rebels clashed with Xuma over a "Program of Action" they had proposed to rejuvenate the ANC. Bitterly opposed by Xuma and the old guard, the program called for strikes, boycotts, civil disobedience, and other forms of active resistance against the white government. In its time, the program embodied revolutionary thinking that scared even the ANC's own leaders.

Just prior to the ANC national conference in December 1949, the three Youth League leaders confronted Xuma in what Sisulu later called "a stormy meeting indeed." They basically blackmailed Xuma, he said, telling him if he didn't support their program they wouldn't vote for him to remain as president. He refused and the three mobilized their supporters to defeat Xuma, rallying around Dr. James Moroka as their last-minute candidate to replace Xuma. In the ensuing showdown, Sisulu, Tambo, and Mandela pulled off their coup. They managed to get Moroka elected and their program adopted. Sisulu was even elected secretary-general, and he made Mandela his de facto deputy to run the organization while he was away on trips. In 1950, Mandela was elected president of the Youth League, and two years later—just eight years after joining the ANC—he rose to become the Congress's deputy president under Albert Luthuli.

At that point, Mandela produced his own "M-plan" (named after himself) to reorganize the ANC at the grassroots level. He created a network of secretive cells to better resist the unrelenting police repression of the ANC's program. Mandela's desire for activism merged with that of a small group of Communist militants to produce a new strategy of armed struggle. According to one member of this original revolutionary cabal, the seeds of revolution were germinated by the Sharpeville massacre on March 21, 1960, during which white policemen shot 69 Africans dead and injured 176 others. The massacre ended the era of peaceful anti-apartheid protest and opened a new one marked by direct confrontation in the streets, townships, and workplaces. The ensuing black rage was shared by a small group of Communists led by Michael Harmel and Arthur Goldreich, who drafted the initial plan for an armed rebellion. Joe Slovo became the chief promoter of the idea and Mandela an immediate supporter of it. Mandela would subsequently become the first commander-in-chief of Umkhonto we Sizwe (Spear of the Nation), the ANC's burgeoning guerrilla army. The initial problem for these activists, however, was that ANC president Albert Luthuli opposed the project, fearing it would impede his chances for winning the Nobel Peace Prize (which he was indeed awarded later that year). So the plan for armed struggle was delayed until December 1961 and was launched with Luthuli's full knowledge but not his formal approval.

Mandela's career as a guerrilla commander was brief, and he was not destined to become the African counterpart of Che Guevera, Mao Zedong, or Ho Chi Minh. He never produced a treatise on how guerrilla warfare should be adapted to the special conditions of South Africa, nor did he ever expound on revolution in the manner of Algeria's Frantz Fanon or Guinea's Amilcar Cabral. Mandela's most important book, *The Struggle Is My Life*, consists of a collection of his speeches and writings together with official ANC pronouncements he helped to draft between the years 1944 and 1964. The book makes interesting reading because one can see the evolution in Mandela's political thinking almost year by year. "The struggle" clearly was his whole life.

Mandela came of age at a time of enormous ferment on the African continent. The national liberation struggle was all-consuming, with scores of French and British colonies gaining their independence just as Mandela was launching the ANC's armed struggle in the early 1960s. African socialism and Marxism were both very much in vogue as "liberation theologies." Algeria was on the verge of gaining its independence after a tough, seven-year-long anticolonial guerrilla war that was, in Mandela's words, "definitely an inspiration." Mandela had gone underground in June 1961 to begin organizing the ANC's armed struggle, which was launched on December 16, 1961, with a series of sabotage acts in cities across South Africa. It was the same initial tactic used by the National Liberation Front (FLN) in Algeria to break out of the sterility of Arab nationalist politics there in 1954. Mandela recounted to me that he led the first group of twenty Umkhonto recruits sent abroad to Algeria and Ethiopia for military training in 1961. He recalled witnessing some of the Algerian battles against the French army, and he still remembered in great detail how the FLN had organized the country militarily as well as its battle tactics. As he would explain to the Pretoria Supreme Court at his treason trial in 1964, he studied "the art of war and revolution" while abroad because he wanted to prepare himself in case the struggle in South Africa "drifted into guerrilla warfare."

After helping to launch the armed struggle, Mandela was chosen by the ANC to publicize its cause abroad. In a speech to a conference of the Pan-African Freedom Movement of East and Central Africa held in Addis Ababa in January 1962, shortly after Um-

khonto's first attacks, he spelled out the ANC's reasons for resorting to violence. His publicity tour also took him to London and
nearly a dozen African countries, where he briefed their leaders on
events in South Africa and sought their support for the ANC's
burgeoning armed struggle.

Still underground, Mandela returned to South Africa that July.
Already a township hero nicknamed the "Black Pimpernel" because he had successfully evaded capture for more than a year by
traveling in various disguises, his luck failed him on August 5. He
was picked up in Natal while, dressed as a chauffeur, he was driving
a car. (His arrest, as it turned out, was the result of information that
an American CIA agent, Millard Shirley, had provided to the
apartheid government. The whole sordid tale of CIA involvement
in Mandela's arrest came out in the American and South African
press—to the great embarrassment of the Bush administration—
just as Mandela was arriving on his first triumphal visit to the
United States in June 1990.) Sentenced that November to five years
imprisonment for incitement and leaving the country illegally,
Mandela was already serving his sentence when, on July 11, 1963,
police raided the ANC's secret hideout at Lilliesleaf Farm in Rivonia, on the northern outskirts of Johannesburg, and seized,
among others, nine top Umkhonto, ANC, and Communist Party
leaders. Mandela would subsequently be tried for treason, sabotage, and conspiracy to overthrow the government alongside his
comrades, among them Walter Sisulu, in what came to be called
the Rivonia trial. On June 12, 1964, eight of the leaders, including
Mandela and Sisulu, were convicted and sentenced to life imprisonment.

In the eight months between the launch of the armed struggle
and his arrest, Mandela did not have time to emerge as a great
guerrilla leader. But the origins of his enormous popularity among
the young doubtless stem from his commander-in-chief role in
those formative months of the ANC's armed struggle, even though
it subsequently failed either to liberate any territory or even organize a single armed confrontation between ANC guerrillas and the
white army inside South Africa. It may have turned out to be a pale
imitation of the Algerian revolution—or, for that matter, the An-

golan, Mozambican, and Zimbabwean ones—but it gave rise nonetheless to a powerful mythology.

Another powerful formative experience in Mandela's early political life was the development within the ANC of methods of action that emphasized secrecy, subterfuge, and centralized decision-making. Relentless government suppression of all black political activity caused the ANC to become a kind of secret society in order to survive. Within two years of taking power in 1948, the National Party passed the Suppression of Communism Act, which it used mercilessly to crack down not just on the Communist Party but on the entire anti-apartheid movement. As a result, Mandela was forced to operate under banning orders throughout most of the 1950s. This meant he was forbidden by law to address groups or participate in political activities; often he was restricted in his travels to the Johannesburg area. Starting in 1956, he was caught up in the first of the government's "treason trials," as one of among 156 activists arrested and charged with conspiring to overthrow the state. The trial stretched over four years, but everyone was eventually acquitted.

After the Sharpeville massacre, the bloody magnitude of which was unprecedented, the government imposed a state of emergency and detained over 20,000 people. It banned entirely both the ANC and the Pan Africanist Congress (PAC), a splinter group that had broken away the previous year in protest over the ANC's acceptance of working with whites and Communists. (The Pan Africanists had been responsible for organizing the Sharpeville protest.) In such a repressive atmosphere, free and open discussion about anything became impossible within the ANC. The result was the emergence of a secretive, centralized, and autocratic style of leadership that was to mark the organization for the next thirty years. These undemocratic tendencies were no doubt reinforced by the Communist Party's influence on the ANC; its doctrine of "democratic centralism" seemed to have become the ANC modus operandi. At the time of Mandela's release in 1990, the ANC was run by a secretive, tightly knit clique of just thirty-five people who for thirty years had made all decisions, without consulting their scattered supporters, from the olympian heights of the National Executive Committee.

Mandela, locked away for twenty-seven years, could hardly be held responsible for the development of this style of leadership. But I had the feeling watching him operate after his release that he had no major quarrel with the organization's secretive, authoritarian legacy. He quickly became very close to, and protective of, the ANC's old guard, which found itself under immediate attack from the new, younger generation who led the United Democratic Front, the coalition of more than 700 groups that could operate legally inside the country, and led the internal anti-apartheid movement from 1983 until Mandela's release. The adulation he was the object of at home and abroad undoubtedly reinforced the authoritarian streak so common in African leaders of his generation. In a sense, he was acting his age, which was totally in keeping with the character of leadership among his contemporaries—men like Kenneth Kaunda in Zambia and Felix Houphouet-Boigny of the Ivory Coast. Mandela's comfort with authoritarianism even led him to reconsider his own youthful opposition to the traditional tribal authorities. "Those who feel that we have nothing to do with chiefs," he told an ANC youth congress in the eastern Transvaal in 1991, "do not know the policy of the ANC and have no idea how to strengthen the organization in the countryside. We should work together with the chiefs and give them the respect they deserve." One couldn't help feeling that Mandela, fifty years on, had mellowed a great deal and had rediscovered his own lost tribal and chieftain roots. There he was handing out advice he had himself rejected at the same age. I came to feel, after following him closely in those first few months, that Mandela harbored a secret yearning to be treated as a chief. The organization he represented, however, was made of his old rebellious mettle and its rank and file had no time for chiefs.

This tension was to surface again and again in various forms between Mandela and the ANC, for he had emerged from prison at a time when Africans everywhere were fed up with autocratic one-man and one-party rule. At home, he faced the highly democratic, decentralized, and consultative politics that the UDF had spawned through close and constant contacts between leaders and followers. He found his freedom of leadership challenged at every turn, as he had little control over township youths or events taking place at the grassroots level. ANC regional leaders in Natal, he was to discover, would dictate whether and when he met with Chief Buthelezi. Other members of the ANC's National Executive Committee would limit his room to maneuver, and even to meet with, President de Klerk. His own obvious preference for dealing with other leaders, be they white or black, on a personal basis to strike deals ran into stiff opposition from both the ANC's rank and file and its top officials.

In thought as in deed, the young Nelson Mandela had crossed the spectrum from moderation to radicalism under the pressure of the National Party's mounting oppression as it proceeded to implement its Grand Apartheid scheme after coming to power in 1948. The 1944 founding manifesto of the ANC Youth League was, in retrospect, a moderate document: its lodestars were African nationalism, a burning faith in the black man's ability to liberate himself, and a rejection of "the wholesale importation of foreign ideologies into Africa." The Basic Policy Document of the ANC Youth League adopted in 1948 continued in the same vein and was even more categoric in its rejection of radical African nationalism as espoused by the Jamaican black nationalist Marcus Garvey. For these youthful firebrands, Garvey's political philosophy amounted to a call for "Africa for the Africans" and "Hurl the white man into the sea." This was too "extreme and ultra-revolutionary" for a Youth League that accepted whites as one of the four main "nationalities" of South Africa. It must be "clearly understood that we are not against the Europeans as such," the 1948 document said, only "totally and irrevocably opposed to white domination."

The government's single-minded pursuit of Grand Apartheid slowly made radicals out of moderates, socialists out of aspiring capitalists, and black power separatists out of racial integrationists. After the government passed the Suppression of Communism Act in 1950 and began persecuting suspected Communists and African nationalists without distinction, one can detect clear signs of a radicalization in Mandela's thinking. Where once Mandela had believed that the Communist Party posed a danger to the ANC and its African nationalist platform (he broke up their meetings, interrupted their recruitment campaigns, and even supported expelling

Communists from the movement), he now saw the party as a strong ally against the white government's wholesale persecution.

It is, of course, ironic that the government's deliberate policy to make no distinction between nationalists and Communists helped to turn Mandela into such an ardent defender of their close alliance, but that is exactly what happened. Walter Sisulu told me that the Suppression of Communism Act was decisive in changing Mandela's attitude toward the Communists. "We regarded right from the beginning that the attack on the Communist Party was in fact an attack on the liberation movement," he said. The two groups forged their alliance by organizing a National Day of Protest on June 26, 1950, the day the Act was promulgated, and on its second anniversary the Campaign for the Defiance of the Unjust Laws provoked the government into taking additional repressive actions that drove ANC and Communist supporters even closer together. Mandela would later proceed to defend the alliance between the ANC and the Communist Party as purely tactical in nature, similar to those alliances formed between the Communist parties and the "freedom struggles" in Algeria, Indonesia, and China. The ANC couldn't afford the luxury of excluding those willing to fight the apartheid system, he explained at the Rivonia trial, and "for many decades Communists were the only political group in South Africa who were prepared to treat Africans as human beings and their equals; who were prepared to eat with us; talk with us, live with us, and work with us." Working with the Communists brought Mandela into close contact with whites who were just as dedicated to the anti-apartheid struggle as blacks were and who were suffering just as much from police repression. This could not help but reinforce his belief that an inclusive multi-racial nationalism was the correct ideology for the ANC to espouse, rather than the exclusive black nationalism that would later motivate the splinter Pan Africanist Congress.

Year by year, moreover, Mandela became more of a socialist in his thinking and intellectually closer to the philosophy of the Communist Party. In an article written for the June 1956 issue of the South African magazine *Liberation*, Mandela claimed that the Freedom Charter (the ANC's official manifesto) was "by no means a blueprint for a socialist state," and failed to "contemplate such profound economic and political changes." Yet the Charter's vision of a new society could not possibly be fulfilled, he said, "unless and until these monopolies are smashed and the national wealth of the country [is] turned over to the people." There had to be an end to the rule of "mining kings and land barons" and "the workers" had to become the principal force upon which the democratic movement was built. He offered a Marxist-style class analysis of the anti-apartheid struggle but called for an alliance of all classes against the apartheid system. The "system" he opposed in his writings included the existing international order, specifically French and British colonialism, but the United States did not escape his attack. Contained within the pages of *The Struggle Is My Life* is an article written in March 1958 entitled "A New Menace in Africa." This was a diatribe against "American imperialism" and a warning to newly independent African nations to beware of the United States, which, he said, "masquerades as the leader of the so-called free world in the campaign against communism." Beware, he wrote, "the American brand of imperialism is imperialism all the same in spite of the modern clothing in which it is dressed and in spite of the sweet language spoken by its advocates and agents."

As to whether Mandela was ever a communist himself, the ANC leader outlined his attitude toward communism and the Communist Party at the Rivonia trial. He denied having been a member of the Communist Party, but explained that he was "attracted" by the idea of a classless society partly because of his Marxist readings and partly because of his "admiration" for early African societies, in which the land had belonged collectively to the tribe. Like many other Third World leaders, he said he had been influenced by Marxist thought but that he differed specifically with communists over their denunciation of Western democracies, professing himself an admirer in particular of British political institutions. "I regard the British Parliament as the most democratic institution in the world," he told the court, yet he was not tied to any particular "system of society other than socialism."

The impression one derives, mainly from this collection of statements made before a white court in the early 1960s, is that Mandela was a sentimental rather than a doctrinaire socialist. He clearly believed that certain key sectors of the economy—the mines, banks, and big industry—should be put under government control and the land redistributed to its former African owners. He was a "visceral socialist" if nothing else, reacting to the massive inequities of South African society. His views were akin to the amorphous "African socialism" of many other African leaders at that time, like Senegal's Leopold Senghor, Zambia's Kenneth Kaunda, and Tanzania's Julius Nyerere. But his socialism was bound to appear far more radical in the South African context because it was aimed at the largest white population on the African continent, one in control of 87 percent of all the land and virtually all the banks, mines, and industries. Upon his release from prison, blacks and whites alike were curious to see whether he had retained his earlier predilection for socialism.

It seemed that Mandela had not changed very much in his views about fundamental economic issues while in prison. He was still a "visceral socialist" and no more of an economist in 1990 than he had been in 1964. The fact that communism was crumbling in Eastern Europe, and Marxism-Leninism a dismal failure in those African countries where it had been the guiding light, took some time to make an impression on his thinking. When Mandela first came out of prison, he was talking just as he had when he went in. At his first press conference, he talked of the need to overhaul the economy to assure full employment and far greater productivity, while at the same time meeting the "question of social responsibility." Asked whether he had changed his views in any way on the need for a radical redistribution of wealth in the country, Mandela responded, without a moment's hesitation, "No. My views are identical to those of the ANC. The question of the nationalization of the mines and similar sectors of the community is a fundamental policy of the ANC, and I believe that the ANC is quite correct in this attitude." His comments that day sent share prices on the Johannesburg stock market plummeting.

Over the ensuing months and years, Mandela softened his comments on nationalization, as did the ANC in its official statements, but this seemed to be more an issue of political expediency reflecting the need to reassure panicky white businessmen, foreign investors, the International Monetary Fund, and the World Bank rather than a fundamental change of heart. Even so, there were repeated lapses. For example, when Mandela addressed the Portuguese community in Cape Town in July 1991 he reaffirmed the ANC's intention to nationalize the big monopolies. State power, he said, would be used to right the wrongs of apartheid, economic as well as political. Many Communist Party members continued to worry, however, that Mandela and the ANC were slowly abandoning their visceral commitment to socialism, and some predicted that the ANC–Communist Party alliance would one day split over this issue. Yet as Mandela spoke time and again about the imperative need for a redistribution of wealth and property, it was unclear whether there was really that much difference between what he was saying and the Communist Party policy of "democratic socialism." His comments to a panel of the World Economic Forum in Davos, Switzerland, in early February 1992 included the following: "Taking some key enterprises into public ownership will itself be a major step towards overcoming the huge inequality in the ownership of our country's wealth." Mandela's interest in seeing the ANC take control of the "commanding heights" of the economy seemed to me as great as that of the Communist Party.

Similarly, Mandela emerged from prison with his empathy for Third World revolutionaries and their various causes unaltered. He went into prison in 1962 as an "anti-imperialist" and he came out in 1990 pretty much the same. When he met Yasir Arafat, the Palestine Liberation Organization leader, in Lusaka, Zambia, two weeks after his release, he hugged and kissed him as if he were a long-lost brother. He further outraged the South African Jewish community by drawing parallels between the PLO and ANC causes. In an appearance on "Nightline" on June 21, 1990, during his visit to the United States, Mandela called Arafat "a comrade in arms." Like the ANC as a whole, Mandela clung instinctively to the old Third World leftist view of the world as one dominated by "American imperialism." His new heroes included not only Arafat but Libya's Muammar el-Qaddafi, Cuba's Fidel Castro, and Iraq's Saddam Hussein. What they all had in common, of course, was their willingness, in one way or another, to stand up against America's world power. When Iraq invaded Kuwait in August 1990, the ANC's first inclination was to take the side of Saddam Hussein. Mandela enraged President George Bush during a telephone conversation the two had shortly before the ground war began by lecturing him on the perils of U.S. policy and telling him that the United States, not Iraq, was at fault.

Mandela also infuriated the Bush administration by taking Qaddafi's side in the U.S.–Libyan feud over the bombing of Pan Am flight 103. Mandela said that the U.S. attempt to extradite two Libyan intelligence agents to stand trial for the 1988 bombing was "intended to humiliate a head of state." The Bush administration tried to dissuade Mandela from visiting Libya in January 1992 because it had "some very strong views" about Qaddafi's involvement in international terrorism. The ANC, however, had equally strong views about Qaddafi, a longtime supporter of its cause who had put several million dollars into its coffers and was providing an airplane for Mandela's tour of North Africa. ANC officials were incensed by the U.S. meddling in Mandela's affairs. "If the United States starts trying to dictate which countries Mandela visits, that's going to cause a lot of problems," ANC spokeswoman Gill Marcus told me. Mandela may have been out of step with American and Western opinion, but he was right in keeping with the majority ANC view.

Another object of Mandela's admiration was Fidel Castro. When he visited Havana in late July 1991, Mandela heaped praise on the aging revolutionary and expressed sympathy for Cuba's valiant struggle against the "imperialist-orchestrated campaign." He also praised the Cuban revolution's "impressive gains," dismissing reporters' questions about human rights abuses in Cuba. "From its earliest days, the Cuban revolution has itself been a source of inspiration to all freedom-loving people," said Mandela. He clearly admired Castro's revolution and its struggle to stay alive despite American pressure. Castro in particular was a hero for Mandela, having sent more than 300,000 troops to Angola to help the leftist government there fight both the South African Army and the U.S.-backed Angolan rebels led by Jonas Savimbi. "We come here with a sense of great debt that is owed to the people of Cuba," said Mandela in a July 26 speech with Castro standing at his side. "What other country can point to a record of greater selflessness than Cuba has displayed in its relations with Africa." Comments like these—repeated in all corners of the earth—made it clear that

South Africa was in for a radical change in its foreign policy if Mandela lived long enough to become its first black president.

The decades in prison had not changed Mandela's political sympathies, but they had brought about some alteration in his character. Mandela had a legendary hot temper in his youth so often on display that practically every book written about him, however flattering, has remarked on it. In prison, however, he gained a mastery over his own emotions that he has seldom lost since. According to a fellow prisoner, Mac Maharaj, Mandela worked systematically to bring his spontaneous bursts of anger under control "for political reasons as well as personal." He succeeded so well that Maharaj was struck by his tendency to bottle up his feelings and keep them hidden from his closest prison friends. This pattern held true after his release, as Mandela remained a very private person.

Mandela was reluctant to talk about his prison experience or how it had changed his outlook on life. I learned from him in March 1992 that much had happened that he never wanted to discuss. He said there had been "a lot of corruption" among the prisoners that involved "food for sexual pleasures," but he never went into the details. He did relate to me, however, one incident. In 1988, while recovering from tuberculosis in a Cape Town hospital, he was offered 500,000 rand (about $180,000) just to have his picture taken. He refused the offer, he said, because he feared it would upset his secret negotiations with the government.

I can remember only once when a few of us reporters succeeded in getting him to reflect back on his prison life at some length. This was during the interview with American reporters he gave at his Soweto home just four days after his release. He told us that he had spent most of the first two years after his capture in solitary confinement, and that this had lasted until after his conviction. Robben Island, where he and six other "Rivonia trialists" were incarcerated, had initially been a very grim experience for him. He described conditions on the small island in the stormy waters off Cape Town as "very harsh and brutal." Although he had never been subjected to physical mistreatment himself, he recounted that "this was happening around me almost daily." Mandela spent many years in hard labor on Robben Island, breaking stones, digging in a lime quarry, and collecting seaweed along its shores. Only in the mid-1970s, after he and his fellow political prisoners had agitated for years over the quality of the food, the lack of proper sporting facilities, and the censorship of reading materials, did conditions improve.

Mandela also told me, in a later interview, that it was on Robben Island that he had learned the virtues of standing fast in dealing with Afrikaners. He related one incident in which he and his prison colleagues staged a slowdown in protest over the work target set for them of loading fifteen truckloads of limestone a day. They succeeded, he said, in getting their quota down to one truckload, and by the time he and four other senior ANC leaders were transferred to the mainland Pollsmoor Prison outside Cape Town in April 1982, they had won most of their demands for better conditions. Mandela and his colleagues would remember this lesson of steadfastness in dealing with Afrikaner authorities when they were pressing for concessions in their negotiations with the government. The only positive side of prison life, Mandela said, was the friendly relationship he was able to develop with some of his jailers. He had discovered that they were the best hope of gaining unofficial favors and improvement in conditions. "We had many friends amongst warders who tried as much as possible to make our conditions as comfortable as possible," he told us. It was the attitude of his jailers that "wiped out any bitterness which a man could have" about losing twenty-seven years of his life behind bars. And it was this lack of bitterness about the whole experience that would always strike me as the most extraordinary thing about Mandela.

Prison was also where Mandela established his lasting authority and leadership over the ANC. Some of Mandela's detractors in the black community argued after his release that it was just an historical fluke that he had emerged as the top ANC leader—they said that another prisoner could just as easily have been selected to dramatize abroad the collective plight of anti-apartheid activists forgotten on Robben Island. Others, like Walter Sisulu, they said, equally deserved the mantle and might well have taken Mandela's place in the international limelight.

But when one looks at the scope of Mandela's career, his selection as the human symbol of the anti-apartheid activists' general plight seems even more of a foregone conclusion. No one, not even his close friend Sisulu, deserved it more. He had already enjoyed a meteoric rise within the ANC leadership prior to his arrest in 1962. He had helped to found the Youth League, becoming its president in 1950 and then deputy national president of the entire ANC two years later. Only successive banning orders, making it impossible for him to attend political meetings, had forced him to resign that post the following year. But the bans had not stopped his political activities, and in 1961 and 1962, there was even discussion among ANC militants of ousting Luthuli as president and replacing him with Mandela.

Finally, the treason trials gave Mandela a platform on which to prove his oratorical skills. His statement in April 1964 at the Rivonia trial, where he defended the ANC's decision to take up arms, established his reputation as an eloquent and cogent spokesman for the national liberation cause. Prison life only confirmed his place as the emerging dominant leader. All accounts by his fellow prisoners described him as the preeminent figure on Robben Island, where Mandela ran what amounted to a political education center for hundreds of youthful black activists arrested in wave after wave of township revolt. He became the accepted arbiter in hundreds of political rows that broke out between ANC members and those who belonged to rival groups. He played the role of political science professor, lecturing on the history of political protest movements around the world. In particular, he attempted to convince the young firebrands of the 1976 Soweto schoolchildren's revolt (most of whom were black power advocates), that historically the main cause of the black man's oppression was not color, but a system of repression stemming from colonial times.

Many followers of the Black Consciousness Movement, who had led the mid-1970s student uprising, left Robben Island converted to the ANC only because of Mandela. Indeed, every indication prior to and during his incarceration was that he would someday assume the presidency even if Oliver Tambo, who had led the ANC in exile, had not had an incapacitating stroke in August 1989.

The real wonder was that Mandela emerged from Robben Island sound of mind and free of bitterness. While I was never able to determine whether his internal spiritual strength derived from religious faith, my impression was that there was a religious component to his spiritual stamina. Mandela was brought up a Methodist and went to a mission primary school, yet I have never heard of him attending church since his release. Certainly there was never any publicity given to it if he did. Charles Villa-Vicencio, a professor of religion at the University of Cape Town, would later interview Mandela about his religious beliefs, and reported that he had found the ANC leader deeply religious, but in the general sense of the term rather than as a devotee of any specific faith. Mandela told Villa-Vicencio that he had "never missed a service" and had "often read the scripture lessons" while in prison. He spoke warmly about the various chaplains whom he had met on Robben Island and from whom he had taken holy communion on a regular basis. "The sacrament gave me a sense of inner quiet and calm," Mandela recalled, but he shied away from characterizing himself as a religious person. "I am not particularly religious or spiritual," he observed. "I am just an ordinary person interested in trying to make sense of the mysteries of life." Mandela said he found the religious experience "beyond articulation," but he had concluded that it was better to live its values rather than just talk about them.

It must have taken a lot of spiritual faith to survive the numbing isolation, loneliness, and slave labor conditions on Robben Island as a mentally healthy person, as Mandela clearly was. In late January 1992, South Africa's prison authorities took me and a few other reporters to the island for a visit to Mandela's tiny cell. It was a sobering experience that brought home graphically the monumental injustice inflicted on Mandela and his colleagues for having dared to oppose the world's most oppressive racial system. Mandela had lived for twenty-one years in a dank, stone-and-cement box of a cell just seven feet by seven feet—barely big enough for a bed, desk, and chair. The barred window looked out on the prison's exercise yard. Somehow, in these cramped confines, Mandela had managed to grow spinach plants that had flourished. This caught the attention of the prison commander, who asked Mandela's secret so that his spinach would flourish as well. Mandela's cell was one of thirty-two located in a special wing of the prison known as the "B-section," reserved for top ANC and other black activist leaders. Looking into that tiny space, I was overwhelmed with wonder that any human spirit could survive intact for so many years. On the wall above his old bed, the current prisoner had hung a tapestry with Jesus Christ's final words before death woven into it: "My God, my God, why have you forsaken me?" I wondered whether during his long years there Mandela hadn't at times uttered the same words of despair.

3

THE
CALVINIST REFORMER

Frederik Willem de Klerk's rise to leadership in 1989 came unexpectedly, and happened literally from one hour to the next. He did not campaign at all to become party leader because there was no time to do so. After President P. W. Botha suffered a stroke on January 18, de Klerk's name surfaced as one of several possible, but by no means certain, choices to succeed the ailing National Party leader. This speculation stemmed from the fact that de Klerk was head of the party in Transvaal Province, a powerful springboard for anyone aspiring to become *hoofleier*, the party's chief, because of its centrality in white politics as the heartland of Afrikaner conservatism, the country's industrial center, and the home of more than 2 million of the country's 4.5 million whites. Still, it is not at all clear that de Klerk would have risen to the presidency had there been time for the reform wing of the party to unite behind a single candidate and mount a proper campaign. The *verligte*, or "enlightened," reformers were gathering strength within the party, and de Klerk was regarded as a leader of the rival camp, the *verkrampte*, or "closed-minded conservative," wing. Circumstances, however, played into de Klerk's hands.

President Botha, at seventy-three, had become a man of unpredictable whims and intolerable dictatorial temperament whom none of his colleagues could stand any longer. After eleven years in office, although he was generally feared or hated he was certainly not respected by anyone in his cabinet. It was entirely in keeping with his capricious nature that, even while recovering from a stroke, he should decide to spring on the National Party the issue of choosing his successor in a way that allowed no time for any of the contenders to rally their supporters.

The occasion was a routine meeting of the party's caucus—the 130 Nationalists sitting in Parliament—in Cape Town on February 2, 1989, just as the new session of the national legislature was about to open. Botha's illness had, of course, raised questions about the party's future leadership, but nobody was truly prepared for what was to happen. Just ten minutes before the caucus was to convene, Botha sent a letter to Jurie Mentz, its chairman, informing him that he was resigning immediately as party leader but would stay on as state president. His letter struck the caucus meeting like an earthquake. Botha was putting the party and the government in a particularly difficult quandary since the state president (formerly the prime minister) had always held the post by virtue of being the National Party's leader. Furthermore, owing to Botha's recent stroke, Constitutional Development Minister Chris Heunis was serving as acting state president, which meant that the country might possibly have a kind of troika leadership—Botha, Heunis, and the new National Party leader (assuming Heunis was not elected). It was an absurd situation, but there was no time to discuss how to resolve the conflict. Parliament was about to open, and the National Party needed a leader to cope with the crucial issues of reform in the forthcoming session.

The caucus immediately took up the issue of electing a new party chief. The reformers fielded three candidates, Finance Minister Barend du Plessis, Foreign Minister Roelof "Pik" Botha, and Heunis, while the conservatives chose to rally around de Klerk. On the first round of voting, the three reform candidates together outpolled de Klerk, by a vote of seventy-one to fifty-nine, but de Klerk had received more votes than any of his opponents alone. Had the reformers had time to work out their differences and choose a single candidate, they would surely have prevailed. As it was, their division was fatal. Pik Botha, popular because of his oratorical skills but with no grassroots constituency, won the fewest votes, only sixteen, on the first round and had to drop out. Heunis fell out on the second round, leaving du Plessis and de Klerk to fight it out.

The final run-off, a straight two-way tussle, should have gone to du Plessis, but reform was not the only issue at stake in the minds of many caucus members. In fact, the most important fissure within the party ran in a direction that had little to do with reform. The hidden fault line lay between those who wanted to restore the National Party's preeminence in policy-making and the "securocrats," the overall security establishment made up of the military, police, and state intelligence which, under Botha's rule, had usurped power and sidelined the party. In this intramural power struggle, de Klerk was very much the "man of the party," while du Plessis, despite his reformist image, was more the man of the securocrats. This explains why Botha, the kingpin of the securocrats, in the end supported the reformist du Plessis rather than the seemingly far more conservative de Klerk. It also explains how de Klerk managed to attract ten additional votes from among those who had previously supported one of the three reform candidates, and thus squeak through to become the winner by the narrow margin of sixty-nine to sixty-one.

The surprise results touched off a frantic quest by the local and foreign media for "the real F. W. de Klerk," as it was immediately assumed that he was now the heir apparent to the presidency. Nobody at the time foresaw de Klerk's emergence as the great white reformer of the National Party. One of the *Johannesburg Star*'s political reporters, Esmare van der Merwe, wrote on election night that "the consensus" among white political leaders outside the National Party was that de Klerk was "too conservative for the challenges currently facing the country." The *Star*'s chief political reporter, Peter Fabricius, predicted that de Klerk would plod along the same road of zigzag reform as President Botha, "with little major innovation." And the *Sunday Star*'s chief political analyst, David Brier, questioned whether de Klerk had the "steel in his teeth," the *kragdadigheid*, or political guts, necessary to carry through on the tough reforms called for. He quoted Helen Suzman, the most outspoken white liberal in Parliament, as saying, "I can't see [de Klerk] removing the foundation stones of apartheid."

One of the rare predictions to appear in print that de Klerk might be the right man at the right time came from the American political scientist Robert I. Rotberg. In an op-ed piece in the March 15 *International Herald Tribune*, he raised the possibility that "just as President Nixon was able to go to China, so Mr. de Klerk could be the leader to go, metaphorically, to Soweto or Lusaka." As it turned out, Rotberg was right, but his prediction went unheeded. Botha himself had gone to Soweto with great fanfare in 1979, and it hadn't made much difference. Little wonder, then, that when de Klerk, in his first speech to Parliament as National Party leader, spoke of his vision of a "totally changed South Africa free of domination or oppression in whatever form," nobody paid too much attention. It just sounded like more empty rhetoric, more hollow Afrikaner promises.

It is easy to make judgments with the benefit of hindsight, but it is nonetheless true that de Klerk's political career prior to 1989 gave no hint that he was anything but a political conservative with a deep faith in the fundamentals of the apartheid system. He was a strong proponent of the "own affairs" concept of government, which stressed each racial community's separateness and its right to its own cultural, social, and political institutions. At the National Party's federal congress in August 1986, it was de Klerk who had given the speech on the party's unshakable commitment to "group rights," a code word for the defense of white privileges and domination. During a debate in Parliament in 1988, he had insisted that the National Party "demands as a basic pattern that [each race's] own residential areas be maintained, that [our] own state schools are not threatened . . . and that this is also done by maintenance of [our] own facilities." William Claiborne remarked in the *Washington Post* that after serving seventeen years in Parliament and holding six different cabinet posts, de Klerk was not associated with a single piece of reform legislation. On the contrary, it was de Klerk who in 1986 had pressed President Botha to insist that Pik Botha publicly retract a statement he had made suggesting that South Africa might one day have a black president under whom he could serve.

De Klerk was also widely believed to have been the decisive influence on President Botha's last-minute decision to back off from announcing any significant reforms in his infamous "Rubicon speech" of August 1985. (South African political commentators dubbed it his Rubicon speech because Botha had been expected to take an irreversible leap toward opening negotiations with black leaders.) However, Robert Schrire, one of South Africa's best analysts of white politics, gave me a different version of the internal struggle over Botha's speech. He asserted that it had been Heunis, not de Klerk, who had convinced Botha to avoid announcing any major policy initiatives at that point.

In any case, it was true that some of de Klerk's actions as education minister between 1984 and 1989 were disturbing to liberals and reformers. He had fought to keep blacks out of white universities, and he had sponsored a bill in Parliament that would have enabled him to use the power of the purse to force universities to crack down on anti-apartheid agitators on campus. The bill passed, but the Supreme Court in the Cape Province subsequently ruled the law invalid.

The South African media also went back to examine the views of de Klerk's wife, Marike, and discovered that on occasion she had spoken like an outright racist. The Afrikaans-language liberal weekly *Vrye Weekblad* unearthed a speech she had given at an old-age home some years earlier, and a summary of her views was republished in the *Sunday Star* of Johannesburg just three days after de Klerk had been elected party leader. Marike had described the three million mixed-raced, brown-skinned Coloured people as "a negative group" of "non-persons" who were South Africa's historic "leftovers." The Coloureds, who constitute about 8 percent of the population, are a racial group unique to South Africa, the offspring of white settlers who had indulged in illicit sexual relations with African women ever since the first Dutchman, Jan van Riebeeck, sailed into Table Bay in April 1652. They were sometimes euphemistically called "God's stepchildren." Marike argued in her speech that it was proper and prudent that a separate voters' roll had been created for them because there had been "great corruption and malpractice" prior to 1948, when the Coloureds had been on the same voters' registration roll as whites. As for the one million Indians living in South Africa, the descendants of imported railway workers, they at least had their own history and homeland, she said, though they still needed to be "supervised a little." Her attitude toward the black population was just as patronizing, but she at least believed they had political rights that should be recognized: "We must now give them political rights so that our political rights aren't threatened because whites remain the leaders in this country . . . and must always be considered first in any solution."

Marike continued to spark controversy after becoming white South Africa's "First Lady." She was held responsible for breaking up the engagement of her son Willem to a Coloured woman, Erica Adams, in February 1992. When their romance made headlines in 1990, Marike was widely reported in the local press as having become livid at the thought of her son marrying a Coloured. Erica recounted to friends that Marike, who sent Willem to study in England to separate the young lovers, "could almost not live with the idea of their affair." The pressure finally proved too much for Willem and he ended the romance.

Marike also raised the hackles of South Africa's feminists with some comments she made in May 1991 while accompanying her husband to the dedication of an International Pentacostal Church in Zuurbekom, outside Soweto. She told the women among the 20,000 assembled blacks that they were "not important. We are the ones who serve, who heal the wounds, who give love" to men. Sharon Lain, national president of the South African Federation of Business and Professional Women, told the local media she was "horrified" by Marike's comments. Helen Suzman asserted that women had more to do than "just being an appendage of their menfolk." Marike was stung by the reaction and still anxious to justify her remarks when I interviewed her in August 1992. She conceded that she was not a feminist herself, but insisted that her message at Zuurbekom had been totally misinterpreted. What she had intended to convey to the women there was their importance in making men into whatever they became. "Women never realize how important they are," she said.

De Klerk's first actions and statements after becoming party leader only seemed to confirm his conservative colors. In a major policy speech to the whites-only House of Assembly on May 18, 1989, he emphatically rejected the idea of a majoritarian system based on one person, one vote, arguing that that would be "unjust toward the electorate of this house and certain other groups and therefore totally unacceptable." He wanted, instead, a political system based on consensus, one that ensured that no group was able to dominate another, obviously meaning black domination of whites. In another parliamentary speech later that month, he reiterated that he was a strong believer in "own affairs" and said that this would have to be the basis of any negotiations with blacks. These ideas all featured prominently as official National Party policy leading up to the elections scheduled for September 6. De Klerk—who became acting state president in addition to party leader upon Botha's resignation in mid-August—prided himself on being one of the authors of the party platform. Only after he had become state president in September did de Klerk raise the hopes of liberals by freeing the first ANC political prisoners and allowing blacks to march through the cities, thus taking his first concrete, and often dramatic, steps toward reform.

For the most part, however, de Klerk kept his motives and future plans obscure. In an interview published in the *Washington Post* on November 26, de Klerk again reaffirmed his belief in the "own affairs" principle and said that any new constitutional arrangement would have to be based on "a balance of power" between "groups." He said he was determined to reach a settlement that would assure there would be no domination of blacks over whites or vice versa. He also rejected repeal of the Population Registration Act of 1950, which classified the population by race, until after a new constitution had been negotiated. Nor did he evidence any remorse over the inequities of apartheid as an ideology or a system. He conceded that apartheid, "as a philosophy," had not succeeded in solving "the problem," as he referred to the crush of the black population in white areas of the country. But he maintained that apartheid had made a positive contribution by creating four independent black homelands and six other self-governing ones.

These were hardly the views of a great reformer. No wonder many South African political analysts remained puzzled about de Klerk. The *Sunday Star* perhaps reflected the general bemusement in a story it ran on May 28, almost four months after de Klerk had become party leader. "Is the real F. W. de Klerk a smiling Jekyll of reform or the grim-faced Hyde of apartheid?" it asked, analyzing his ambivalent behavior under the headline "Will the Real F.W. Please Stand Up."

I was as interested as my local colleagues to fathom who the "real de Klerk" was. My first personal encounter with him was at the cocktail party the state president holds for foreign correspondents at the opening of Parliament every year. The one held in 1990 came on the Thursday following his historic February 2 speech to Parliament, three days before Nelson Mandela's walk to freedom. It was an incredibly exciting time for everybody, and I was convinced that de Klerk was another Gorbachev in the making. After all, he had just shown an impressive boldness of decision and the readiness to take enormous political risks. I easily discovered other seeming parallels between the Soviet and South African leaders. It was not just that they both happened to be bald and in their fifties, de Klerk then fifty-three and Gorbachev fifty-nine. De Klerk, like Gorbachev, was offering a refreshing new style of leadership to his party and his country. Both represented a younger generation far more conscious of the media's power and usefulness, and both were aware of how to exploit it to project an appealing public persona to the outside world.

As soon as I saw de Klerk in action, he immediately struck me as a consummate politician. He was smiling and at ease as he worked the room. Cigarette in hand, chatting freely to one group of reporters after another, he answered every question thrown at him without a trace of hesitation. If his intention had been, as we expected, to mark a sharp contrast between his style and that of his predecessor, he had succeeded. Botha had been remote and uncommunicative, often openly hostile if a reporter happened to ask a touchy question. De Klerk was unflappable.

After listening to a number of conversations between de Klerk and other veteran correspondents, I decided to ask him what was on my mind. What did he think of the comparisons being drawn between himself and Gorbachev? Did he see himself playing the same kind of innovative, even iconoclastic, role in South African history? Without a second's hesitation, he dismissed the comparison, insisting that he was not acting on his own initiative the way Gorbachev had done; the reform program he was launching had been agreed upon earlier by the entire National Party leadership. The whole cabinet had discussed and approved the measures he had just announced, he told me. They were not "his" ideas, he insisted. They stemmed from changes under way in Nationalist thinking since at least July 1986, when the party had adopted its new concept of "power-sharing" aimed at finally incorporating the black majority into the political system. De Klerk seemed determined to convince me that he was only the point man and spokesman for his party, not an innovator on a solo flight.

His reply startled, even disappointed, me to some extent. He seemed too anxious to belittle himself and his own accomplishments. He struck me as overly modest, perhaps falsely so, for a man who had just delivered a speech reversing forty years of his own party's history, policies, and practices. Nonetheless, his responses made me think in a new way about de Klerk and his role in the unfolding reform process. I began looking into how the National Party had been changing over the past few years and how de Klerk himself had related to that change. My reassessment was spurred by an observation the rebel Afrikaner writer Rian Malan made in his excellent book, My Traitor's Heart, which I happened to read shortly afterward. The person who had struck Malan as the Gorbachev of South Africa was P. W. Botha, the very man everyone had just discarded into the dustbin of history as a stodgy, out-of-date autocratic ruler. Not only did Botha share with Gorbachev "the same sallow jowls, the same balding pate and a similar tendency to wag their fingers," remarked Malan, "both men inherited ideological sclerotic regimes and launched tentative reforms in the teeth of stiff opposition from vested interests and ideological purists." With Malan's and de Klerk's own comments in mind, I began reexamining the roots of the seemingly irreversible reform process now under way in my quest for "the real de Klerk."

F. W. de Klerk grew up in a family of Afrikaner politicians for whom the National Party had been the center of gravity for three generations. His great-grandfather, Jan van Rooy, had been a senator. His grandfather, Willem de Klerk, was a clergyman who had been active in party politics his entire life. His father, Jan de Klerk, was a senator who had served for fifteen years in the cabinets of three prime ministers, including Hendrik Verwoerd, the architect of Grand Apartheid. Jan de Klerk had also been president for seven years of the now defunct Senate. F.W.'s uncle by marriage was Prime Minister J. G. Strijdom, an uncompromising white suprema-cist who had led the campaign in the late 1950s to establish South Africa as an independent republic outside the British Common-wealth. In other words, the de Klerk family had been intimately involved in establishing the whole apartheid political system that its present scion was now proposing to dismantle. The de Klerk family history was distinctive in another aspect as well. They be-longed to the smallest of the three branches of the Afrikaner estab-lishment Dutch Reformed Church, the Gereformeerde Kerk, also commonly known as the Dopper Church. The Doppers, or funda-mentalists, were reputed to be the most attached to church dogma, the purists and conservatives of the Dutch Reformed Church. In a book he wrote about his brother in 1991, Willem de Klerk de-scribed F.W. as "an Afrikaner Calvinist" whose political values were grounded in a religious morality. Willem claimed that religion also explained his younger brother's strong conviction that the Afrikaners had to maintain their own culture, language, and his-tory in order to preserve their own identity, though the other Dutch Reformed groups seem just as attached to this notion. If de Klerk did harbor a religious conviction about the need to preserve the Afrikaner identity, this might help to explain his stout defense of "own affairs" even as he was launching his dramatic reform program. Yet it was abundantly obvious that many whites who were not religious at all believed just as passionately that each race should have its own separate institutions.

Marike de Klerk explained another aspect of the Dopper Church that gave me further insight into that strange and distant Afrikaner world of religious-political idealism. She impressed upon me that the Doppers were actually more liberal than the other Dutch Re-formed churches because they had been the first to become multi-racial. The Doppers held that each congregation was an autono-mous decision-making body and free to integrate or not, "according to its own circumstances." In this manner, the Doppers had taken the controversy out of the issue of racial integration and removed it from the national church leadership's agenda. "That's what we're looking for in the constitution as well," she added, referring to the government's insistence on community group rights. But not every Dopper congregation had decided to become multi-racial, and whether they were really any more liberal than the other Dutch Reformed sects was seriously questionable: in January 1991, the Gereformeerde Kerk's national synod came out in favor of continued segregated education, citing the "differences in life-style" of South Africa's various ethnic groups. This was just part of apartheid's old "own affairs" philosophy disguised in new language. Altogether, it seemed to me that a deeply religious Dopper, as de Klerk was portrayed by his wife and brother, could easily harbor inherently ambiguous feelings about reform: he might be able to perceive the injustices of apartheid on a religious basis, but still be driven by a political imperative to preserve the Afrikaners' separate identity.

De Klerk's Dopper affiliation also explained in part another attitude that would later cause considerable controversy: his steadfast refusal to agree that apartheid had been a "sin." De Klerk faced a lot of pressure to make a public confession to this effect. South Africa's greatest playwright, Athol Fugard, told a group of us foreign correspondents over lunch one day that "as long as he doesn't say, 'I'm sorry, forgive me,' I can't believe him." I once asked de Klerk what he thought about the debate raging within the Dutch Reformed Church—and indeed, within the entire white community—over whether apartheid should be considered a "sin" requiring a formal "confession." He became emotional and defensive, saying that he did not feel any need to apologize for apartheid. Verwoerd and its other Afrikaner forefathers had done their best to advance the interests of the black majority. Apartheid wasn't inherently wrong, he said, and no "evil" intent toward the black population had ever motivated its architects; the homeland system, promising blacks their own independent states with full political rights, simply had not worked out.

South Africa's apartheid masters did their best to separate as much of the black population from the white nation as possible until the economic, social, and political costs became prohibitive.

The scheme that was envisaged gave each of the ten main African ethnic groups its own homeland, which in stages would develop into a fully independent state. By 1981, there were four "independent" homelands—Transkei, Ciskei, Venda, and Bophuthatswana—and six other "self-governing" ones, all heavily dependent on South African government financing for their survival.

De Klerk's total lack of recognition that there was anything inherently morally wrong with apartheid shocked me, but it did help to explain something that had struck me all along about his speeches: the absence of any attempt to justify, or argue for, his reforms on moral grounds. He seemed to have no moral imperative steering him in what he was doing. Unlike Gorbachev, de Klerk never engaged in "de-Stalinization" within the National Party, which would have required the renunciation of apartheid's founding fathers and their ideology. He didn't defend his predecessors publicly, but mostly remained silent and tried to ignore the whole problem of the morality, or lack of morality, in a system based on strict racial segregation. On one rare occasion, after his victory in the March 1992 white referendum, the president gave his version of apartheid as an "idealism" that in practice had gone wrong. "What started out as idealism in the quest for justice," he said, "could not attain justice for all South Africans and therefore it has to be abandoned."

It was not until October 9, 1992, that de Klerk publicly offered an "apology," but not a "confession of sin" about apartheid. At a speech in the small Afrikaner town of Winburg, he said: "For too long, we clung to a dream of separated nation-states when it was already clear that it could not succeed. For that we are sorry." But, he quickly added, apartheid had not been evil by intent. "Yes, we have often sinned . . . But that we were evil, malignant, and mean— to that we say no." Altogether, the motivation behind de Klerk's great reforms was not the belief that apartheid was inherently wrong, evil, or sinful; it had a utilitarian impetus—it had simply failed to work.

Despite de Klerk's ambiguous public pronouncements on apartheid, there was arguably no person better suited to lead the reform process within the National Party. He was, after all, a true, blue-blooded Nationalist and a son of the Afrikaner "establishment." Though de Klerk's family had never been particularly wealthy, like the Kennedys or Rockefellers, they were nonetheless typical of the modern, urbanized Afrikaners whose power derived mainly from holding political office and controlling the machinery of state. De Klerk's father had been a schoolteacher in Mayfair, a working-class district of Johannesburg when the future state president was born on March 18, 1936. The boy's early life saw constant changes of address as his father was transferred from school to school; F.W. himself attended seven primary schools in seven years. Jan de Klerk quit teaching in 1945 to become first a trade union official and then a National Party secretary in the Johannesburg regional office. His two sons literally grew up on the hustings with their father. At age twelve, F.W. found himself counting returns in the 1948 election that brought the National Party to power.

F.W. was later sent to an Afrikaner boarding school in Krugersdorp, outside Johannesburg, for his high school education, where he distinguished himself as a debater and a Latin scholar. He attended Potchefstroom University for Christian Higher Education, the most prestigious college run by the Dopper Church, where he got his B.A., and then a law degree in 1958. Like his elder brother, he plunged into student and National Party politics on campus. He was elected vice president of the Students' Representative Council, an executive member of the Afrikaanse Studentebond (an Afrikaner youth organization), and editor of the university newspaper.

He was also, according to no less an authority than his wife, quite a ladies' man. Marike told me that F.W. was extremely sensitive to "beautiful things" in the world, with an almost artistic temperament that attracted women then and was still evident thirty-five years later. She ascribed this special quality to his upbringing: his mother had wanted a girl as a second child but was given another boy. "He grew up as an only child with his mother," she told me, because Willem was eight years older and his father was often absent from the house. Marike and F.W. first met when they were both students at "Potch," under hardly propitious circumstances. Her boyfriend at the time had made her go to a university rag, or dance, in a homemade car that would start only when it was pushed. The boyfriend showed up with a few friends, including F.W., who after pushing the car a few times with her in it failed to ignite the motor. Marike, feeling humiliated by this treatment, became furious, and fled the car, her boyfriend, and his friends. The upshot was that F.W. came to her later to present his apologies and a box of chocolates. "He asked my pardon and handed over the chocolates," she said. "And when he got home to his residence, he told his roommate that tonight he had met his wife." Marike surmised that it was her anger that had attracted him. The university lovers were married in 1959, when she was twenty-two and he at twenty-three was fresh out of law school and still unemployed and penniless. In fact, Marike had to pay for her wedding ring, their honeymoon, and all their living expenses for the first two years of their marriage.

After serving an apprenticeship in a Pretoria law firm, de Klerk in 1961 bought his own practice in Vereeniging, a town in the industrial heartland of the Transvaal thirty miles south of Johannesburg. He was highly successful as a lawyer there, but he cut short his career in 1972 when the National Party, with which he had remained active since his student days, asked him to run for Parliament. He accepted and won, beginning at age thirty-six what was to be a meteoric rise through the party ranks. Barely six years later, he was selected by Prime Minister John Vorster to serve as minister of posts and telecommunications. It was de Klerk, Marike told me, who masterminded the circumvention of international sanctions to purchase the country's first digital phone system, along with the guarantee of spare parts to keep it running.

Over the next eleven years, de Klerk went on to hold five other cabinet posts. He was a generally bland technocrat at first, and only began attracting public notice after becoming education and home affairs minister in 1984. As education minister, he became a target of the anti-apartheid movement because the only reform of the educational system he would entertain was an equalization of spending for white, black, and Coloured schoolchildren. Even this "separate but equal" approach was vetoed by President Botha. Marike de Klerk reckoned that her husband first emerged into the political consciousness of the white community around 1982, when he became National Party chairman for the Transvaal Province following the defection of Andries Treurnicht and the twenty-one others who immediately walked out in protest after the idea of sharing power with nonwhites, even the Coloureds and Indians, was raised in a tricameral Parliament. De Klerk's job was to stop the hemorrhage of National Party members into Treurnicht's new Conservative Party, and he seems to have acquitted himself well, but only by highlighting his own conservative views.

De Klerk became chairman of the ministers' council in the House of Assembly in 1985, and eighteen months later the Leader of the House, the equivalent of the Speaker in the U.S. House of Representatives. What stands out in his political curriculum vitae is that de Klerk made his way up the party and government ladders without becoming tainted by any scandal and never having held any "security" cabinet positions. (He thus never belonged to President Botha's coterie of securocrats.) Altogether, his cabinet career had left no strong impression on anyone outside inner Afrikaner circles. Robert Schrire, who has studied de Klerk closely, observed that he was never very energetic or forceful as a minister, and certainly not "a detail man," preferring to leave the running of the various departments he oversaw to his subordinates.

The man who led the National Party's momentous break with its own ideological past was not de Klerk but his predecessor, P. W. Botha, who had come into office in 1978 and remained there for eleven years. For it was during Botha's presidency that the irrevocable split in the National Party resulted in the formation of the rival Conservative Party. Though the split was wrenching, it at least had the beneficial effect of allowing the National Party's own internal "reform" process to go forward. The first step was the establishment in 1983 of the tricameral Parliament that gave separate houses to the Coloured and Indian communities. Then came the adoption in 1986 of a new party platform accepting what was for the National Party the revolutionary notion of "sharing power" with the black majority. The party also gave up the apartheid dream of segmenting South Africa into ten independent statelets, calling for an "undivided South Africa" and "one citizenship" for all South Africans, black or white. In terms of Nationalist thinking, acceptance of these ideas meant turning the party's back once and for all on Verwoerd's Grand Apartheid scheme of spinning off the black population into separate homelands, leaving whites in control of 87 percent of the land and almost 100 percent of its mineral resources. It was a choice of integration rather than segregation, unity rather than division, and it had all happened under Botha's iron-fisted rule over the party. If these changes were the outcome of a slow collective process of reform thinking under way within the party's inner circle, the fact remained that without Botha's consent they could never have gone forward.

By the mid-1980s, however, Botha had turned into a crotchety autocrat with a reputation for savaging his critics and snapping at his colleagues that became so bad he was nicknamed "the old crocodile." Throughout this period of transition in Nationalist thinking, de Klerk played a modest but increasingly central role within the party's inner sanctum. F.W., like his wife, dated the change in his role to his election as Transvaal leader in 1982. He told his brother that from that point on, he became an active participant in "the design, adjustment, development and renewal" of policy. But there is no evidence to show that de Klerk was "a closet reformer" who played a major role behind the scenes in reformulating National Party thinking about apartheid. He was a follower, not a leader; a lawyer, not a free-thinking visionary. He was good at assessing his colleagues' arguments and reform proposals rather than putting forward his own measures.

The real ideological innovators seemed to have been men like Gerrit Viljoen, the former head of the secret Broederbond, the Afrikaners' ideological think tank (or, literally, "Brotherhood" of Afrikanerdom's leading intellectuals, politicians, and educators who had once guided the party) who served as de Klerk's first constitutional affairs minister; Chris Heunis, Botha's chief reform thinker; Stoffel van der Merwe, who held various ministerial posts in Botha's cabinet while popularizing American and Western theories of power-sharing in multi-racial societies; and Piet de Lange, head of the Broederbond after Viljoen. Schrire, who has interviewed de Klerk on several occasions, said he was always struck by the president's lack of familiarity with constitutional models and issues. He found him "profoundly ignorant" about such things as the Swiss constitution and how Swiss cantons worked, even though the Nationalists had seized upon Switzerland as a model in formulating their own negotiating proposals in 1991. He also felt that de Klerk had never carefully thought through the constitutional implications of "group rights," the notion that initially held sway among Nationalist reformers until their own party turned multi-racial in 1990. For example, how could de Klerk both defend ethically or racially based communities and promote multi-ethnic political parties? Altogether, Schrire found the state president a "profoundly nice" person but also "profoundly ordinary."

By virtually all accounts, de Klerk owed much of his popularity in the National Party to his congenial personality. While he had a lawyer's way of analyzing problems and events, he was never abrasive or confrontational. Always good humored and friendly, he sought compromise and reconciliation instead, according to one of his closest colleagues, Dawie de Villiers, the National Party leader in the Cape Province. His brother described him in his early adulthood as hail-fellow-well-met in character, "a joker and the soul of every party." This fit Marike's own description of him as "something of a ladies' man."

De Klerk has taken particular pride in being a good "team player." The team in his case was the National Party, while for Botha and the securocrats it had been the military-security complex. His brother called F.W. "Mr. National Party," so dedicated was he to that institution. I asked de Klerk in an August 1992 interview why, given his reputation as a conservative, he had decided to stay with the National Party rather than join the Conservatives in their breakaway movement. De Klerk said the image created of him as a conservative had not "done me justice." He had always defended reform efforts within the party, he said, and always "placed the emphasis on the absolute necessity that any solution in South Africa must afford full justice to all the people of this country." The party had been going through "a deep self-analysis" ever since 1978 and had finally decided on a fundamental change away from its apartheid policies. It had been Botha, he said, who had made power-sharing the "formula for the future and I wholeheartedly supported him in that." He had never "for a moment" considered leaving the National Party. "I was part of the internal reform process of the National Party and always enthusiastic about the need for fundamental reform of our policies." His *verkrampte* reputation, he said, stemmed from his leading role in trying to hold back the conservative tide in the Transvaal, and his need to convince those of uncertain party faith not to switch allegiances. Marike said her husband always wanted to work from within to change the party, so, she said, "nobody knew on the outside what his views were except to be loyal." A less sympathetic view of de Klerk's cabinet career was offered just after his election as party leader by the *Weekly Mail*, which found that it bore a striking resemblance to the career of the new American president, George Bush. De Klerk, like Bush, was "a man who has left no footprints." Nobody could really remember what he had done in most of the cabinet posts he had held. The general consensus of his colleagues was that de Klerk was "solid but unimaginative; of unquestionable integrity but not inventive; powerful but cautious." Schrire later summed up de Klerk to me as "a classic over-achiever," a man who had done far better than anything that his personality, career, or public statements would have indicated.

De Klerk first displayed his prowess as an exceptionally astute politician in how he handled relations with P. W. Botha, who for a little more than six months lingered on as state president while no longer National Party leader. There was no precedent for such a sharing of executive powers, and the autocratic Botha was not an easy man to deal with. The two disagreed on when elections should be called, and even over whether de Klerk should travel abroad. De Klerk let the pressure build up within the party leadership against Botha without seeming to be the instigator of the revolt. Within six weeks of de Klerk's election as party leader, the entire party caucus had risen up against Botha.

The crisis came to a head in mid-March when Botha, still recovering from his stroke and temporarily suspended from exercising his powers as state president, announced that he was resuming his presidential office. The National Party's highest body, the federal council, and the parliamentary caucus both voted in favor of his resigning the presidency instead. Botha refused to budge, and in a nationally televised interview on March 12, he vowed to stay on until the next general election—which he intended to postpone for a full year. "I don't believe in usurping the Lord's work ahead of time," he said. A day later, the party caucus delivered a stunning rebuke to Botha, unanimously adopting a resolution that it would be in the best interest of the country if Botha stepped down and de Klerk took over. Still, the "imperial president" refused to listen, and his stubbornness only increased support for de Klerk, who found himself under extremely heavy pressure to challenge Botha head on. Confrontation, however, was not de Klerk's preferred style of combat; he used the support he had consolidated within the party to force Botha into a compromise that called for the elections in September 1989 instead of March 1990.

The final showdown between de Klerk and Botha came in August over whether de Klerk should make a trip to Lusaka to meet Zambian President Kenneth Kaunda. In the expectation that he would be the next state president, de Klerk wanted to begin the process of building new bridges to black Africa, starting with the so-called frontline states, those immediately to the north of South Africa. Botha was dead set against de Klerk's trip, even though the party leader had the full support of the cabinet. For Botha, Lusaka was the den of "the enemy," since it was the headquarters of the African National Congress, against which he had battled for virtually all of his presidency. It was "inopportune," he said, for de Klerk to meet Kaunda on the eve of a general election that the ANC was seeking to disrupt.

The cabinet, however, was unconvinced, and every minister let it be known that Botha had become a major political liability to the party and that his continued presence posed a danger for its victory over the Conservatives in the September 6 elections. It was de Klerk, however, who spoke first, saying, "We believe, therefore, that the least painful solution for you, for the National Party, and for all of us would be that you move to the Wilderness and say that you have decided to appoint an acting state president from now until after the election." Wilderness, an aptly named oceanside resort 275 miles east of Cape Town, was the location of Botha's private residence. According to his own account of that last stormy cabinet session, Botha rejected a suggestion that he use his poor health as an excuse, saying he was not going to leave "on a lie." So when he did leave, on August 15, 1989, he did so spitting venom at his colleagues and warning de Klerk to get his relationship with

God in good order for what was coming. De Klerk was named acting president.

The National Party emerged from the September 1989 elections with a thin margin of victory. It attracted only 48 percent of the total 2.2 million white votes, the first time in thirty years that the Nationalists had received less than an absolute majority. The party was now a minority within the white minority. Though they retained control of Parliament, they had lost twenty-seven seats. The Conservative Party, dead set against any reform, loomed large over the white political landscape, its thirty-nine seats making it the official opposition in Parliament.

De Klerk, however, saw that there was another way of looking at the outcome. The National Party, after all, had won a higher percentage of the white vote in the 1989 election than it had boasted upon taking power in 1948. Yet that 41 percent plurality had been sufficient to implement the sweeping legislation that first codified apartheid. In addition, this time the National Party had an ally for its reforms in the relatively liberal Democratic Party, formed earlier in 1989, which had gained 21 percent of the vote and 33 seats in Parliament. The two parties together had nearly 70 percent of the white electorate behind them and controlled 126 of the 166 seats in the white house of Parliament. De Klerk could argue, as he often did in the months and years ahead, that he had a solid white mandate to introduce sweeping reforms.

4

CROSSING THE RUBICON?

The annual opening of Parliament in late January or early February is always an elaborate ceremony. The president delivers a speech that is the equivalent of an American president's State of the Union message to Congress. The wives of cabinet ministers and their guests all attend, dressed in their Easter Sunday finery, including brightly colored wide-brimmed hats, briefly turning the Parliament grounds in downtown Cape Town into a scene reminiscent of the annual British fashion displays at Ascot and Henley. The government holds a week of briefings by its top cabinet ministers for foreign correspondents, and the president presides at a cocktail party where he talks casually with his guests for two hours. It is the only time of the year when the government formally puts itself and its policies on display for the world to see and question.

In 1990, everybody knew the opening of Parliament was going to be a very special occasion in the history of South Africa. The new state president had promised a "New South Africa, a totally changed South Africa," upon his election in September, and his office had put out the word that he intended to set forth his reform program in his address to Parliament. Hundreds of foreign newspaper, radio, and television reporters began flooding into the country, and visas, normally extremely difficult to obtain, were suddenly available for the asking. It was de Klerk's grand debut on the

72

international scene and he seemed determined not to disappoint his global audience the way P. W. Botha had in August 1985 with his famous Rubicon speech.

This time the world expected de Klerk to announce, among other reforms, that Nelson Mandela would at last be set free. On that account, the world had been bitterly disappointed before by South Africa's white leaders. In fact, great expectation followed by bitter disappointment had long been the norm. William Claiborne, my predecessor as the *Washington Post's* correspondent, had reported periodically on Mandela's "imminent release" for four years but ended his tour of duty without ever seeing him set free. Still, this time the buildup seemed to have been carefully orchestrated and the scene set for just such an announcement. Botha had astounded whites, blacks, and the world alike by meeting Mandela the previous July 5 at his presidential offices in Cape Town, and then announcing that he had done so.

De Klerk, too, had already done his share of astounding in the six months of his presidency. On September 13, the day before his formal installation as state president, he granted permission for more than 20,000 anti-apartheid activists to march through the streets of Cape Town. This was such an extreme alteration in government attitude toward permissible opposition activity that everyone immediately sensed a change in the political wind. Then, on October 15, he released all the remaining Rivonia trialists except Mandela, along with two leaders of the United Democratic Front and the Pan Africanist Congress. Their release was followed by the granting of permission for ANC followers to hold a welcome-home rally seven days later in the huge Soccer City Stadium outside Soweto. The stadium, which holds 80,000 people, was packed.

In a society where black political activity had been taboo for decades, the very occurrence of such events was precedent-setting. And it didn't stop. On November 16, at the start of the South African summer, de Klerk announced that the Separate Amenities Act, which enforced racial segregation in public facilities, was to be scrapped, and he dramatized the change by opening the beaches to all races. Twelve days later, he scuttled the National Security Management System, the machinery of police and military repression set up by President Botha to hold the anti-apartheid movement in check. Then, on December 13, he met with Mandela to take his own measure of the man and begin laying the groundwork for the kind of personal relationship that would be necessary if a nego-tiated settlement were to be undertaken. Like Botha, sending a signal, he let it be known that the meeting had taken place. This set of initial measures quickly won for de Klerk the image at home and abroad of being another Mikhail Gorbachev in the making.

Such was the atmosphere of high hopes and great expectations in which de Klerk addressed Parliament on February 2, 1990. It had been exactly one year since his ascension to leadership of the National Party. As it turned out, de Klerk not only lived up to the expectations, but exceeded them. His speech was truly a watershed in South African history. Even the best-informed Western diplo-mat in the country, Britain's Sir Robin Renwick, was surprised by the sweep of the reforms de Klerk announced that day in a calm, sure voice that seemed almost to play down their scope and signifi-cance. It is even more remarkable that de Klerk kept his decisions a secret from just about everybody. He had not told his own National Party leadership what he intended to announce that day, though the cabinet had already discussed and generally approved at an informal *bosberaad,* or party brainstorming session held in the bush, the release of Mandela and other possible reforms in Novem-ber 1989, not long after the fall of the Berlin Wall. But de Klerk's "bush palaver" had dealt in generalities. It was left up to de Klerk to choose the timing and sequence of the reforms everyone knew had to come.

The state president drafted most of his address the previous day after receiving input from various ministers, none of whom saw the final text. They couldn't have reviewed it even if they had wanted to, for de Klerk didn't finish writing it until well after midnight. He finally went to bed about 2 A.M., and was back in Parliament nine hours later to deliver his address.

With the world listening to his speech, thanks to CNN and other direct international coverage, de Klerk set the scene for his momen-tous announcement with these words:

> The general election of September the sixth, 1989, placed our country irrevocably on the road to drastic change. Underlying

this is the growing realization by an increasing number of South Africans that only a negotiated understanding among the representative leaders of the entire population is able to ensure a lasting peace. The alternative is growing violence, tension, and conflict. That is unacceptable and in nobody's interest. The well-being of all in this country is linked inextricably to the ability of the leaders to come to terms with one another on a new dispensation. No one can escape this simple truth.

On its part, the government will accord the process of negotiations the highest priority. This aim is a totally new and just constitutional dispensation in which every inhabitant will enjoy equal rights, treatment, and opportunity in every sphere of endeavor—constitutional, social, and economic.

De Klerk's cascade of reform announcements came in no coherent pattern or order as he skipped from one issue to another. He began by suggesting that it was time for a new era in South Africa's relations with its black African neighbors, and then switched to the four nominally independent homelands, suggesting they should be incorporated back into South Africa.

Next came human rights and the need for a bill of rights justifiable before an independent judiciary. But the rights of minorities, "national entities," and other groups also had to be guaranteed, he said. Meanwhile, the death penalty was being suspended—and all executions halted—until new procedures were adopted to limit its application and guarantee the condemned every chance to appeal a sentence.

After discussing the need for structural changes in the economy, to reduce the size and role of the government and enhance those of the private sector through privatization of state companies, de Klerk finally got to the crux of his speech: the process of negotiating a settlement with South Africa's black leaders and the obstacles in the way. He intended to sweep away all the latter by:

1) lifting the ban on the ANC and Umkhonto we Sizwe, the Pan Africanist Congress, and the South African Communist Party, as well as ending restrictions on the free activity of thirty-three other organizations;
2) releasing all those arrested or imprisoned for merely belonging

to all these parties and organizations, plus 374 people imprisoned under emergency security rules;

3) reforming the emergency security laws to limit the length of time for holding anyone in detention to six months, and to ensure detainees access to lawyers or doctors of their own choosing;

4) lifting the nationwide state of emergency, except in Natal Province, as soon as possible;

5) abolishing the emergency media regulations that restricted coverage of black political activities; and

6) repealing the Separate Amenities Act of 1953, which provided the legal basis for so-called petty apartheid, segregating public facilities that included restaurants, buses, parks, beaches, toilets, and even fishing grounds.

De Klerk left his announcement about Mandela's release for his grand finale. He noted the need to get negotiations for a peaceful settlement under way as soon as possible, and argued that Nelson Mandela "could play an important part." The government had made a firm decision, he said, to release Mr. Mandela "unconditionally" and would do so "without delay."

The state president ended his proclamation with dramatic flair:

> History has thrust upon the leadership of this country the tremendous responsibility to turn our country away from its present direction of conflict and confrontation. Only we, the leaders of our people, can do it.
>
> The eyes of responsible governments across the world are focused on us. The hopes of millions of South Africans are centered on us. The future of South Africa depends on us. We dare not falter or fail.

With his speech, de Klerk had set the stage for the wholesale destruction of Grand Apartheid, the normalization of black political activities, the end to the apartheid police state, and the start of negotiations with the country's black leaders. He was opening up a breathtaking landscape of a new political order before all South Africans, but this time for blacks in particular.

His justification for releasing Mandela was a masterpiece of political rhetoric. Mandela had an important part to play in the unfolding of a peaceful political process, and the black leader had already declared himself willing to make a "constructive contribution." This was a formula devised to get around Mandela's refusal to renounce violence, meaning armed struggle, one of the conditions for his release that P. W. Botha had set down years earlier. The other was that the ANC should break up its alliance with the Communist Party. Mandela had always refused to accept these conditions. De Klerk had carefully stated that Mandela's release was "unconditional." What this meant in political code was that he had given up trying to extract from Mandela commitments to end the ANC's armed struggle or to break its alliance with the SACP.

De Klerk was just as crafty in his choice of words in his discussion of the economy and economic reforms. His terminology made it seem as if he were addressing the World Bank and International Monetary Fund rather than the South African Parliament. He used words like *structural adjustment* and *privatization* and *deregulation* and talked of restricting government expenditures and shrinking government control over the economy. "We still persist with the implementation of the required structural adjustments," he said. He even seemed to have an eye on Washington, where the Reagan and Bush administrations had made a fetish of supply-side economics. De Klerk promised that his government would "give particular attention to the supply side of the economy."

De Klerk was fully aware that what he was announcing would come as an enormous shock to his white constituency, brought up to believe that the ANC was a godless, communist organization, not to mention the Communist Party itself. So he had included a long justification for his actions, defending them on security and political grounds. The government could afford to unban all these organizations, he said, because of the collapse of any support for their cause from the Soviet Union and Eastern European communist countries. This meant that they were no longer as much of a threat to the internal security of the country as they had been in the past. In addition, the attitude of the ANC toward negotiations with the white government had changed; it now was demonstrating "a preference for peaceful solutions." The lifting of the bans on anti-apartheid organizations did not signal any change in the government's tough attitude toward law and order, he assured whites, nor a change in its intention to deal firmly with "terrorism" and political violence. The state of emergency would be ended "as soon as circumstances justify it," but not a day earlier. But there were solid political reasons for legalizing opposition politics: "It is time for us to break out of the cycle of violence and break through to peace and reconciliation. The silent majority is yearning for this."

The president announced no firm date for Mandela's release, but said he wanted to bring "this matter to finality without delay." He reminded his national and international audience that it was normal to have a certain time lag between a government's decision to release a prisoner of Mandela's stature and his actual freedom because of what he called "logistical and administrative requirements." Mandela was no ordinary prisoner and hadn't been for some time; there were "factors" in the way of his immediate release, including "his personal circumstances and safety." Before the closing words of his speech, de Klerk appealed to the country's black nationalist leaders to end their recourse to "violence" now that they were to be allowed free political activity. "Walk through the door and take your place at the negotiating table together with the government," he said. "The time for negotiation has arrived."

Outside the Parliament building, de Klerk's speech brought to a standstill an anti-apartheid demonstration by several thousand blacks. The crowd quietly dispersed as news of the ANC's unbanning spread. It was suddenly registering in the minds of all South Africans that de Klerk had just opened the floodgates to a new era in their country's history. He had gone much farther than anyone had expected, simultaneously announcing reforms that he had been expected to unveil sequentially over a number of months. An announcement about the release of Mandela was the only news everybody had expected, together with the unbanning of the ANC. But legalizing the South African Communist Party and even Umkhonto we Sizwe was totally unexpected. Whites were in a state of shock; blacks in one of disbelief. The long-term implication of what the state president had announced was the end of the old apartheid order, an end to the white monopoly of political power, land, privilege, and jobs. Could de Klerk really mean this?

The white Conservative Party, dedicated to defending apartheid, exploded, saying that de Klerk had no electoral mandate to do what he was doing. The Conservatives' claim was true; de Klerk had neither sought nor received support for such reforms during the 1989 election campaign. In fact, he had excoriated the liberal Democratic Party for its contacts with ANC "terrorists." The Conservatives demanded a new white general election, to be held immediately, to test support for de Klerk's reform program.

Anglican Archbishop Desmond Tutu seemed to sum up the black reaction when at a press conference that afternoon he said that de Klerk's speech seemed just "incredible" to blacks. "What he has said has certainly taken my breath away," he said, and it was time to "give him credit. I do." The ANC, whose top officials were in Stockholm visiting the organization's ailing president, Oliver Tambo, was not quite ready to do that. Still, it had to concede that the reforms de Klerk had launched were at least "progressive." The United Democratic Front "happily welcomed" the speech and conceded grudgingly "the boldness of some of the steps." But the black population did not wait for its leaders' approval to celebrate. The speech sent tens of thousands of blacks pouring into the streets of Cape Town, Johannesburg, and Durban to applaud what they regarded as the harvest of the first fruits of their long struggle for freedom. They again danced their *toyi-toyi* in the streets and shouted at the top of their lungs, "Amandla, Awethu": Power to the People.

De Klerk more than fulfilled all foreign expectations as well. He had already established himself as a master politician, one who knew how to use the media, timing, and dramatic effect to his maximum benefit and wrap his message in Western democratic terminology to please an international audience. He had carefully crafted his speech to meet all the world's demands of white South Africa over the previous three decades. A careful examination of his announced reforms showed that he had kept a close eye on the 1986 Comprehensive Anti-Apartheid Act passed by the U.S. Congress, which had imposed sweeping economic sanctions on South Africa and had spelled out five conditions to be met before any sanctions were lifted. These included the freeing of Mandela and all other persons imprisoned for their political beliefs; a legalization of political activities for blacks; the scrapping of the main legislative pillars of apartheid; and the opening of good faith negotiations with black leaders for a nonracial democracy. De Klerk had clearly put his government on a course toward fulfilling these conditions and similar ones imposed by the European Community.

Despite the euphoria, no one could agree as to whether change in South Africa was now "irreversible." The ANC cautioned against celebrating too soon, and urged the international community to keep the sanctions in place and thus maintain pressure on de Klerk. Indeed, many of the ANC's demands had not yet been met, such as the freeing of all political prisoners and the return of some 20,000 to 40,000 exiles. Nor had de Klerk at any point specifically accepted black majority rule. Moreover, some aspects of his address were deeply troubling to blacks, especially his insistence on the need for the protection of the rights of "minorities and national entities." Blacks knew these as code words for the white minority in any future black-ruled state.

Just as disturbing to many blacks were de Klerk's statements on economic policy, with his heavy emphasis on privatization and a cutback in government spending. Though all the black nationalist groups saw an imperative need for increased government expenditures on housing, schooling, and welfare, to overcome the legacy of apartheid and more than three centuries of white exploitation, de Klerk seemed to be abdicating his responsibility for these core issues. At the same time, blacks recalled that previous attempts at privatization had always resulted in the dismissal of tens of thousands of blacks from their jobs. The ANC and other groups were deeply suspicious; by touting privatization just as blacks were about to gain national power, the white government (it seemed) was simply trying to shift control of the economy to white-run private companies.

Despite these suspicions of de Klerk's true intentions, it was hard to see how de Klerk's or any future white government could ever again ban the ANC, the PAC, or the Communist Party. Any attempt to close the floodgates that had been thrown open would almost certainly provoke a mass uprising such as Eastern Europe had witnessed in 1989. Nor would the international community stand for a re-banning of the political opposition groups without harsh reprisals. No longer could the South African government wield the impressive array of security laws it had spawned to crush all opposition activity. The infamous Suppression of Communism Act would have to be scrapped now that the Communist Party was legal.

De Klerk was now routinely compared to Gorbachev, but the most striking parallel between the reform under way in South Africa and that in the Soviet Union was its unpredictability. In time, reform in the Soviet Union would lead to the total destruction of the Communist Party, as Gorbachev lost control of the reform process and was finally swept away by the forces he had unleashed. It was unclear in February 1990 what fate awaited de Klerk or Gorbachev, both of whom were ringing the death knell of the old order without knowing whether they could keep the resulting political forces under control.

From the beginning, there was a basic misunderstanding about what de Klerk intended when he used the word *reform*. Most local and foreign reporters just assumed that by unbanning the ANC and releasing Mandela, de Klerk was recognizing the historical inevitability of black majority rule. During the week of press briefings after his February 2 speech, his cabinet colleagues reinforced this impression with their constant harping on the need for ironclad guarantees for "minority rights" in any new constitution. This suggested strongly that the National Party had finally accepted blacks as the country's future ruling majority, with whites the political minority. But de Klerk, the long-time supporter of "own affairs," had also made it clear in an earlier speech as party leader that he was not ready to countenance black majority rule. In his February reform speech, he had carefully qualified his support for a bill of individual rights by saying minorities and "national entities" also needed guarantees. The new constitution had to take into account South Africa's "national composition" and "heterogeneous population." This meant, he stated plainly, that no racial group should be in a position to dominate another. He did not go any farther at that point to elucidate what he meant, but the intent was clear—he would not accept black domination even though whites comprised only 10 to 12 percent of the total population. In the excitement over his other announcements, no one paid much attention to this part of his speech. But it would soon become clear that all these terms were code words for a very special notion of how South African society should be reordered.

De Klerk and his National Party saw the New South Africa developing along the model of Switzerland, with separate "cantons" for each ethnic group. Each "national entity" had to be recognized, protected, and allowed its own institutions, just as the cantons of Switzerland did for its German, French, Italian, and Ladina populations. The result would be a loose confederation, in which the "white canton" could pretty much rule itself under a weak central government. De Klerk was far too clever to put forward such a controversial vision of a multi-racial society in February 1990. But this was "reform" of a very special kind, aimed not at giving blacks full majority rule but at precisely the opposite—containing their political power and control over the white minority. Within this context, the government's new economic policy of privatization also took on new meaning; it was part of the government's plan to decentralize all power, political and economic, away from the powerful central government the National Party had built up over four decades of absolute rule. This was not just de Klerk's individual vision of the New South Africa, it was that of the entire National Party's *verligte* leadership.

With de Klerk's speech on February 2, and Mandela's release nine days later, the scene was set for the last grand struggle over the dismantling of apartheid and the birth of a new order in the richest nation of Africa. The scene was also set for the final great battle between black African and Afrikaner nationalism. Both nationalisms had come to be divided internally by different visions of the future and by parties fighting for power and leadership of their respective communities. White Afrikaner nationalism was irrevocably split between its *verligte* and *verkrampte* wings. Diehard believers in the old apartheid order gravitated around Andries Treurnicht's Conservative Party, while those who felt the imperative need for some kind of reform belonged to de Klerk's National Party. Diehard white separatists were subdivided into various right-wing splinter groups proposing various last-ditch schemes for a new white homeland.

African nationalism was no monolithic movement, either. It was divided in at least three ways over differing visions of South Africa's society and polity. Mandela's African National Congress advocated the need for a nonracial nationalism, a melting pot of all the races working in partnership to build a multi-party democracy. The rival Pan Africanist Congress believed in pure black nationalism, meaning black control over the economy and government unfettered by white hands. And Chief Buthelezi's Inkatha Freedom Party propounded a form of "tribal nationalism," insisting that the Zulu "nation" be given special recognition and status. Buthelezi was far closer to the National Party's multi-ethnic view of South Africa, and its call for federalism to accommodate ethnic diversity, than to either the ANC or PAC in their demands for a strong unitary system.

Mandela and de Klerk, the two towering figures expected to reconcile this land of shattered nationalisms, held radically different visions of the New South Africa. Mandela wanted to reincorporate the ten nominally independent or self-governing homelands into a single united and strongly centralized state. His program was not overtly socialist, but it did provide for government control of the key sectors of the economy and the eventual redistribution of white wealth. His vision of the African nation and government had been the one commonly held ever since the former French, British, and Portuguese colonies had first gained their independence in the late 1950s. The first generation of African leaders had tried to forge nations and nationalisms out of loose collections of disparate tribes bound together by artificial colonial borders. They had also sought to establish African control over whatever modern economic sector the colonial powers had bequeathed to them. Their preferred ideology for accomplishing this difficult task had generally been either African socialism, Marxism-Leninism, African nationalism, or just plain statism. But the general drift in thinking about nation and state was very much the same, and the outcome after thirty years of independence had proved disastrous—autocratic one-man rule, the disintegration of government, the withering away of the state, and economic catastrophe.

De Klerk and his constitutional draftsmen would cite again and again the explosion of ethnic nationalisms in Eastern Europe to justify their vision of a multi-ethnic, federal nation, warning of grave consequences if South Africa's ethnic and racial diversity were not recognized and accommodated. But this vision was all too reminiscent of the old Afrikaner apartheid ideology to be acceptable to the country's black nationalist groups, who viewed it as one more clever Afrikaner scheme designed to keep as much power as possible in white hands.

Holding diametrically opposed views of the state, government, and society, Mandela and de Klerk each had to lead a fractious community toward a fabled New South Africa. Yet even as early as February 1990, their stated goal of national reconciliation seemed as distant and almost as mythical as the quest for the holy grail.

5

ANC, INC.

Ben Turok, an old-time militant Marxist, had long harbored doubts about the ANC. He was sure that one day, under pressure from the World Bank, the International Monetary Fund, and political realities, the Congress would jettison its commitment to socialism. So when Nelson Mandela stood up at the ANC's May 1992 policy conference to argue that nationalization should be set aside as an option, his worst fears seemed about to be confirmed. Turok, a white man in his sixties, had been one of the proud authors of the ANC's 1955 Freedom Charter, particularly its brief economic platform, which had stressed the movement's unequivocal commitment to nationalization. "The mineral wealth beneath the soil, the banks and monopoly industry shall be transferred to the ownership of the people as a whole," it said. "All other industries and trade shall be controlled to assist the well-being of the people." In 1992 the Charter was still formally the ANC's guiding ideological beacon, considered a sacred document by many of its leaders. But the pressures on the ANC leadership to abandon its socialist plank had become enormous. The de Klerk government, the country's four gigantic business conglomerates, the IMF and the World Bank, and virtually all Western governments were preaching free-market economics and urging privatization of South Africa's scores of state-owned companies. With the economy crumbling and the need for foreign investment enormous, the ANC as the likely future government could not just ignore these pressures.

Nationalization was so sensitive an issue that Mandela had formed a committee of senior officials under his chairmanship to rework the wording of ANC economic policy. He was putting his prestige and his considerable powers of persuasion on the line to scuttle the nationalization option. Mandela related to the policy conference his own experience in February at the World Economic Forum in Davos, Switzerland, where he had been counseled even by Communist China's representatives not to follow the road to socialism. He had been humiliated, he told the roomful of ANC policy-makers, to witness President de Klerk and Chief Buthelezi receiving a much longer round of applause than he had from the world's top business and financial representatives.

Turok finally stood up to take issue with Mandela. He was in a unique position to do so, having resigned from the South African Communist Party years earlier in protest against its Stalinist methods and rigid thinking. After assuring Mandela that he had the greatest respect for him, Turok started raising some embarrassing issues. He wanted to know how Mandela and the ANC could turn their backs on the Freedom Charter, and he predicted that there would be an enormous hue and cry when militants in the ANC and its labor union allies saw that nationalization had been abandoned, even as an option.

At first Turok was greeted with dead silence. "There was suddenly a lot of tension in the room," recalled one participant. Then, slowly, several others began standing up to add their voices to Turok's protest. Faced with this spontaneous outburst of opposition, Mandela did an amazing thing: He got up and told the conference that he had "reconsidered" and was withdrawing his proposal to drop nationalization as an option. It would remain in the text of the ANC's economic policy statement. The final wording read that the state would "consider increasing the public sector in strategic areas through, for example, nationalization, purchasing a shareholding in companies, establishing new public corporations or joint ventures." Not for the first time, or the last, had Mandela been defeated on a major policy issue.

◆　◆　◆

One of the least understood aspects of Mandela's leadership quandary—at least by observers from afar—was the constant challenge to his authority within his own movement. He spoke with such Moses-like authority at rallies and press conferences that many outsiders found it difficult to believe that he might not genuinely possess the political power he projected through his voice, demeanor, and gestures. But a closer inspection of the ANC in action revealed the enormous pressures on Mandela and the intrigues under way to sideline him.

The authoritarian streak in Mandela's personality aroused deep indignation and opposition among his own lieutenants, who set out to curb his independence and autonomy of action. Whether the issue was a policy, personnel, or organizational matter, the ANC leader had to battle to assert his authority, and he was often outmaneuvered. Mandela seemed at times like the giant Gulliver pinned to the ground by a mass of Lilliputians. Yet this war of attrition waged by those around him was not his only problem, for Mandela was also at war with himself over the issue of leadership. On the one hand, Mandela not only spoke like Moses, he acted as if he expected to be obeyed like Moses. On the other hand, he professed to believe strongly in the principle of "collective leadership." In reaction to a statement made by National Union of Mineworkers general secretary Cyril Ramaphosa, he told one visitor to his prison quarters shortly before his release that he had no intention to just "come out and take over the ANC's leadership." In his first post-prison speeches, he insisted time and again that he was a loyal and disciplined member of the ANC and was totally under its orders.

Yet Mandela had emerged from prison to find the ANC in the midst of a triple crisis of identity, leadership, and organization. It had been a "national liberation movement" waging an armed struggle for thirty years, but now the white South African and Western governments suddenly expected it to lay down its arms, disband its guerrilla army, and convert itself into a normal political party. Naturally, there was tremendous resistance to such an instant conversion within the ranks of the ANC; many militants firmly believed that the struggle should continue unabated until whites handed over power for good. Imperative to achieving this objective was the maintenance of a broad "movement" encompassing South

Africans of all races, ethnic groups, and ideological persuasions. There was also great opposition to turning the ANC into a "party," which would imply abandoning the armed struggle and drawing up a platform of specific economic and political goals. Even Mandela dreaded the prospect of having to define what the ANC stood for other than general "liberation"—the African majority winning the right to vote and taking power just as it had already done elsewhere on the continent. When he visited the offices of the *Washington Post* during his trip to the United States in June 1990, Mandela described the ANC as akin to the "Parliament of the African people," little more than a kaleidoscope of groups with vastly different political beliefs. "Some are conservatives. Others are liberals. We are united solely by our determination to oppose racial oppression," he said. There could be "no question of ideology" with the ANC, he continued, "because any question approaching ideology would split the organization from top to bottom." It was a remarkably frank assessment of the ANC's "identity crisis" and would remain valid for years to come.

This ideological confusion was accompanied by wrangling over the ANC's future leadership. De Klerk's unbanning order had created scramble for position and power among former political prisoners, exiles, internal activists, and underground operatives. The ANC resembled a holding company, or a gigantic conglomerate made up of many subsidiaries, each with its own leaders, "corporate" interests, and turf to defend—"ANC, Inc.," if you like. There were the exiled old guard, forming the temporary National Executive Committee (NEC); the new generation of activists from the mid-1980s who had given birth to the United Democratic Front (UDF); the independent labor union leadership grouped within the Congress of South African Trade Unions (COSATU); regional and township leaders; and the South African Communist Party.

The old guard consisted of the small group that had run the ANC from Lusaka, Zambia, without challenge or questioning from the rank and file. After thirty years in exile, people like ANC President Oliver Tambo and Secretary-General Alfred Nzo were unknown personalities in the townships, but were mostly just names shouted in slogans and seen on posters. This external leadership was closed, secretive, and distant. The NEC members—nine of them in 1969, thirty in 1985, and thirty-five in 1990—had for decades made all decisions on their own and had never been exposed to the questioning and criticism of the mass of their followers inside South Africa. Upon his release, Mandela quickly became identified with this group. Tambo, the victim of a stroke, was partially paralyzed and barely able to walk on his own, let alone lead the ANC. Mandela was made an honorary member of the NEC immediately and was then named deputy president. Everyone knew that Mandela's eventual appointment as president was just a matter of time. But until the ANC was able to convene its national conference in July 1991, the old guard tried to consolidate its power around Mandela but came under enormous criticism for a multitude of past and current mistakes.

The main challenge came from the UDF, whose leaders had remained inside South Africa and had fought the day-to-day battle against the repressive apartheid security machine. They resented the old guard's attempt to take over the new ANC leadership being established inside the country as well as the outside ANC's authoritarian style. While the UDF as an organization was shortly to disband, its leaders were integrating themselves into the new ANC structures and were thus in direct competition with the old guard for posts and power. An umbrella organization, the UDF had always maintained a highly decentralized and participatory leadership style, with literally hundreds of township leaders in constant contact with their followers. The UDF's democratic traditions, stressing local initiative and much grassroots discussion of any campaign, strike, or boycott undertaken, clashed with the secretive, autocratic behavior of the old guard. Mandela, authoritarian by temperament yet democratic in principle, immediately found himself torn between these two styles of leadership, especially once the two groups found themselves in sharp competition for the top positions after the ANC's unbanning.

Part of the UDF, yet separate in structure, were the labor unions, whose power had grown steadily, but independently, from the ANC since the mid-1980s. Cyril Ramaphosa was the most visible leader of the union movement. He had made his career and reputation as a tough negotiator in the 1987 mineworkers' strike, one of the largest in the country's history. Ramaphosa had already helped launch COSATU, the first black labor confederation, in 1985. COSATU always identified itself with the ANC and its goals but had never operated under the orders of the Lusaka leadership. After 1990, however, it formed a "tripartite alliance" with the ANC and the Communist Party to coordinate a common policy against the de Klerk government. In many instances, the ANC found itself adopting the militant tactics, such as national strikes and mass marches, of the labor movement.

It was not just at ANC headquarters in Johannesburg that Mandela's authority came to be challenged. Like the whole of the National Executive Committee, he would discover that he could exercise only limited influence over the ANC's fourteen regional offices and practically none at all over its roughly 750,000 members. "Regional autonomy" soon came to mean that the regions sometimes imposed their own immediate concerns onto the ANC national agenda. The decentralized UDF-led struggle against apartheid within the country gave rise to scores of local and regional leaders who came to have their own independent power bases. Men like Harry Gwala, with a base in Pietermaritzburg in the Natal Midlands region, and the Reverend Allan Boesak of Cape Town, a UDF founder and former president of the World Alliance of Reformed Churches, were regional powers unto themselves over whom the ANC leadership had little authority.

The most blatant example of this phenomenon occurred in the Midlands, Gwala's "fiefdom." Gwala at first glance seemed an unlikely leader, for he was totally paralyzed in the upper part of his body due to a prison illness, his arms hanging limply at his sides. He could walk and talk, but not much else. Yet he was a proud modern-day Stalinist, whose uncompromising militancy was idolized by the ANC youth. Gwala proudly defended Stalin and advocated head-on confrontation to eliminate Chief Buthelezi's Inkatha Freedom Party from the whole Midlands, even from the whole of Natal Province if possible. Gwala believed, and publicly said, that Inkatha "warlords" ought to be killed. He even wanted to organize a march to occupy Buthelezi's headquarters in Ulundi, a plan that was sure to cause massive bloodshed.

Whether he was directly responsible, the fact remained that professional "hit squads," nominally belonging to Umkhonto we

Sizwe, operated in his area and had succeeded in wiping out scores of middle-ranking Inkatha officials. Gwala publicly argued that the quickest way to establish peace throughout Natal was to win the war against Inkatha. His notion of a "peaceful solution" was to cite several Midlands areas that had become totally peaceful because his supporters had killed or chased away all Inkatha members. Having imparted his hardline attitude toward Inkatha to much of the ANC rank and file, Gwala made it impossible for Mandela or the National Executive Committee to make any peace overtures toward Inkatha unless he was first consulted and convinced that they were worthwhile.

The most important faction of ANC, Inc., was the South African Communist Party, which functioned less as a subsidiary than as an independent corporation under the same interlocking directorate. Under the ANC's long-standing policy permitting "dual membership" and "dual leadership," any ANC activist could be a member or leader of another political organization, be it the Communist Party, a labor union, a church group, or a "civic association" (one of the many small anti-apartheid groups organized in the townships during the 1980s that later became local institutions of government). In practice, the Communists made the fullest use of this policy, using the leadership roles in both organizations to move ANC positions more in line with those of the SACP. In the struggle for influence over the ANC, the Communists had the advantage of being enormously popular within the black community, enjoying a revolutionary mystique out of proportion to its real accomplishments in the anti-apartheid struggle. Joe Slovo had the standing of a white folk hero for millions of blacks, with scores of squatter camps and township streets named after him. His popularity was no doubt due in part to the government's demonization of him as the allegedly evil Communist genius behind the black liberation struggle. Next to Mandela, Slovo was probably the best known and most popular ANC leader returning to the country in the wake of de Klerk's unbanning order.

Slovo's high standing was in many ways an outgrowth of the general attraction to socialism among many in the black community, who equated apartheid not only with white oppression but with capitalism as well. Naturally, black majority rule came to be equated with socialism as well as freedom, and many of the best and the brightest among the country's black intellectuals, youth, and labor union leaders joined the SACP after its unbanning, defying the international pronouncement of the death of communism and "the end of history." "We say loud and clear that history has not ended," Slovo proclaimed at the party's Eighth National Congress in December 1991. "The corpse they are trying to bury is not true socialism."

Not only did communism flourish at the dawning of the New South Africa, but its proponents were extremely influential within ANC councils at all levels, from the National Executive Committee to township branches. Many of the ANC's chief negotiators in the constitutional talks with the government were either former or active Communist Party members, and no single group had more weight than the SACP in devising the tactics and strategy for dealing with the de Klerk government. Communists were in the forefront of every militant activity undertaken by the ANC, from the formation of "self-defense units" within the townships to the promotion of various "mass action" campaigns and major demonstrations. Their espousal of revolutionary tactics to bring down the government had enormous appeal for the township militants because it offered an outlet for their pent-up frustrations and anger. Yet, surprisingly, the party had no identifiable ideology or political strategy. In the classical terms of the French Revolution, South African Communists were both "Jacobins" and "Girondists," radicals and moderates. The party was also filled with "romantic revolutionaries" and advocates of "people's power" through grassroots democracy. About the only universally held idea was a vague notion of a revolution carried out in phases, the initial goal being a "national democratic revolution" in alliance with the ANC, the primary thrust of which was to be the transfer of power from the white minority to the black majority.

It quickly became evident that the Communists, individually if not collectively, were destined to play a critical role in the "new ANC" taking shape after February 1990, just as they had in the "old ANC" over the previous four decades. There was no hope of understanding the internal dynamics and ever-changing tactics of the ANC without delving into this fascinating symbiotic relation-ship, which had developed in their common struggle against apart-heid.

The history of the ANC–Communist Party alliance is a textbook example of how a repressive government can make close allies out of potential rivals. Created in 1921 and initially largely a white labor-oriented organization, the SACP grew to become a driving force of the anti-apartheid movement after it was outlawed in 1950. Its influence on the ANC proved to be enormous, helping the organization to launch its armed struggle in 1961 and providing it with cadres, organizational skills, and strategic thinking. President P. W. Botha unceasingly castigated the SACP as the alleged master-mind behind what he called the ANC's "total onslaught" against the white apartheid state. Botha had always insisted that the ANC break its alliance with the SACP as one of his conditions for releasing Mandela and starting negotiations with the ANC. In two years of private talks with the government before his release, Man-dela had steadfastly refused. De Klerk finally decided not only to drop it, but also to unban the Communist Party as well as the ANC. Given de Klerk's own deep-seated prejudices against all things communist, his decision must be seen as one of his most courageous steps and a major shift in attitude by the white govern-ment toward its political foes. But de Klerk did not stop hammer-ing away at the ANC–SACP alliance; he sought by every means possible to provoke discord and division between the two. Joe Slovo became the focal point of de Klerk's continuing anti-commu-nist crusade.

With his white hair, twinkling eyes, soft voice, and habitual red socks, Slovo looked more like a benign grandfather or Santa Claus than a communist theorist or guerrilla military strategist. But his engagement in the anti-apartheid movement, like Mandela's, was total. The son of poor Lithuanian Jewish immigrants, Slovo had come to South Africa in 1926 when he was nine years old. His father had been a van driver and so poor that Joe was forced to quit school in the ninth grade and go to work to help the family survive. He volunteered for the Army when World War II broke out, and served in Italy with South Africa's Sixth Armored Division. After-ward, he took advantage of a special war veterans' grant to study law at the University of the Witwatersrand in Johannesburg, having been admitted even though he had never graduated from high school. He proved a brilliant law student, but his real interest was politics, particularly the Communist Party, which he had joined in 1942. His connection to the party grew stronger after his marriage in 1949 to Ruth First, daughter of SACP treasurer Julius First. Both found themselves on the "honor roll" of the first 600 people blacklisted when the government passed the Suppression of Communism Act in 1950. Four years later, Slovo—like Mandela, Sisulu, and countless others—was banned, meaning that he could no longer attend public gatherings or engage in political activity. Nonetheless, he continued his activities clandestinely. It was in these postwar years, when both the Communists and the ANC were fighting an increasingly repressive apartheid government, that he struck up a relationship of mutual admiration with Mandela, who was also a law student at Witwatersrand. "We got on. I would say we were even friends at that point," Slovo recalled in 1992. But there was also much that still separated them. "We had our political differences," reminisced Slovo. "He came from a black consciousness origin, while the party was the only one that had non-African members and leaders."

White Communists like Slovo played a major role in changing Mandela's thinking about cooperating with whites, for their devotion to the cause was undeniable. As one of the 156 anti-apartheid activists arrested in 1956, Slovo served as part of the defense team in that first famous treason trial, which dragged on until March 1961 and ended in no convictions. Later that year, Slovo and other white Communists helped Mandela launch the ANC's armed struggle. Slovo was not one of the original guerilla leaders but served first as one of its chief propagandists and later strategists of the armed struggle. Only because he was on an external mission at the time did Slovo avoid being arrested at Lilliesleaf Farm in July 1963.

During his twenty-seven years in exile, Slovo remained in the forefront of the ANC's liberation struggle, as a member of its supreme Revolutionary Council, and, starting in 1984, as Umkhonto's chief of staff. From London, Moscow, Maputo, Dar es Salaam, and Lusaka, he helped put together a political and military alliance between the Communist Party and the ANC that was often contentious but ultimately unshakable. Slovo quickly gained the reputation for being "Moscow's man" in the liberation movement; he was the gatekeeper for the arms, money, training, and diplomatic support flowing from the Soviet Union to the ANC. He was also regarded as one of those most responsible for the Stalinism and slavish pro-Soviet foreign policy that had won the SACP such a dubious reputation. But in Mandela's eyes, this didn't matter much; Communists like Slovo were first and foremost good allies who steadfastly stood by the ANC.

In fact, Slovo often risked his life in the deadly cat-and-mouse game with apartheid's secret assassins and the South African Defence Force's numerous air and commando raids on ANC bases in Zambia, Botswana, and Mozambique. While never succeeding in killing him, the army's "dirty tricks" department did manage to assassinate Ruth First, who was blown apart by a parcel bomb in August 1982. The ANC leadership's collective respect for Slovo was made manifest in 1985 when he became the first white person elected to the ANC's National Executive Committee. The following year he took over the key position of Communist Party general secretary, slowly devoting more and more time to party rather than ANC matters, a transition made explicit in April 1987 when he stepped down as Umkhonto's chief of staff.

In time, Slovo would be joined by many fellow Communists in the high councils of the ANC, thanks to the dual membership and dual leadership policies. Though Mandela doggedly defended the practice (on the grounds that the ANC and the Communist Party had worked together closely for forty years and were true and trusted allies), critics claimed dual membership was being exploited by the Communists to indulge in their classic tactic of infiltrating non-Communist organizations in preparation for their eventual takeover. President de Klerk did his best to dramatize the potential dangers of the dual membership policy to the ANC, warning Mandela that the Communists had become such an integral part of his organization that the ANC and SACP resembled a scrambled egg. He tried again and again to convince the ANC president to unscramble that egg, but he never succeeded.

◆   ◆   ◆

The alliance character of the ANC posed enormous problems for Mandela and imposed sharp limitations on how much influence he could hope to exercise. His efforts to take control of the organization and shape the direction of its policies met with increasing resistance. He ran head-on into a grassroots militancy that he had apparently been unaware of during his years in prison. He could not dictate to COSATU, the Communist Party, or the civic associations, for they remained independent bodies and formed strong lobbies inside the ANC to press their own particular agendas. Mandela found himself leading and speaking in the name of a kind of "rainbow coalition" of autonomous and semi-autonomous groups. This coalition included an incredible array of Catholics, Protestants, and Moslems as well as Communists, capitalists, and union militants. Little wonder, then, that he would encounter enormous difficulty making his voice heard and his authority felt.

Mandela's first attempts at exerting leadership were, in fact, embarrassing failures. He discovered that the admiring followers who listened to him in rapt attention and total silence paid no heed to the content of his sermons. An early example of this came in Durban on February 25, 1990, just two weeks after his release. At least 100,000 people, almost all Zulus, came to see and hear him pound home the imperative need to end the fighting between ANC and Inkatha supporters in Natal Province. South Africa stood on the threshold of a new era, but Natal was "in flames, brother fighting brother in wars of vengeance and retaliation." He made a stirring appeal to all Zulus to lay down their arms: "Take your guns, your knives, and your *pangas* and throw them into the sea. Close down the death factories. End this war now." His wise counsel fell on deaf ears. Neither his followers nor those of Chief Buthelezi were interested in making peace; in fact, the conflict in Natal soon escalated to new heights of death and destruction.

At that same rally, Mandela the statesman artfully sought to appease Buthelezi by praising him for his steadfast refusal to hold talks with the white government so long as it kept him in prison. Mandela wanted to deal with Buthelezi directly, chief to chief, and thereby bring an end to the fighting. Whether he was dealing with de Klerk or Buthelezi, he clearly preferred "personal diplomacy," a contemporary version of old-style African chiefs getting together to decide matters of war and peace for their respective tribes. Unfortunately, he was shortly to discover that his own unruly "tribe" would not put up with such old-fashioned tactics.

On Friday, March 29, after another spasm of violence hit Natal, Mandela and Buthelezi announced that they would meet the following Monday outside Pietermaritzburg at a mountain hamlet called Taylor's Halt. There was no time to stand on ceremony when people were dying, Mandela said, defending his decision to meet the Inkatha leader. "We must unite," he said. The mere announcement of the meeting, arranged by the two leaders' aides, infuriated the top local leaders, particularly Harry Gwala. Even the moderate regional UDF leader Archie Gumede was enraged. While Gwala favored direct confrontation to wipe Inkatha off the face of the political map, Gumede told me he thought the meeting was simply ill-prepared and premature. Meeting at Taylor's Halt, he said, was like asking Mandela to walk into the lion's den, since it was deep inside Inkatha-controlled territory. Furthermore, Gumede was furious that it had been arranged without consulting him.

So Gwala, Gumede, and another UDF leader, Dilisa Mji, went to see Mandela at his Soweto home early the next day. They counseled him strongly against going to Taylor's Halt to meet Buthelezi, arguing that it would only boost the Zulu chief's prestige and convince him that violence paid handsome political dividends. Though Mandela went ahead with his planned trip to Pietermaritzburg the following Monday, he never saw Taylor's Halt or Buthelezi. Instead, Gwala's men took him just outside the city to the site of the latest fighting in Imbali township. There he was shown the charred remains of an ANC supporter and introduced to the enraged families of the latest victims. Gwala and Gumede had taught Mandela a lesson he would never forget: He could not ride roughshod over the wishes of ANC regional leaders. And he was about to learn another lesson as well—that the personal diplomacy with which he hoped to engage de Klerk was held in deep suspicion and was bitterly resented by ANC followers and leaders alike.

6

STEPPING STONES
AND STUMBLING BLOCKS

B y comparison to Nelson Mandela's ordeal of leadership,
President F. W. de Klerk's experience was relatively smooth.
He ruled over an incredibly disciplined, hierarchical, and
homogeneous political organization—a real Tammany Hall–style
machine. For over forty years, the National Party had been a party
of lemmings ready to follow its leader over any political cliff without much questioning. In 1990, even with its recently conferred
status as a minority party, the NP, as it is commonly called, was
united in its membership and its thinking.

Unlike Mikhail Gorbachev, who at the time was fighting a losing
battle against hardline conservatives to reform his Communist
Party, de Klerk did not have such elements to battle inside the
National Party—they had all left to join the breakaway Conservative Party in 1982. Throughout the momentous reforms de Klerk
implemented in 1990 and 1991, not a single National Party member
of Parliament defected to the Conservatives. Furthermore, de
Klerk did not have to struggle to get the notion of "reform" accepted as did Gorbachev: the National Party had been flirting with
the idea of reforming apartheid since the late 1970s, and various
measures had already been implemented under P. W. Botha. In
fact, by the time de Klerk became NP leader in February 1989, he

took over a party poised for more reform and headed for power-sharing with blacks. In many senses, de Klerk was the Boris Yeltsin rather than the Gorbachev of South Africa. The question was: Would he pursue reform all the way to its logical conclusion of yielding power to the black majority?

The NP, then, unlike the ANC, was not at sixes and sevens ideologically. Nor was it a coalition of squabbling factions loosely hung together in a "movement." The National Party was theoretically a federal party made up of four autonomous regional bodies corresponding to the country's four provinces—Natal, the Cape, the Orange Free State, and the Transvaal. Though its membership figures were not a matter of public record, the NP's Stoffel van der Merwe put the figure at "over 100,000." It appeared, however, that many whites regarded themselves as "Nats" in the same vague way Democrats and Republicans do in the United States: They were registered members of the party but did little from one election campaign to the next. The party held four separate provincial congresses annually, and occasionally met in a single federal congress to discuss and approve vital issues. The four provincial party leaders all had separate regional power bases and were thus strategically placed to become frontrunners in the race for state president on those rare occasions of a change in leadership. In fact, so "federal" in formal structure was the NP that not until 1992 did it establish a national headquarters outside Pretoria and appoint a secretary-general.

In daily practice, however, the NP seemed extremely centralized, certainly when compared to the ANC. Under Botha, decision-making had become so centralized that his was dubbed the imperial presidency. Botha sidestepped his own party as the instrument of control and used instead a State Security Council made up of the so-called securocrats, mostly Army, intelligence, and security officials but also his closest ministers. Under the council was a National Security Management System that extended down to the white town and black township level and basically ran the country by implementing Botha's policies, particularly toward the black population, and taking responsibility for all security matters. The NP was reduced to a rubber-stamp operation; decisions were made elsewhere.

When de Klerk took over, he made a point of restoring the badly emasculated National Party as the locus of decision-making. In the first years of his presidency, the focus of power was the cabinet, whose members (the number changed constantly but was generally around sixteen) were all senior NP officials, including the four provincial leaders. De Klerk, anxious to distinguish his leadership style from Botha's, revived the NP's role and went out of his way to emphasize collective decision-making within this small power elite. Though Botha had started the practice, de Klerk became famous for his *bosberaads*, informal meetings of the entire cabinet that took place at isolated vacation resorts. At these brainstorming sessions, which usually lasted two or three days, major decisions about negotiations with the ANC were made. The *bosberaad* held in November 1989, for example, had discussed and approved the general outlines of de Klerk's reform program, leaving the timing and sequence of reforms to the president.

Once the cabinet reached a decision, the Party Caucus would usually be called together to be informed about that decision. The caucus included all ninety-three NP members of Parliament, making it even larger than the ANC's National Executive Committee. While the caucus was not a decision-making body, it did act as a sounding board and fed back to the NP leaders the mood of the white constituency.

De Klerk's use of the cabinet as his center of operations assured a degree of collective decision-making on government and party issues. There were times, however, when the circle of decision-makers was even smaller and was restricted to his closest advisers, who seemed to form a kind of kitchen cabinet. Its members changed somewhat, and different cliques exercised more influence with de Klerk depending on whether the issue concerned constitutional negotiations, foreign affairs, economic issues, or security matters. De Klerk's closest adviser on constitutional matters was Gerrit Viljoen, former head of the secret Afrikaner Broederbond (which had extensive ties to the NP) and constitutional affairs minister in 1990. Another close adviser and friend was Dawie de Villiers. He was the party's chairman in the Cape Province and de Klerk's heir apparent, for the Cape was eclipsing the Transvaal as the party's main base of power. (The Conservatives had made significant inroads in the Transvaal.) Many South African analysts regarded de Villiers as a political lightweight, but he had de Klerk's confidence and the two socialized regularly and played golf together. Then there was foreign affairs minister Pik Botha, who had held the post since 1977. Botha educated de Klerk in the skills of diplomacy and the art of selling his reforms abroad. But he was also invaluable inside the party in dealing with the Conservative challenge because of his fearlessness and his flair for colorful language. The fourth minister of considerable weight was Kobie Coetsee, minister of justice since 1980 and the man who had played a major role in the negotiations with Mandela before his release. Coetsee was also party chairman in the Orange Free State.

Younger members of the ruling elite around de Klerk included Stoffel van der Merwe, minister of education in 1990; Barend du Plessis, finance minister; and Roelof Meyer, deputy minister for constitutional affairs and one of the party's rising stars, having served in three deputy ministerial posts since 1986. He would prove exceptionally adept at dealing with ANC negotiators.

De Klerk's inner circle had a number of things in common. First, they were all "blue-blood" Afrikaners dedicated to the cause of their people's survival and continued presence in government through power-sharing. Second, they had all served in P. W. Botha's cabinet as ministers or deputy ministers. Third, in National Party terms, they were all, with the exception of Coetsee, regarded as *verligte*, or "enlightened" reformers. Fourth, they all believed strongly in the preeminence of the party, not the security establishment, in decision-making. None was regarded as a securocrat, though Meyer, who had served as deputy minister of law and order during the massive 1986 government crackdown on the anti-apartheid movement, and thus had been actively involved in the nationwide network of Botha's security management system, might well have been considered a reformed securocrat. But after the unbanning of the ANC, he became one of the most liberal NP thinkers. He was the first National Party negotiator to say publicly that protection of group rights could no longer be part of the National Party's platform in the negotiations for a new constitution. Whites, to defend their interests, he said, would have to depend on political parties that were likely to be multi-racial as the basic unit of the new political order. Meyer's progressive views would gain greater currency as the negotiations wore on.

Despite de Klerk's rhetoric of collegiality, the NP was still a highly centralized, undemocratic, and elitist organization. Basically, a coterie of a dozen or so people drew up plans and made decisions on their own. The rank and file was never called upon to debate the great issues of the day, remaining passive and accepting of whatever new direction the NP leadership took.

One example of this docility is that de Klerk never sought, or received, a specific mandate from his party to open negotiations with the ANC, let alone write a new nonracial constitution. In fact, the National Party had won the September 1989 elections by campaigning *against* negotiation with "terrorists." It had indulged extensively in negative advertising against the liberal Democratic Party for its advocacy of negotiating with the ANC; a famous campaign poster meant to scare white voters into supporting the NP featured Democratic Party leader Wynand Malan meeting with Joe Slovo outside the country. Yet, within less than a year of that election, the Nationalists would be holding talks with the same "terrorists," including Slovo, inside the country. The Nats, though, followed de Klerk's about-face without a murmur, not even asking for a special party congress to discuss the abrupt shift in course. The only hue and cry came from the opposition Conservative Party.

Three contemporary lessons in reform shaped the thinking of de Klerk and his strategists as they began their search for a settlement to the South African conflict: Zimbabwe (known as Rhodesia until 1980), Namibia, and the Soviet Union. Zimbabwe, in their minds, was a case study of what happened when a white minority stubbornly and foolishly fought the tide of history instead of seizing the initiative to negotiate the best deal possible. De Klerk believed that Ian Smith, the white Rhodesian prime minister, had made "great mistakes." "When the opportunity was there for real constructive negotiation, it was not grasped," the president remarked on February 4, 1990. "We must not make that mistake. We are determined not to repeat that mistake."

On the other hand, the lesson de Klerk drew from the negotiations over Namibia's independence was quite different: never allow outside mediators to dictate the pace and substance of the negotiations—in other words, don't lose control over the process. Gerrit Viljoen put it succinctly when he addressed the National Party's Transvaal provincial congress in November 1989: "The negotiation process will take place between South Africans in South Africa. There is no need or role for foreign mediators." This conviction—that direct negotiations constituted the best course—had been behind the government's decision to undertake secret exploratory talks with Mandela while he was still in prison.

The white reformers drew another lesson from Namibia, namely, that elections based on proportional representation, and not a winner-take-all system as in the United States, could prevent one's main adversary from gaining a commanding majority and could set the stage for power-sharing in a coalition government. SWAPO, the nationalist organization that had won Namibia's 1989 independence elections, had obtained less than 60 percent of the vote and concluded that a coalition with its political enemies was in the best interest of national reconciliation and the country's political stability. De Klerk and the National Party hoped to obtain a similar outcome in South Africa, and the election in Namibia proved that it was possible. Furthermore, after three years of independence, Namibia also proved that a black majority and a white minority could cooperate to make a coalition government function successfully.

Uppermost in the minds of de Klerk and his National Party, however, was the Soviet Union. The collapse of communism had tipped the balance of power in their favor because the ANC had suddenly lost its main source of arms, political support, and ideological inspiration. Briefing foreign reporters four days after de Klerk's historic speech to Parliament, Viljoen summed up the implications of the dawning of a New World Order in these terms: "Our situation has changed fundamentally by what has happened in the international field, in Eastern Europe, Russia, and in several African states recently. The total effect of all these things puts the threat posed by the South African Communist Party and the African National Congress in an entirely new context."

Later, and for very different reasons, the example of the Soviet

Union under Mikhail Gorbachev would come to haunt de Klerk. Gorbachev had unleashed forces that he proved totally unable to control and that eventually became his undoing. De Klerk believed that Gorbachev's fall resulted from his own indecisiveness; he vowed not to make the same mistake.

The negotiations for a New South Africa proved to be a very messy process filled with delays, misunderstandings, unfulfilled agreements, and endless complications. The whole nation lived on an emotional roller coaster, traveling from peaks of great expectation to canyons of despair over repeated deadlocks and back again. There was never to be a single great leap across the South African Rubicon, but rather a series of "stepping-stones" that had to be created along the way. "The method that one follows when the river is very wide is to jump from stone to stone. If you try to do it all in one jump, then you land in the middle of the river," warned Stoffel van der Merwe, who served as one of the NP's initial negotiations strategists. (The party and government had separate delegations and negotiators though they talked from the same script.)

The beginnings of the negotiation process resembled the initial probings of age-old adversaries at the start of another round of war. Neither side knew what to expect. De Klerk and Mandela both had to work hard to overcome a series of initial obstacles that included everything from the outbreak of the worst political violence since the mid-1980s to such legal niceties as the granting of temporary indemnities to the ANC's exiled leaders to return home. Because of bureaucratic delays on both sides, the first exiled leader, ANC intelligence chief Jacob Zuma, did not arrive back until March 21 to engage in what were supposed to be secret preparatory talks with the government.

A portent of things to come was the ANC's decision on March 31 to postpone the first official ANC–government meeting because of the March 26 massacre in Sebokeng township, about twenty-five miles south of Johannesburg, in the industrial heartland of the country. The police had opened fire without warning on a crowd of ANC protesters, killing at least 11 and wounding more than 400 others. Many had been shot in the back as they were fleeing.

Mandela, whose leadership was already being challenged inside the ANC, was obliged to speak out, warning de Klerk that the state president could not "talk about negotiations on the one hand and murder our people on the other."

Complicating matters further, the ANC balked at having to sit at the same table with law and order minister Adriaan Vlok, while the government choked at the idea of Joe Slovo being present. It took a three-hour nighttime meeting in Cape Town between de Klerk and Mandela on April 5 to finally get the so-called talks about talks back on track.

The historic first meeting of the old adversaries took place May 2–4 in a surrealistic atmosphere. The location chosen for the *indaba*, or round table, was Groote Schuur, the mansion of South Africa's first colonial governors located at the foot of Cape Town's majestic Table Mountain. Cecil Rhodes, the nineteenth-century British founder of Rhodesia, had lived there, as had the infamous architects and builders of apartheid, D. F. Malan, J. G. Strijdom, Hendrik F. Verwoerd, and John Vorster. Small wonder, then, that some ANC delegates felt they were being led into a trap; only half jokingly, they recalled the story of famous Voortrekker Piet Retief, who, in 1838, had naively led seventy unarmed men into the cattle *kraal* of the Zulu king Dingaan to discuss a treaty for a vast tract of land in Natal, only to end up massacred.

The ANC deliberately chose its delegation of nine men and two women—seven blacks, two whites, one Coloured, and one Indian—for the purpose of making a statement about its vision of a new multi-racial leadership for South Africa. The government sent out quite a different message with its delegation—nine people who were all white, all men, and all Afrikaners. These conflicting messages didn't spoil the occasion, however. For all present, participants and observers alike, it was an unforgettable experience. Reporters watched in fascination as the likes of Joe Slovo and Joe Modise, commander of Umkhonto we Sizwe, exchanged their first words of greeting with their long-standing Afrikaner enemies. (While reporters were excluded from the meeting, they were able to watch members of the delegations interact as they arrived at and left each session, and occasionally shared coffee breaks while both sides leaked profusely.)

The first day was devoted to the airing of the bitter history of the conflict. Mandela explained that the ANC had always cherished the hope of a peaceful negotiated settlement and had only taken up arms when this avenue was closed off by white intransigence. De Klerk, for his part, defended the National Party's long quest for a system of separate countries for blacks and whites, though he conceded that it had failed and might even have gone astray in its application.

On the second day, the ANC's international affairs chief, Thabo Mbeki, emerged from the closed meeting to tell a media luncheon that he and his ANC colleagues had discovered that their white counterparts "did not have horns" after all and that they could talk, exchange jokes, and dine together amicably. Mbeki, we learned later, had quipped to Pik Botha that he was looking forward to having him as his deputy in a new multi-racial cabinet. For his part, Botha was overheard commenting to one ANC delegate that as far as he was concerned the two sides were now sailing "on one boat together." Furthermore, their boat was surrounded by "sharks to the left and right that are not going to distinguish between us when we fall overboard."

At the end of the three-day affair, all the delegates gathered on the back lawn of Groote Schuur for a group picture that epitomized the changes under way: old enemies politely standing together and chatting about what united rather than separated South Africa's blacks and whites. Both sides talked optimistically about the prospects for a settlement, national reconciliation, and national unity. As Mandela remarked, the very fact of the meeting was "sobering in its implications." It heralded, he suggested, the end of the "master and servant" relationship between whites and blacks.

Later, at a joint press conference, a beaming Mandela and a delighted de Klerk sat side by side, expressing their confidence in the future. "I have not the slightest doubt that the state president means what he says," Mandela said, referring to de Klerk's expressed commitment to "a vote for all" in the New South Africa. "I have no doubt whatever about [the president's] integrity." These views were shared by the entire ANC delegation, he assured the media that day. De Klerk and his colleagues waxed equally rhapsodic, saying that they had been thoroughly impressed by Mandela's dignity, graciousness, and remarkable lack of bitterness. Mandela had spoken their language, de Klerk said, that of a settlement where there would be no losers and everyone would emerge a victor.

Still, shades of the bitter contest to come darkened even this first encouraging encounter. Before the press conference was over, de Klerk and Mandela found themselves suddenly engaging in sharp exchanges over whether it was time to lift international sanctions against South Africa, and over the ticklish issue of "minority rights." The state president, of course, felt that sanctions were no longer necessary and should be lifted, while Mandela strongly disagreed and called on the international community to keep them in place. De Klerk then remarked that while he was not "ideologically obsessed" with the notion of group rights, he wanted a constitution that would recognize "the reality of the existence of groups in South Africa." Mandela couldn't let this comment pass unchallenged. "The concept of group rights," he said, "gives the impression of apartheid in disguise." De Klerk ended the exchange with an offhand comment that would prove all too true: "You can see that long debates lie ahead when we come to real negotiations." But at least the two sides were finally sitting down and talking together. The ice had at last been broken, even if there was still little common ground.

The substance of the first agreements reached, contained in what was thereafter called the Groote Schuur Minute, reflected the thinness of this common ground. Both sides pledged to work for an end to the climate of violence and committed themselves to "a peaceful process of negotiations." They agreed to set up a joint working group to resolve the multiple obstacles standing in the way of the start of constitutional negotiations. These obstacles included, the minute stated, the release of political prisoners and the granting of immunity from prosecution for those involved in the struggle both inside and outside South Africa, particularly ANC National Executive Committee members. In addition, the government committed itself to revising all security legislation to allow for the normalization of black political activities and to the lifting of the state of emergency.

In the text of the minute, one could clearly detect the preconditions each side was laying down for the start of substantive negotiations toward an overall settlement. The ANC demanded that the government first lift the state of emergency; allow the 20,000 to 40,000 political exiles to return home; release all political prisoners; scrap all apartheid and repressive security legislation; and grant permanent immunity from prosecution to its negotiators and senior officials. The government, for its part, insisted that the ANC declare an end to its armed struggle; demobilize its guerrilla army; disclose the whereabouts of its arms caches; and transform itself from a liberation movement into a normal political party.

The most immediate problem both sides faced was reaching an understanding on what constituted a "political prisoner" and who should benefit from any amnesty or immunity from prosecution. The initial deadline set for resolving this issue, May 21, saw a draft agreement actually drawn up, but it then underwent numerous amendments, revisions, and delays. They found they could reach no agreement on what the term "political prisoner" meant, and therefore who should be included in any amnesty or immunity. This initial difficulty over terminology was a harbinger of far worse things to come. Unable to resolve this legalistic tangle, the government would force the ANC to proceed on a laborious, time-consuming case-by-case basis, reviewing whether whatever "crime" allegedly committed had been "politically motivated." The two sides would gnaw over this first bone of contention for more than two years. Terrible precedents had been set at Groote Schuur in this very first "minute"—precedents stemming from a lack of clarity over words, and misunderstandings over presumed agreements, that would come to haunt their future negotiations.

The next stepping-stone in the peace process was reached in Pretoria on August 6, 1990, when delegates met again to discuss the recommendations of the working group set up at Groote Schuur. This time, the meeting between de Klerk and Mandela was overshadowed by a crisis of confidence as to whether the ANC was ready to end its armed struggle.

On June 7, de Klerk had met one of the ANC preconditions for negotiations by lifting the nationwide state of emergency, leaving only Natal, the center of much of the violence, under special law.

De Klerk then asked for a reciprocal gesture of good faith from the ANC, namely some statement of intent about permanently ending its armed struggle. This issue was largely symbolic, as Umkhonto had proved totally ineffectual; it had never fought a proper battle against the South African Defence Force or even fielded a large number of commandos and saboteurs inside the country. But de Klerk had become infuriated in late July when his security forces arrested about forty members of Umkhonto connected to a plot for a nationwide insurrection called Operation Vula.

Consisting of a network of secret cells in Natal Province, Vula, "the opening," had been established in 1988 as the ANC's last attempt to revive the flagging armed struggle. It had never gotten off the ground, but the government used its discovery of the dormant revolutionary plan to pursue its own strategic aims of trying to drive a wedge into the heart of the ANC–Communist Party alliance. De Klerk immediately insisted that Joe Slovo, who had been mistakenly identified as a Vula commander, be excluded from the negotiations. In fact, Slovo's presence became the object of a test of wills between de Klerk and Mandela. The more de Klerk insisted that Slovo be excluded from the talks, the more Mandela insisted that he be present. The more de Klerk harped on the SACP's supposed evil influence over the ANC, the more stubborn Mandela became in defending their alliance. However ambivalent he may have sometimes felt about the party's role, Mandela remained steadfast in his loyalty to the Communists; he had no intention of abandoning them now, after they had stayed the course for forty years, just to please de Klerk.

Though Slovo remained on the ANC team, the confrontation over Operation Vula helped the government to extract a firmer commitment to ending its armed struggle from Mandela and the ANC at the Pretoria meeting. In the Pretoria Minute, as the second accord was called, the ANC agreed immediately to "suspend," though not end, its armed struggle. In return for this major concession, the government undertook only to "consider the lifting of the state of emergency in Natal as early as possible" and to "review" the Internal Security Act with a view to amending all restrictions on free political activity.

As it turned out, Mandela and de Klerk had once again signed an accord over which there was, in fact, little agreement. The two sides had not been able to determine what constituted "related activities," so they established another joint working group to wrangle over the meaning and report back by September 15. The Pretoria Minute also tried to clear up some of the misunderstandings over the Groote Schuur Minute. It set forth "target dates" for the release of some political prisoners and the granting of indemnities to others accused of minor "crimes" such as leaving the country illegally. Some were to be freed by the end of 1990, and the last supposedly "not later" than April 30, 1991. The government refused the ANC's request, however, that it grant all anti-apartheid activists a blanket amnesty to speed up the process, and insisted that those seeking immunity from prosecution enumerate themselves what crimes they thought they might have committed. In other words, exiles were obliged to incriminate themselves before they could return home.

The Pretoria Minute provoked a furor within the ANC. Mandela and his negotiators came in for enormous criticism from the rank and file for having agreed even to "suspend" the movement's armed struggle without extracting a comparable concession from the government. The reaction was so strong that the ANC National Executive Committee, sensing the angry mood, decided to postpone until July 1991 the organization's first national conference held inside South Africa for more than thirty years. It was probably a wise decision. The depth of suspicion that Mandela was leading the ANC toward a "sellout" of the struggle was made manifest in the militancy of a substitute three-day "consultative conference" held in mid-December 1990 to discuss the negotiations and other issues.

At that conference, the test issue was whether the ANC should modify its policy toward sanctions and support a new approach of phasing them out as de Klerk implemented the reforms they were demanding. Even as the conference opened, the twelve-nation European Community voted to ease its ban on new investment in South Africa. The idea of a phased lifting of sanctions seemed to make sense in the circumstances, and Mandela supported this approach wholeheartedly. In this stand he was joined by Thabo Mbeki, the ANC de facto foreign minister and one of its most influential officials. On the first day of the conference, ANC President Tambo, semiparalytic though he was, appeared to admonish in his faltering voice the 1,600 delegates that "trite slogans" were no longer sufficient and that the time had come to reevaluate "the advisability of the retention of sanctions." A draft document circulated to delegates had also warned that the ANC faced "international marginalization" unless it took the initiative to propose a "well-considered program for the de-escalation of the sanctions campaign."

Tambo's proposal was met with an angry outcry that neither he nor Mandela had anticipated. The next day, ANC militants (led by Communist Party members) pushed through a special resolution insisting that the entire sanctions package be maintained unchanged. To the enormous embarrassment of Tambo, Mandela, and Mbeki, the resolution received an overwhelming vote of support. Reporters were excluded from that session but were later shown a video of delegates cheering wildly after its adoption.

As if this rebuke to his authority were not enough, Mandela also had to endure the criticism leveled by one delegate after another against his "personal diplomacy" with de Klerk as well as the ANC's negotiations with the government in general; ANC militants just could not understand why he kept calling de Klerk a "man of integrity." In his closing speech, Mandela bemoaned the fact that he had heard "hardly a word of praise" for any of the National Executive Committee's members and only "serious reservations" that they should be holding talks with the government at all. He readily conceded that he and the NEC had been remiss in their duty to keep the membership informed about their contacts and agreements with the government. He said he accepted the criticism "without qualification" and promised to make "radical adjustments" to the ANC style of leadership. But he also insisted on his right to maintain contacts with de Klerk and his government. He simply could not go back to a consultative conference every time he, or the NEC, had to sort out a problem or resolve a conflict.

The delegates' general hardline stance set off alarm bells in the ANC's headquarters and in Pretoria. De Klerk began to wonder whether Mandela really was in control of his own organization and capable of delivering his constituency to a peaceful settlement. A serious divide was indeed opening up between the ANC leadership under Mandela and the membership over the central issue of negotiations with the government. The conference had served to crystallize the growing unease within the militant mainstream that behind its back Mandela was striking secret deals and making compromises with de Klerk. Clearly, Mandela was facing a grass-roots rebellion that was going to make his task of negotiating a settlement exceedingly delicate and difficult.

De Klerk's reaction to Mandela's predicament was to squeeze more and more concessions out of a shaky ANC leadership on the fate of its armed struggle and the so-called "related activities" of its military wing. A series of unpublicized meetings between officials from the two sides led to a third agreement. This one was called the D. F. Malan Accord, after the Cape Town airport (named for the post–World War II prime minister) at which it was signed on February 12, 1991. The government extracted from the ANC the understanding that it had "suspended" its armed struggle on "the presumption" that "there would be no return to armed action." The ANC agreed to cease the infiltration of men and arms into the country; to stop the creation of further clandestine structures and all military training inside South Africa; and to end all attacks by arms, explosives, or bombs. The ANC also accepted the principle that in a democratic society no political party or movement should maintain a "private army." In addition, the ANC agreed that it was "vital" that control be exercised—by whom was not made clear— over Umkhonto cadres and arms caches inside South Africa. There was even to be a phased process to demobilize Umkhonto guerril-las and to "legalize control over the arms." All this was supposed to be accomplished "forthwith" and "as speedily as possible" under a joint government–ANC liaison committee. In return, the only concessions the ANC extracted from the government this time were an acknowledgment of the ANC's right to "express its views through peaceful demonstrations" and a promise to investi-gate reports of security force involvement in the political violence.

    Yet another bone of contention had been created and a su-premely discordant accord signed between the ANC and the government. It seemed that the de Klerk government, ever anxious to extract whatever it could, was blind to the noxious consequences of proceeding to negotiate in such a fashion. The results were always the same. The D. F. Malan Accord, just like the Groote Schuur and Pretoria minutes, would remain mostly a dead letter and the subject of continuous dispute. And, like the others, it could only compromise the chances of reaching a larger, overall settlement to the South African conflict.

The April 30, 1991, deadline for the release of all political prisoners and the return of exiles would pass, with hundreds still awaiting release and thousands awaiting repatriation. The ANC chose to interpret all its commitments regarding the fate of its military wing as dependent on sufficient progress in the constitutional negotiations. It refused to acknowledge that Umkhonto was any more a "private army" of the ANC than the South African Defence Force was of de Klerk's National Party.

Wittingly or not, de Klerk was making matters worse for the ANC moderates led by Mandela, who were at least ready, even anxious, to negotiate a peaceful resolution. Instead, he was pursuing a myopic strategy of going for maximum short-term gains at ANC expense, seemingly oblivious to the eroding effect this tactic was having on prospects for obtaining a larger settlement.

Though frustrated by his inability to keep his troops in line, and saddened by de Klerk's faint-hearted commitment to embrace change, Mandela nonetheless forged ahead in his quest to secure political power for his people. But, to his dismay, he found the violence in the townships bedeviling every step of the negotiating process. Chief Buthelezi often described this general collapse of law and order as a "low-intensity civil war," but as 1990 turned into 1991, it became clear that the KwaZulu leader was intent not on dousing the flames but on turning up the heat.

7

THE END OF
THE HONEYMOON

The most contentious figure on the South African political
landscape after February 1990 was, without a doubt, the
would-be leader of the Zulu nation, Chief Mangosuthu Gat-
sha Ashpenaz Nathan Buthelezi, head of the Buthelezi clan from
Mahlabatini and Prince of Kwaphindangene, among his many
other titles. His was also the most complicated personality, one
palpably dominated by an insatiable appetite for power and an
overweening ambition to be recognized as the equal of Nelson
Mandela. Falling far short of that mark and feeling himself mis-
treated as the "ultimate leper" by the mainstream nationalist movement, Buthelezi became increasingly intractable and belligerent, to
the point where he loomed over the peace process as a calculated
spoiler. In his determination to impose himself as a national leader,
he became, arguably, his own worst enemy.

He was also Mandela's nemesis, the one African leader Mandela
could not find a way to deal with successfully even though he
realized Buthelezi promised too much trouble to ignore. Essentially, Mandela was caught between his own initial inclination to
make peace with Buthelezi and enormous pressure from ANC, Inc.
to declare all-out war against him. Whether to make peace or war
remained for Mandela an unresolved conundrum. So Mandela,

114

buffeted by the conflicting forces and counsels around him, wavered back and forth between the two approaches, encountering equally limited success in each direction.

Buthelezi, ten years younger than Mandela, was probably the most unpleasant politician on the African continent—suspicious, unpredictable, touchy, and so easily offended that normal journalistic questions often provoked blasts of cold fury. He seemed almost to enjoy the role of odd man out, being difficult, different, and contrary just for the sake of emphasizing his importance in his frustrated quest for legitimacy. Buthelezi harbored a sense of superiority that bore no relationship to how others perceived him. He acted and talked as if he had been the central figure in the South African black liberation struggle for decades and as if it were high time everyone else acknowledged his enormous contribution. For example, he told me during an interview in May 1990 that he had been solely responsible for Mandela's release and for bringing the government around to accepting negotiations with the ANC. Behaving as if he were some kind of unsung national hero, Buthelezi was constantly offended by the fact that nobody seemed to appreciate what he felt he had done for Mandela, the ANC, and the country.

Chief Buthelezi's haughtiness undoubtedly stemmed from his pride in being a member of the royal family of one of Africa's great warrior tribes. He never let anyone forget that he was related to the great nineteenth-century Zulu king, Shaka, the builder of the mightiest black empire and army in southern Africa, through his maternal great-grandfather, King Cetshwayo, son of Dingaan (Shaka's half-brother), who defeated the British at the Battle of Isandlwana in 1879. Urged on by his strong-willed mother, Princess Magogo, Buthelezi saw himself as a modern Shaka out to restore the glory and honor of the Zulu nation.

Another of Buthelezi's many character flaws was his inability to come to terms with the political consequences of his own carefully calculated decisions and actions during the long anti-apartheid struggle. Unlike Shaka, this Zulu chief had totally rejected armed struggle. So there was no way that Buthelezi, never having spent a day in jail, could hope to enjoy the national and international prestige of Mandela, who had sacrificed twenty-seven years of his life to the cause. Buthelezi's political organization, the Inkatha Freedom Party, had few, if any, martyrs to the liberation struggle whose praise Buthelezi could sing, while the ANC had hundreds. (Inkatha had been founded in 1975 as a cultural movement to project Buthelezi onto the national scene. Whether or not it had the nearly two million members it claimed, there was no doubt that it commanded the allegiance of hundreds of thousands and could mobilize thousands of "shock troops" to wage its battles.)

The effect of all these frustrated dreams of national glory was to create a politician who was amazingly thin-skinned and unable to deal with the thrust and parry of everyday political life. Any insult to him became an insult to his nephew, the Zulu king Goodwill Zwelithini, to the royal Zulu house, and to the entire Zulu people. When it suited his purposes, Buthelezi would wrap himself in the mantle of King Goodwill, and demand that he be treated with practically the same royal respect. He clearly thought of himself as more than just the king's prime minister, the position his paternal great-grandfather, Chief Mnyamana Buthelezi, had held in the court of King Cetshwayo. Rather, he presented himself as the sole political leader of the Zulu nation, and he treated King Goodwill the way a ventriloquist does his puppet, putting his own words in the latter's mouth.

Buthelezi's prickly personality was often on display during interviews and press conferences. He preferred making speeches to answering questions. When reporters went to see him at his headquarters in Ulundi, the capital of the KwaZulu homeland in Natal Province, he often prepared long written statements he would read out through his lowered glasses in front of his entire cabinet. When the time came to ask questions, a reporter had to avoid offending his many sensibilities or risk a tirade that often turned into a personal attack. When Buthelezi was really perturbed and the reporter was white, he would resort to accusing him or her of racism, offering a reply such as, "I know you think all blacks have curly hair, wide noses, and think alike. But that's not how we are."

Yet getting Buthelezi to spell out his own views was no simple task. Ambiguity seemed to be a hallmark of his thinking, one that he had honed to a fine art. He would often go off on a tangent and so obscure the issue that a reporter would be at a loss to understand what he had really meant to say. He also deliberately avoided answering questions about his own, or Inkatha's, role in the political violence against the ANC. Buthelezi always held himself blameless and maintained that he was totally devoted to high Christian principles and Martin Luther King–style nonviolence. He assured reporters endlessly that he had never sat in on any meeting of Inkatha or the KwaZulu government where the use of violence was even hinted at as a way of promoting their political ends. But Buthelezi was not only prime minister of KwaZulu and president of Inkatha, he was also chief of police—and his police officers and their men were deeply involved in Inkatha's political struggle. Given the strict hierarchy and discipline within Inkatha, it was unbelievable that he knew nothing about what his lieutenants were doing and had no hand in their resorting to violence.

Buthelezi's sanctimony rang all the more hollow in light of his insistent appeals to Zulu ethnic pride and warrior traditions when exhorting his followers to stand up and fight the ANC. Sometimes he would use the name of King Goodwill to get his message across; sometimes he would issue statements on behalf of the *amakhosi*, or local Zulu chiefs; and sometimes he would speak out himself.

The first time I witnessed his manipulation of the ethnic factor to arouse Zulu passions occurred in March 1990. On the night of March 24, a set of resolutions taken by the "Amakhosi of KwaZulu" came across the South African Press Association wire in my bureau. They were intriguing because they came straight from Buthelezi's office in Ulundi. Their importance was underlined by a reference to the fact that they had been adopted after a speech by the king in the presence of Buthelezi, "the political head of the Zulu nation." The resolutions constituted a call to war. Every *inkhosi*, every chief, was ordered to rally together his *indunas*, or headmen, to "maintain the dignity of their Zulu communities" by dealing with the ANC challenge "from positions of strength." No *inkhosi* was to give any ground to the "youthful rabble imported by political parties." Those chiefs and headmen living in urban areas where the ANC challenge was the greatest were ordered to rally their supporters to uphold "Zulu values." To the initiated, these were all buzz words and barely coded orders to go on the attack.

Four days later, thousands of heavily armed Inkatha supporters laid siege to ANC strongholds across the Natal Midlands region around Pietermaritzburg. March 28 was said to be the worst single day of fighting since 1987, with more than 100 homes set alight the first day. But the violence continued, and over the next week, at least 80 people were killed and hundreds of others wounded. Altogether, over 200 homes were destroyed and 12,500 people made refugees. Buthelezi's "Zulu nation" had responded to his call. Yet he continually denied that he had had anything to do with fomenting the violence.

Buthelezi did regularly raise the specter of violence but in such a way that he could not be accused of exhorting his followers to engage in such activity. Violence, he said, would just spontaneously erupt in the country if for some reason he and Inkatha were not part of a political settlement. It was as simple and impersonal as that, and obviously not his fault. He repeatedly made reference to the civil wars in Angola and Mozambique as a warning to the ANC not to try to ride roughshod over Inkatha or impose its own constitutional solution over his wishes. The coming civil war in South Africa, he warned, would make those in the two neighboring countries look like "child's play," for there could be no democracy in South Africa unless the support of the "Zulu-speaking minority" was sought and received. In effect, he was saying that he would unleash a civil war that would disrupt a future ANC–dominated government if he did not like the constitution.

Buthelezi posed an enormous dilemma for those interested in seeing South Africa develop an authentic multi-party democracy, for he was profoundly anti-democratic in the way he ran his own Inkatha Freedom Party. Basically, Inkatha was a one-chief party, and the chief behaved more like a Zulu king or tribal patriarch than a modern-day politician. Nor was there anything "democratic" about the politics of KwaZulu. Inkatha was the only party represented in the KwaZulu legislature, and it and the government were so tightly entwined that KwaZulu resembled the typical single-party African state: Party, state, and leader were one. Far from being a democrat, Buthelezi belonged to the same class of authoritarian rulers as Mobutu Sese Seko of Zaire, Hastings Banda of Malawi, and Daniel arap Moi of Kenya. At Inkatha's annual national conferences, basically exercises meant to regenerate enthusiasm and support for his leadership, his word went unchallenged.

Buthelezi openly promoted another profoundly anti-democratic tendency—Zulu ethnic nationalism. More than any other black South African politician he was responsible for the "ethnicization" of the country's politics at the difficult dawning of a new democracy. While the ANC tried to move away from the apartheid concept of a South Africa made up of many ethnic minorities, Buthelezi sought to perpetuate the notion. He even praised P. W. Botha for stating that "South Africa is a country of minorities." Buthelezi was constantly harping about "the Zulu nation" and exhorting Zulus to defend their culture and heritage. Far more than any other South African leader, he clearly manipulated the ethnic factor to try to consolidate his own power base. Though Inkatha attracted a small number of whites, Indians, and Sotho-speaking people, it remained essentially a Zulu operation, with its headquarters in Ulundi, its leaders drawn from the Zulu chief classes, and its support primarily coming from the Zulu people. Its local and regional leadership depended on traditional Zulu *indunas*, some of whom were sent off to the hostels (housing for migrant workers, mostly single men) around Johannesburg to ensure military-style discipline among Inkatha's followers. Even Inkatha-dominated hostels were organized into traditional Zulu fighting units, the basic one being the *impi*. Ethnicity may well still be an inherent factor of modern politics, but as the sole determinant it bodes ill for multi-party democracy, as events in Eastern Europe and Yugoslavia have so clearly illustrated. Yet Buthelezi remained its prime promoter in South Africa.

The exasperating reality for South African liberals and others interested in the emergence of a real multi-party democracy was the absence of any serious alternative to Buthelezi's Inkatha as a countervailing political weight to the ANC. The white liberal Democratic Party was far too small, and there was no Christian or Social Democratic black party in the making. The two other major black parties, the Pan Africanist Congress and the Azanian People's Organization, seemed determined to stick to hardline opposition politics, even though the polls showed little support for this. Without

Inkatha's willingness to stand up to the ANC, South Africa would undoubtedly have been headed for a de facto one-party system, with the ANC assuming the old role of de Klerk's National Party in controlling every branch of government. But the presence of Inkatha introduced an element of real uncertainty, for a coalition between Inkatha and the National Party could create serious opposition to the ANC in a new Parliament. Opinion polls taken between 1990 and 1992 showed Inkatha drawing anywhere from 3 to 12 percent of the vote—hardly enough to catapult Buthelezi into the president's office, but perhaps enough to make him a valuable ally for de Klerk. Buthelezi was not afraid to play this card in his dealings with Mandela.

The relationship between Mandela and Buthelezi had been extremely stormy from the start. As young men, they had been friendly; Buthelezi was once a member of the ANC Youth League, and was even expelled from Fort Hare University in 1950 for engaging in one of its boycotts. He was fond of reminding Mandela that he had initially become KwaZulu's chief minister with the express encouragement of the ANC, which had wanted to use Buthelezi to put the brakes on the wheel of the government's policy of setting up "independent" homelands. He had likewise consulted the ANC before launching Inkatha, and the ANC had again given its assent. In fact, the two organizations had enjoyed cordial relations from 1975 until 1979, acting as anti-apartheid allies, albeit increasingly uneasy ones. Buthelezi craved Mandela's blessing to establish his legitimacy in the ANC political community, but Mandela's main interest was not in boosting Buthelezi's standing but in curbing the violence undermining the ANC.

According to Buthelezi, the origins of the ANC–Inkatha split stemmed from his meeting in London in October 1979 with Oliver Tambo. Inkatha by then claimed a membership of 300,000, and Buthelezi was demanding outright ANC recognition of its status as "a dominant force in the country." The ANC, however, was under pressure to break with Buthelezi because Inkatha had opposed the 1976 Soweto revolt against the Afrikaner education system; its members had actually fought against those participating in the uprising. More to the point, the ANC was seeking to establish itself as the sole legitimate spokesman of the anti-apartheid struggle, and

Inkatha loomed as an obstacle to this objective. The policies of the two organizations were also clearly heading in opposite directions. Buthelezi later claimed that he had tried to convince the ANC president at their London meeting to abandon its armed struggle and hold talks with the Botha government. If this was the case, it was hardly surprising that the two had come to a parting of the ways and that the ANC thereafter regarded Buthelezi as a "tool" of the apartheid regime.

The Zulu leader fostered this antipathy by putting forth a political platform deliberately calculated to be the exact opposite of whatever the ANC stood for at any given time. The ANC had always advocated sanctions against South Africa as a way of pressuring the government to make concessions; Buthelezi in turn opposed them, arguing that their effect on the economy and on blacks was disastrous. The ANC attempted to carry out an armed struggle; Buthelezi defended nonviolence and negotiations. The ANC had a socialist-flavored economic policy; Inkatha's was distinctly capitalist-oriented. The ANC was a proponent of a strong, centralized state and government; Buthelezi insisted that the only form of government possible for South Africa was federalism. The ANC wanted to do away with the ten black homelands as soon as possible; Buthelezi insisted they be kept to form the nuclei of future "states" in a federal government. The ANC wanted to hold democratic elections as soon as possible to determine the relative strength of each political party; Buthelezi wanted to postpone them. The ANC went out of its way to avoid talking about ethnicity and minorities; Buthelezi constantly championed their importance in South Africa and contemporary world politics. Whenever the ANC and its allies called for a national strike to pressure the de Klerk government, Inkatha opposed it. About the only points in common between the ANC and Inkatha were that the ten homelands should be reincorporated into a single South Africa; that elections should be held on the basis of proportional representation to assure all parties representation in Parliament; and that an alliance with whites was desirable.

The ANC accused Buthelezi of defending policies and principles that were identical to those of the de Klerk government, seeking to discredit him as a puppet of the white establishment. While it was often true that Buthelezi took positions identical, or at least similar, to those of the government, he usually had his own very good political reasons for doing so. For example, Buthelezi favored federalism in order to preserve a regional power base for himself in KwaZulu. He sought to postpone elections as long as possible because they were likely to reveal his lack of large-scale national support and therefore would diminish his political influence. He was likewise opposed to an elected constituent assembly and interim government—even after de Klerk came around in support of these bodies—because he would be whittled down to his real political size. Buthelezi played up ethnicity and the importance of minorities not to please de Klerk and the whites so much as to mobilize his own shrinking power base.

Moreover, on closer inspection, Buthelezi was not the pliable prop of apartheid the ANC made him out to be. He had refused to accept "independence" for KwaZulu; he had led the struggle to prevent the Ingwavuma district in Natal from being incorporated into Swaziland; and he had repeatedly rejected negotiations with the white government unless Mandela were released from prison. P. W. Botha hated Buthelezi because of his obstructionism to his apartheid plans, and Buthelezi cleverly manipulated that hatred to promote his stature at home and abroad. Buthelezi was no one's fool. In fact, he proved an extraordinarily clever political manipulator of those who wanted to use him for their own ends.

ANC propaganda portraying Buthelezi as a puppet who would cease to exist if the struts and strings of the apartheid system were pulled away may have provided sweet music for its supporters, but it also led the ANC into numerous delusions and miscalculations about how to deal with him. The ANC instinct was to resort to strong-arm tactics. It tried to discredit Buthelezi by launching a major propaganda war against him, and when that didn't work, the ANC mobilized a one-day national strike against Buthelezi and his KwaZulu homeland on July 2, 1990—the first time such a tactic had been used by one black group against another. It had little visible effect.

The unbanning of all anti-apartheid groups in February 1990 had given rise to an explosion of pent-up political fireworks, inevitable after thirty years of police suppression. Despite the government's delaying tactics, thousands of political exiles returned home and thousands more poured out of the prisons. A new era had dawned, with the ANC and the Communist Party suddenly allowed to operate freely all over the country. Even the commanders, officers, and soldiers of Umkhonto we Sizwe could operate legally. Some Umkhonto members became active in helping to establish the largely autonomous "self-defense units" in townships and squatter camps dominated by the ANC; others joined the ANC struggle against Inkatha. Though the ANC had agreed to "suspend" its armed struggle in mid-1990, the smaller, more militant Pan Africanist Congress did not; in fact, its armed wing, Poqo, stepped up its "liberation struggle" and adopted a super-militant line in a bid to draw followers away from the ANC.

While all this was going on, the government's security forces remained totally unchanged: the police force responsible for maintaining apartheid over the decades, the mysterious Army Military Intelligence Department, expert in "dirty tricks" against the government's enemies; and the secretive military Civil Cooperation Bureau (CCB), a leftover "death squad" operation that had waged open warfare against the ANC. The political struggle between the government and the ANC did not suddenly end; it just changed form and arena. But the ingrained animosity of these security forces toward the ANC remained as great as ever.

Added to this volatile mixture of conflicting forces was a veritable deluge of Soviet-made AK-47 rifles coming in from Mozambique. Ironically, many of these guns were simply being recycled, since the South African security forces had provided thousands of them to rebels fighting the Frelimo government there in the 1980s. The rebels, as well as unpaid government soldiers, found a lucrative trade in gunrunning across the border. Everyone from ordinary bank robbers and carjackers to the ANC's self-defense units, Poqo hit-and-run commandos, and Inkatha warriors were using these former "weapons of liberation" to further their respective causes.

All those active in the South African "killing fields" around Johannesburg and in Natal—and there were plenty of participants—became experts in exculpating themselves of all blame for the violence. They passed responsibility back and forth, each seeking desperately to have the blame fall on someone else. The government immediately blamed the political violence on either the "black-on-black" power struggle between the ANC and Inkatha, Communist machinations inside the ANC, or the ANC's various "mass action" campaigns. The ANC, for its part, claimed it was all the fault of either the unreformed security forces; apartheid's "surrogates" like Chief Buthelezi or Brigadier Oupa Gqozo of the Ciskei; or a mysterious "third force" of renegade right-wing extremists operating from within the police and army. Inkatha attributed it principally to the ANC's drive to eliminate Buthelezi and his KwaZulu government from the political arena. The country's academics sought to apportion the fault among various social, economic, and political conditions beyond the control of any political faction. The violence, they said, was the product of apartheid, economic depression, a deeply racially divided society, the traumatic changes inherent in the transition of power from the white minority to the black majority, or some combination of these factors. There was truly a bewildering smorgasbord of culprits and causes to choose from.

The central nagging question remained, however, of whether the government was helping in any way to stir up the violence. Were the security forces really making a determined effort to curb it, or were they simply allowing it to flow forth? The main allegation of the ANC, and the black community in general, was that the security forces, commanded by the same cold warriors as before, were either stoking the volcano themselves or were helping others to provoke "eruptions" deliberately in order to strengthen the government's political position.

In part, the police and the government's attitude of callous indifference grew out of the Afrikaners' view of African society. The police seemed to just shrug off the violence as the "natural" consequence of an Afrikaner-imagined historic rivalry between the Zulus and Xhosas. The two ethnic groups, South Africa's largest (Zulus numbered about seven million and Xhosas in the Transkei and South Africa hardly less) had both fought the white colonial invaders in different parts of the country, but they had never clashed with each other over land or king. Yet the general Afrikaner perception was that Inkatha was "the Zulu party" and the ANC "the Xhosa party." The unquestioned assumption was that the Zulus, a proud warrior nation, would never submit to "Xhosa rule" and would resist to the end its imposition. The fighting, therefore, was inevitable. Afrikaner police officials, military officers, academics, and average citizens all propounded this view despite the fact that there was no historic precedent of Zulus and Xhosas fighting each other, and that in Natal Province, Zulus were on both sides in great numbers. While it was true that in the townships around Johannesburg the fighting had become highly "ethnicized" along Zulu-Xhosa lines, this was largely the result of Buthelezi's exploitation of Zulu pride to rally the migrant Zulu workers to his side.

The Afrikaners, moreover, had their own political reasons for their affinity for Inkatha and its followers. The Afrikaner establishment had always appreciated Buthelezi's insistent theme of the Zulu "nation" because it served to confirm the multi-ethnic makeup of South Africa and the "right" of each group to recognition and protection of its special, separate identity. The ANC was the Afrikaners' enemy, as it wanted to obliterate the concept of separate homelands for each ethnic "nation" and form what the Afrikaners as well as Inkatha saw as a Xhosa-dominated centralized government. Viewed from this peculiar Afrikaner angle, the Inkatha battle against the ANC could only be regarded as a boon to the Afrikaner quest for an ethnically based federal solution. The violence could easily be ignored if it advanced that cause.

By the middle of 1990, it had become clear that the Inkatha-controlled hostels had become the centers of the perpetual explosions of violence rocking the townships. Either ANC supporters were attacking them, or Inkatha members were launching raids into the townships from them. Starting as early as March 1990, at the time of the attacks around Pietermaritzburg, the ANC began raising the issue of their closure, or their conversion from single-men's dorms to family units. The hostels would remain a central topic of all ANC–government negotiations regarding the violence over the next two years.

Inkatha operated each hostel as an urban fortress to expand its zone of influence into the surrounding areas. Inkatha would bring in traditional *indunas* to organize the hostel inmates, as the dorm residents are called, into Zulu fighting units that could be mobilized at a moment's notice. Once its hold over a hostel was consolidated, Inkatha would systematically send out small raiding parties to attack and intimidate residents in the adjacent streets until they had established an entire Inkatha-controlled district around the building.

De Klerk, however, remained extremely hesitant to crack down on these hostels, largely because of his own ambiguous policies toward the ANC and Inkatha. He couldn't decide whether Chief Buthelezi should be treated as a potential ally against the ANC or as an obstacle to an alliance between his National Party and the ANC. If the NP party opted for an electoral strategy of building an anti-ANC coalition of moderate black, Coloured, and Indian groups, Inkatha would then play a large role in its success. Buthelezi, after all, hated the ANC far more than the National Party did and like de Klerk was an avid proponent of federalism. If he wanted to have Buthelezi on his side, de Klerk could not overlook his wishes, and the chief was adamantly opposed to all the ANC proposals for fencing in, phasing out, or converting the hostels.

Mandela felt that de Klerk bore a heavy personal responsibility for the violence, and said so publicly and repeatedly. In his words, "either President de Klerk has lost control of his security forces or he is conniving with them." As Mandela saw it, de Klerk never made a serious effort to try to rein in his own security forces. De Klerk again and again would promise to "investigate" the cases brought to his attention, but would then do nothing. Mandela said that he had warned de Klerk, even before he was released from prison, that the violence would become a problem for their relationship if it were allowed to get out of control. "No amount of moderation or logic on the part of any liberation leader will be able to convince people not to get out of hand," he had warned de Klerk. The president had at his disposal a security establishment that had successfully suppressed the liberation struggle for three decades. Those same security forces had the means to curb the violence if they really tried, according to Mandela. Of course, it was also true that if de Klerk had employed the same methods as the government to suppress the violence against the anti-apartheid struggle, Mandela and the ANC would have been just as critical.

Mandela's slow but progressive disenchantment with de Klerk over the violence began in July 1990, with the first major clash since his release between the ANC and Inkatha in the Johannesburg region. The fighting in the black township of Sebokeng marked the start of the Inkatha offensive to establish itself as a political party in the townships all around Johannesburg and in the Vaal Triangle to the south. It happened in the wake of the ANC's July 2 nationwide strike against Buthelezi. In this boiling political atmosphere, the ANC obtained information that Inkatha was going to stage a big show of force in Sebokeng on July 22 that was likely to end in an attack on ANC supporters there. ANC lawyers wrote two letters to Minister of Law and Order Adriaan Vlok as well as to the two commanders of the Transvaal police force, pleading with them to cancel the Inkatha rally. Mandela said that at first there was no response from any of them, though he did eventually receive assurances that the police stood ready to forestall any violence. But Inkatha would be allowed to hold its rally despite the high potential for an explosion.

So Inkatha went ahead with its plan, busing in its supporters from Johannesburg's hostels, armed to the teeth with their "traditional weapons." Predictably, fighting did break out, and around thirty people were killed, mostly ANC supporters. The next day, Mandela went to the Sebokeng morgue and then visited the hospital to express his solidarity with the survivors. After all his attempts to prevent the violence, he was understandably furious.

On July 24, he went to see de Klerk, seeking an explanation for the police's inaction. An angry exchange ensued. "I said, 'You were warned beforehand. You did nothing about it. Why?' " Mandela later recounted. " 'Why is it that there have been no arrests? In any other country, where thirty-two people had been slaughtered in this way, the head of state would come out condemning the matter and giving his sympathies to the next of kin. Why have you not done so?' " De Klerk's answer, according to Mandela, was "absolutely ludicrous." The president tried to deflect Mandela's criticism by noting that police reinforcements, even helicopters, had been sent to Sebokeng. He conceded, however, that these measures had been taken not on the day of the Inkatha rally, but the next day, to protect Mandela during his visit to the Sebokeng morgue and hospital. As for the police's failure to intervene to stop the trouble, after repeated warnings, "de Klerk just had no answer," according to Mandela.

This head-to-head confrontation between Mandela and de Klerk over Sebokeng was followed the very next month by a government decision to change the "Zulu code" of Natal Province. The changes specifically permitted Zulus to carry "dangerous weapons" to political rallies for the first time. The government "proclamation," dated August 31 and signed by de Klerk himself, stated that "no black shall carry an *assegai* [spear], sword stick, battle axe, stick shod with iron, staff or sharp-pointed stick or any other dangerous weapon" except in a specific number of circumstances. Among those listed was the bearing of such weapons if a person could "prove that he had the bona fide intention to carry such dangerous weapons in accordance with traditional Zulu usages, customs or religions." Clearly, the major beneficiary of this decree could only have been Inkatha, the vast majority of whose members were Zulus.

Mandela said that the proclamation was a sobering eye-opener for him about de Klerk's behavior: "It served his own political objectives. I realized the game he was playing." The Legal Resources Center, a human rights monitoring group, led the outcry against the proclamation, forcing the government to defend its provocative decision. The decree took effect September 30. But ten days later, the government issued a statement that constituted a masterpiece of doubletalk and subterfuge. It had only changed the Zulu code in order to maintain better law and order, and any questioning of de Klerk's aversion to violence was "preposterous." The old Zulu code had become "archaic" and "too rigid" to apply effectively. The revised code was far better because it would now be up to the individual to prove he had "bona fide intentions" in carrying dangerous weapons to a rally. Buried at the bottom of the statement was the punch line: The code had been altered, it said, because to take "extreme measures in terms of which the Zulu nation is strictly disarmed in all circumstances of any traditional weapons would simply add fuel to present frustrations." Zulus would suffer "a loss of dignity," and the result would be a "further increase in rage and violence." In other words, the government was arguing that it was acting to curb the violence by allowing Inkatha members to carry dangerous weapons in public!

The furor over these changes to the Zulu code was followed in November by a massive Inkatha attack on an ANC stronghold, the squatter camp of Zonkizizwe on the East Rand outside Johannesburg. "Zonkizizwe," Mandela noted with irony, means in Zulu, "place where all nations are welcome." The attack ended in the rout of all residents and a total Inkatha takeover of the camp. Mandela said that he again went to see de Klerk, as well as Vlok, to ask why no action had been taken to restore the shacks to their rightful owners. De Klerk, he said, seemed totally unaware of the incident. But Vlok was "very bold and slightly rude to me," asking, " 'Who owned the land anyway on which your people were living?' " To Mandela, that seemed secondary to the main question of the police inaction. In fact, the local authorities had made the land available for squatters generally, and were even trying to get others from another violence-torn camp to move there. De Klerk promised Mandela to investigate the matter but he "never came back to me." Mandela said he brought up Zonkizizwe with de Klerk again and again, but never got a reply.

The fighting between ANC and Inkatha supporters escalated steadily during the last months of 1990, with Inkatha seizing by force more and more hostels around Johannesburg and turning them into its strongholds and operation centers. The ANC was doing as much in the squatter camps, so the fighting tended to center either on these camps or in the hostels.

Mandela had initially tried to resolve this crisis with Inkatha through old-fashioned, personal diplomacy, but Harry Gwala and the other hardline regional ANC leaders in Natal had already vetoed that idea in March 1990. A Buthelezi-Mandela summit finally did take place on January 29, 1991, but so much blood had flown across Natal by then that the chances of diffusing the accumulated enmity were slim.

Buthelezi, acutely aware that he was facing political marginalization and desperately seeking recognition for himself and Inkatha, seized upon the occasion to vent his political spleen, opening old wounds and airing his own grievances. He dug up old statements made by ANC officials as far back as 1985 vilifying him as a "ban-

tustan chief" and "collaborator" with the racist apartheid government, rereading them aloud to all assembled for the summit at
Durban's Royal Hotel. He went on and on, reading page after page
of insults and cataloguing all the political differences that still separated Inkatha from the ANC. He warned that if the ANC continued to demand an elected constituent assembly and interim
government "it can only lead to disaster for us all."

The summit could well have ended in total disaster if Mandela
had not intervened to counsel other members of his delegation to
remain calm and not respond in kind. In his own speech, Mandela
went out of his way to appease Buthelezi, thanking him for his
contribution in securing his release from prison, and underlining
the common goals of their two organizations. The summit ended
with the signing of what was supposed to be a peace agreement
setting forth a code of conduct for dealing with each other, calling
for an end to the violence and creating joint committees to deal
with the violence on the ground. But there was no real will on
either side to implement the agreement, and it quickly became
soaked in blood.

In March 1991, Inkatha moved into Alexandra, the only black
township inside the city limits of Johannesburg. Forty-five people
died there in three days of fighting March 8–10. Affidavits of alleged police collusion with Inkatha kept piling up at ANC headquarters: Residents in Alexandra as well as other strife-torn townships recounted incident after incident in which they claimed to
have seen police vehicles transporting Inkatha supporters or white
policemen actively participating in attacks on ANC squatter camps
or township homes. By the time the government belatedly sent in
police and army reinforcements to quell the fighting, and finally
declared the township an "unrest area" a few days after the worst
killing was over, Inkatha members, many brought in from outside,
had succeeded in seizing control of the Madala Hostel. This was a
huge, fortresslike building sprawled across the top of the main hill
overlooking the entire township and thus a strategic asset. It
housed 2,000 to 3,000 migrant workers, originally from a variety of
ethnic groups. When the fighting finally subsided, nearly all the
remaining residents were Zulus and all were Inkatha members.

Having gained this foothold in Alex, Inkatha decided to hold a big rally on March 17 to mark its arrival in the township and the creation of a new branch. To the astonishment of everybody, the police allowed Inkatha to proceed with its demonstration even though it was still an "unrest area" and tensions were running high. Anticipating trouble, a number of foreign correspondents showed up early the morning of the rally to witness what would happen. To our surprise, we found that the police were allowing Inkatha supporters from Soweto and other townships to be bused in by the hundreds to augment the size of the crowd. Even more incredible, after stopping a few of the new arrivals armed with a motley array of "traditional weapons," the police finally gave up and let them all come into Alex armed with spears, pangas, knobkerries, and war clubs. General Johan Erasmus, the commanding police officer that day, told us he was going to request that all arms be handed in, but he never did. "We of course don't approve of those pangas at all," he commented at one point, with a big smile. His only reply when asked why he had allowed the rally at all in the prevailing tense conditions was, "They might as well get it over with."

The rally and an ensuing street march almost turned into a pitched battle between the 5,000 Inkatha supporters and the ANC residents; word reached the already aroused crowd that two Inkatha members who had lost their way had been hacked to death deep inside the township. We found their bodies in the middle of the road near the township's stadium, where the ANC was holding its own rally; they had been stabbed and stoned to death. With the help of army reinforcements, Erasmus just barely managed to keep the incensed Inkatha crowd from taking its revenge on the Alex residents. Six people died that day, but the toll could easily have been far higher.

All this directly affected Mandela; he was besieged with desperate pleas for help, yet found himself unable to obtain any assistance from de Klerk or his ministers. The final straw was a massacre in Daveyton, east of Johannesburg, on March 24. As in Sebokeng the year before, police opened fire on an ANC demonstration, this time causing at least twelve deaths. It was becoming clear to Mandela that the entire country would first have to concentrate on curbing the violence before any constitutional negotiations could get under way.

◆ ◆ ◆

When Steve McDonald, an official of the Colorado-based Aspen
Institute, went to Cape Town's airport on April 3, 1991, to pick up
Nelson Mandela, he found the ANC leader in an exceedingly angry
mood. They were on their way to a symposium organized by the
institute for members of the U.S. Congress and their aides, and
Mandela was a featured speaker. De Klerk, he said, had betrayed
his trust, spurned his requests for help, and done nothing to curb
the violence in the townships. Behind closed doors at the colonial-
style Mount Nelson Hotel, Mandela continued his tirade against
de Klerk during a three-hour question-and-answer session with
twenty-one stunned American senators and congressmen. He listed
by date, and recounted in great detail, the various occasions over
the past year when he had asked de Klerk for help in rendering
justice to the latest ANC victims of the township violence. An
American diplomat present at that session remembered that Mandela had used the word *connivance* three times when referring to de
Klerk's role in the violence.

The next day at lunch, de Klerk came to address the same group
of Americans. When he was asked by several congressmen about
Mandela's complaints, de Klerk at first didn't seem to take them
seriously. But as more and more questions were raised about the
specific incidents Mandela had cited, the president began to realize
the seriousness of his problem. McDonald recalled that at first de
Klerk had seemed truly unaware that his personal relationship with
Mandela had deteriorated. But the reality was that Mandela had
undergone a fundamental conversion in his attitude toward the
state president. Because the Aspen Institute meeting was a private
gathering, not a word of what had transpired appeared in the local
or foreign press. It was not until November of that year that their
falling-out became visible as Mandela went public with one denunciation after another of his fellow peacemaker.

In tracing where and when the "special relationship" between
these two leaders crumbled, it becomes clear that the main cause
was the pervasive violence ravaging the fabric of the peace process.
By refusing to answer the ANC leader's pleas for help, de Klerk had
undermined Mandela's credibility and standing within the black
community. Mandela seemed to have come to the conclusion that

the president's inaction indicated that de Klerk had betrayed his trust and was exploiting his goodwill for purely personal political gains. He had made a fundamental error of judgment about de Klerk and had been duped into believing the two of them had similar agendas and objectives in mind. Mandela felt he had been used by de Klerk, whom he had been defending as an honest reformer.

The fallout from Mandela's change of attitude was felt immediately. On April 4, the same day de Klerk was learning about Mandela's disenchantment with him from the American congressmen, the ANC's National Executive Committee began a two-day meeting devoted to the escalating violence, at which Mandela confessed his initial misjudgment of de Klerk. He had been wrong to call him "a man of integrity," for he had come to realize that de Klerk had a different agenda from the ANC's and that he was a cunning, shrewd, and callous adversary. He had tried to get through to de Klerk but had failed. The skeptics, he admitted, had been right.

Mandela then presented the NEC with a formal apology for misleading them. Suddenly, he was the "hawk," calling for the suspension of all contacts with the government until it did something concrete to dampen the violence. At the end of the meeting, the NEC issued an "ultimatum" to de Klerk in the form of an open letter, putting the president on notice that if he did not act to curb the violence by meeting seven ANC demands, the talks about talks would be over. The demands seemed absolutely fanciful at the time, calculated to assure a deadlock. They included firing Defense Minister Magnus Malan and Law and Order Minister Adriaan Vlok; outlawing the carrying of dangerous weapons at public meetings; dismantling all Army counterinsurgency units; closing down the migrant workers' hostels; and establishing an independent commission of inquiry to investigate complaints of police misconduct. The ANC also wanted a purge from the police force of all officers and men implicated in various incidents of violence. It gave the government until May 9 to meet these demands.

Many local and foreign political analysts as well as most government officials interpreted the ANC "ultimatum" as an excuse to postpone the start of constitutional talks with the government until after the ANC's national conference that July. The ANC did not have its own house in order yet, the reasoning went, and a new leadership, empowered to negotiate with de Klerk, was expected to emerge from the elections at the conference. That may well have been among the reasons for the ANC's sudden tough attitude toward the government. But it seemed more convincing that without Mandela's change of attitude there probably would not have been a breakdown in the peace process at that point. This would be only the first of many major crises over the violence, which before long would destroy Mandela's fading trust and faith in de Klerk.

8

THE SORROWS OF
NELSON MANDELA

"Ladies and gentlemen, I hope you will appreciate the pain I have gone through."

Such were the final words of anguish blurted from the lips of Nelson Mandela on April 13, 1992, the day he announced his separation from his wife, Winnie. It was a terribly sad moment for the Mandela family, the African National Congress, and the whole black community. The marriage of South Africa's most visible couple had finally fallen apart. The ailing Oliver Tambo, whose wife, Adelaide, had introduced Nelson to Winnie back in 1957, was at his side, along with Walter Sisulu, his oldest and closest friend. Nelson's voice seldom trembled, but it did that day as he read a prepared statement at the ANC's headquarters in downtown Johannesburg. Every television camera in the city seemed to be there, recording a historic event long expected and more than a year in the making.

Everyone knew Nelson and Winnie had never enjoyed a normal married or family life because "the struggle" had always come first. Nelson reminded reporters of this as he began reading his statement, which was full of praise for Winnie and her unstinting devotion to him during his long years in prison. She had endured the hell of apartheid's jails, innumerable bannings, and daily persecution at the hands of the police for nearly three decades; she had kept alive his memory and that of the black nationalist cause in the darkest days of the struggle. "Her tenacity reinforced my personal respect, love, and growing affection," he said. "My love for her remains undiminished." Unfortunately, "tensions" had arisen between them owing to differences over "a number of issues." Nelson did not elaborate, but every reporter there knew what he was referring to. They had both agreed that it was in their best interest to separate, he said. He would, nonetheless, continue his unstinting support for her during what he called "these trying moments in her life." The press conference ended in an awkward silence, with Nelson rising suddenly from the table and uttering those last few words of private pain. Nobody there doubted they were true.

Two days later, it was Winnie's turn to face the media. She spoke with tears in her eyes and a voice that was at times faltering: "My husband has been the focus of my life and my love throughout our marriage and continues to be so," she said. "Nothing can make me waver in my commitment to my organization, to my husband, and to the oppressed and impoverished people of South Africa." The political fallout for her came immediately. Winnie announced she was resigning as head of the ANC's Social Welfare Department, claiming she had become the victim of a "campaign of vilification," referring to her court conviction the previous year for her role in the kidnapping of four Soweto youths. She insisted that she was innocent and that other charges of political and personal misconduct leveled against her by the local and foreign media were totally false. Nonetheless, she acknowledged that the allegations had created a "difficult situation" for the ANC, her husband, and herself.

Few tears were shed for Nomzamo Zaniewe Winnifred Mandela over the separation. They were all for Nelson. The overwhelming sentiment within the ANC, shared by much of the black community, was that the long-suffering martyr of apartheid had now fallen victim to his own wife's political and sexual machinations. He had been duped by the very woman he had longed for in prison and had initially idolized after his release. Their separation was a poignant reminder that great leaders often lead tragic personal lives because of their commitment to larger causes. Mandela seemed philosophically resigned to this fate. He told guests attending the wedding reception for his daughter Zindzi, in late October 1992, that it seemed to be the destiny of famous freedom fighters to see their family lives "totally destabilized." His certainly was.

Married in June 1958 in the midst of his first treason trial, Nelson and Winnie had hardly ever lived together except as two myths and symbols of the struggle. Nelson went underground in April 1961, had been arrested and jailed in mid-1962, and had then been sentenced to life imprisonment in June 1964. As a result, he and Winnie had spent less than four of the thirty-four years of their formal marriage together, two before his detention and two after his release. It had been a marriage, conceived on the battlefield of the anti-apartheid struggle, that had finally become another of its victims. He had hardly known his daughters by Winnie, Zeni and Zindzi, or they him. He reflected on the sad state of his own family life in that moving speech at Zindzi's wedding: "We watched our children growing without our guidance and when we did come out [of prison], my children, for example, said: 'We thought we had a father and one day he'd come back. But to our dismay, our father comes back and he leaves us alone almost daily because he has now become the father of the nation.'" Mandela said he had often reflected on whether the struggle had been worth the loss of a normal family life but had always concluded, "It was, it is, the correct decision that we should commit ourselves."

In the spring and summer of 1991, Mandela faced two new major setbacks to his authority—the public shaming of his wife and the loss of his control over ANC, Inc. He emerged from these twin ordeals a far lonelier figure, with only his faith in his mission to carry him forward. De Klerk had already deeply disappointed him, and his hopes for a close, special relationship with South Africa's white leader had been dashed. Now it was the turn of his wife and the ANC to slip from his grasp.

Of all the challenges to his leadership that Mandela faced after returning to freedom, none was more debilitating than dealing with his own wife. Winnie not only proved to be Nelson's emotional Achilles' heel, she became one of the principal causes of the erosion of his moral and political authority within the ANC. The

question of what to do about Winnie turned into a major controversy within the National Executive Committee, just as it had in the
United Democratic Front before Nelson's release. It put Nelson to
another kind of leadership test that he was slow to meet because he
was blinded to the truth by his strong feelings of guilt for having
left Winnie on her own for so long. In the end, only Nelson could
resolve the dilemma Winnie posed for him and the whole ANC,
but it took him almost two years to come to terms with Winnie's
dark side and to liberate himself from his guilt.

In the process, a lot of political damage was done both to himself
and to the ANC as Winnie ruthlessly exploited his guilt to resur-
rect her own political career. Nelson allowed himself to be caught
up in her political intrigues aimed at positioning herself to become
South Africa's Corazon Aquino. He even endured in discreet silence the sexual escapades that had become the talk of the nation.
Not until Winnie's extravagant misbehavior had become too much
even for him to tolerate did he yield to the pressure from distraught
ANC officials, who worried that she was corrupting the entire
ANC leadership and tearing apart its Women's League.

The fate of the Mandela marriage became a topic of speculation almost from the day Nelson was released from prison. On
February 15, 1990, the *Johannesburg Star* carried interviews with
several British psychologists who predicted rough times ahead.
Nelson and Winnie had not lived together long enough to cement
a strong emotional bond, these analysts said. The two had lived
separate lives for far too long. They would both find they were
living with "a complete stranger." Winnie's love would be "one
of reverence, not passion or desire," similar to the kind of emotion a devotee felt for "a saint or martyr," opined one psycholo-
gist, David Lewis. He also predicted that Winnie would have a
massive emotional readjustment to make as she found herself
relegated to the sidelines when her own international notoriety
was eclipsed by Nelson's far greater fame. Time was to prove
these predictions all too true. Winnie would demonstrate her
total inability to make that readjustment or others. As her devious and deviant conduct became all too obvious to everyone, the
general view within the ANC and the black community was that
Winnie was to blame for the breakup of the Mandela marriage,

though living with a myth who was also a human being could not have been easy for any woman.

Winnie never learned from her own mistakes or came to understand when she had gone too far. Even after Nelson's release, she continued to regard herself as a political untouchable, standing above not only the apartheid laws of the land but the discipline and rules of her own organization. So, until their separation, we were treated to the ugly spectacle of her manipulation of Nelson to serve her own political ends, inflicting enormous emotional pain on Nelson and political damage on the ANC. Winnie was driven by a lust for power so great that even Nelson became only a pawn in her schemes. The irony was that she might have had it all if she had played her cards more carefully and been less aggressive and abrasive. Winnie had everything necessary to become the first first lady of a black-ruled South Africa. It was a position that would have assured her place in history. She even had an outside shot at becoming president, riding to power on the certain explosion of public sympathy for Nelson at his death. She blew it all.

Winnie could not control her worst impulses, her need for immediate gratification, be it political or sexual. She behaved like an *inlokhasi*, a she-elephant, as she was called by some of her township admirers. But she was a maverick one, determined to bull her way past any obstacle that stood in her way. She was voracious in her appetite for power, posts, and privileges within the ANC, getting herself elected to half a dozen executive positions. To all appearances, Winnie had developed a split personality. She was capable at times of enormous generosity, civility, and caring for the victims of the political violence. Often she was the first—sometimes the only—ANC official to rush to comfort those who had just lost family members and homes in the latest incident. The flip side of her personality was that she had a vile temper and turned on friends as well as foes without notice and with only the slightest cause. Nobody was spared her outbursts of uncontrollable anger. She even once slapped the face of Thabo Mbeki, head of the ANC international affairs department, because he thwarted her. Her trial in early 1991 revealed a woman who had become incredibly hardened and had indulged, apparently with relish, in outright township thuggery. There was a great deal of evidence that she had approved of, and possibly ordered, the numerous murders of her real and imagined foes. And she had gathered around herself an incredible collection of township thugs, wayward youths, and sycophants, while those of good character and intention who tried to help her usually found themselves tainted by the association.

There were all kinds of theories as to the cause of her misbehavior: schizophrenia, alcoholism, prolonged persecution, or megalomania. I had always wondered what role the American and British media had played. The foreign press had built her into the personification of the apartheid struggle, giving her a martyrlike image in the eyes of the world. It had then destroyed that saintly image as it reported more and more often on her township activities. Had this fall from media grace somehow affected her mentally? I was convinced that a similar experience had affected President Anwar Sadat of Egypt, whom I had watched become progressively hysterical in the final months before his assassination by Islamic fanatics in October 1981. Sadat couldn't understand why the Western media had taken to questioning his judgment and criticizing him for his harsh crackdown on a growing Islamic opposition at home. The criticism became a mirror into which he could not look after years of being the object of American hero worship. Like Sadat, after enjoying a martyr's status, Winnie couldn't cope with the rising tide of public criticism of her behavior. Whatever the cause, or combination of causes, Winnie Mandela by 1990 appeared to be truly mentally ill. Driven by an uncontrollable desire for power and attention, and hardened by confrontation with the authorities, she became bent on her own self-destruction. In the process, she corrupted everything and everybody around her. But most unforgivable was her callous exploitation and public humiliation of Nelson, the very man she claimed she had always idolized.

Most "Winnie watchers" seemed to agree that the turning point in her life came in May 1977 when Winnie—who had lived under banning orders almost continuously since 1962, as well as spent seventeen months in solitary confinement—was summarily sent into banishment in the small Orange Free State *dorp*, or village, of Brandfort, located in the heart of Afrikaner redneck farming country. Winnie's plight evoked tremendous sympathy, and the sympathy quickly became admiration as she dared to challenge the apartheid laws of separate lines for blacks and whites at the local post office and grocery store. She even managed to organize a strike of farm workers from the confines of her hovel in the black township of Phathakahle just outside Brandfort.

If her will to defy the apartheid system was fortified by her experience in Brandfort, something else snapped in her psyche there. These eight years of isolation and lonely struggle took their toll on her mental balance. Reporters who covered her activities before and after her stay in Brandfort stated emphatically that she had returned to Soweto in August 1985 a markedly different person. Part of her problem at that point may have been alcoholism. But she had also become embittered and paranoid, no longer able to distinguish foe from friend after years of dealing with intrigues, police informers, and betrayals by those around her.

Winnie had left Brandfort, breaking her banning order, after her two-room house was ransacked by youths probably acting at the instigation of the local police authorities. She used the incident to boldly defy the authorities to stop her from returning to her own home on Vilakazi Street in Soweto's Orlando West district and got away with it. So she settled back down into township politics just as resistance to the apartheid system was about to take a powerful upward surge. Many of the townships tried to establish "liberation zones," setting up neighborhood street committees led by teenagers ready to take on the police with rocks, sticks, and firebombs. South Africa's resistance fighters came up with their own horrific style of punishment—necklacing—to deal with police informers, or *impimpis*. Winnie in turn became infamous for her May 1986 statement, "With our boxes of matches and our necklaces, we shall liberate this country." Less than a year after her return, in June 1986, the government declared a state of nationwide emergency.

It was in this atmosphere of township insurrection and intensive police repression that Winnie gave birth to what was to become her undoing, the Mandela United Football Club. Naming soccer clubs after popular anti-apartheid leaders was the rage of the township at the time. And Winnie the social worker and political activist was taking in homeless youth on the run from the authorities. Forming a club under her patronage was thus nothing out of the ordinary, but there was clearly a fine line in those tumultuous times between social, political, and criminal activities. Gangs of *tsotsis*, teenage thugs, often extorted protection money and laid down their own law in their neighborhoods in the name of "the struggle."

A good account of how Mandela United was founded and slipped from playing soccer to playing revolution was published in the London *Independent* on September 21, 1990. Lerothodi Ikaneng, a founding member, told the newspaper that Mandela United had emerged in 1986 out of Winnie's efforts to end the fighting between two rival gangs of about twenty "comrades" each. The gangs agreed, at Winnie's suggestion, to bury the hatchet and form a football club under her auspices. Some of them went to live in the backyard room of a second Mandela home in Soweto's Diepkloof Extension. Ikaneng said the club actually played a few games before turning to political and criminal activities. In late January 1987, those club members living at Winnie's home were arrested in connection with the first of many shootings. Things became worse for the club when Winnie sought to use its members as "enforcers" to extend her own political influence across Soweto. Under her auspices, and the iron fist of "Coach" Jerry Richardson, they held a kangaroo "people's court" that judged and sentenced their victims, sometimes to death. The *Independent* found evidence linking Winnie and her football club to the killing of sixteen Soweto residents, mostly teenagers. By the time Winnie went on trial in early 1991, four members of Mandela United were sitting on death row in Pretoria's main prison, including "Coach" Richardson, in connection with twelve of those murders.

It took the slaying of a fourteen-year-old township resistance hero, "Stompie" Moketsi Seipei, to bring matters to a head. Leaders of the anti-apartheid mass democratic movement had been paralyzed in their efforts to deal with Winnie, who had gained the stature of "Mother of the Nation" in the black community. A kind of conspiracy of silence had developed around Winnie and her football club; hardly a word was reported in either the local or foreign press about their increasingly wayward activities because it was feared that such criticism would serve only to discredit the anti-apartheid struggle. Nomavenda Mathiane, a black woman reporter writing for the now defunct periodical *Frontline File*, was the only reporter who dared to raise any questions locally about what the Mandela United Football Club was really up to. William Claiborne of the *Washington Post* was one of the few foreign correspondents who reported early on about the questionable activities around Winnie. On February 26, 1987, the *Post* published his story relating how the Mandela's Orlando West home had been stoned by black youths the day before. The stoning was carried out by students of the Daliwonga High School in retaliation for having been chased off a disputed soccer field by members of Winnie's football club. Claiborne reminded readers that this had not been the first sign of popular discontent with Winnie. She had been pelted in Cape Town the previous December with soft drink cans, litter, and sand thrown by a crowd that had become infuriated when she gave her blessings to an unpopular local woman just convicted of murdering her husband.

Stompie's murder broke the wall of silence protecting Winnie. He and three other youths had been kidnapped from a Methodist Church manse in Orlando West not far from the Mandela home. This time Winnie was taking on the church, which happened to have an excellent record for supporting the anti-apartheid movement. Though a Methodist herself, she had become embroiled in a quarrel with the church pastor, Paul Verryn, who also had a group of homeless youth staying with him. Winnie made the mistake of taking seriously the allegations of her friend Xoliswa Falati, the housemother at the manse, a woman who later turned out to be seriously mad. Falati told Winnie that Verryn was molesting a number of the boys staying with him and that something had to be done to save them from his sodomy.

So Winnie told Falati and Richardson to organize their "rescue," which they did on the night of December 29, 1988, bringing four frightened youths to the backyard of Winnie's Diepkloof home. There the four were interrogated and beaten mercilessly by club members to wring "confessions" from them about Verryn's alleged homosexual activities. Stompie came in for special treatment because he was believed to have become an *impimpi* for the police. He barely survived his "interrogation," only to be taken away three nights later by "Coach" Richardson and knifed to death. His body was found on January 6, 1989, in an empty Soweto field. The next day, Kenneth Kgase, another of the kidnap victims, escaped while on "guard duty" outside the Mandela home. He immediately alerted Methodist Church elders to what had happened to him and his three friends. The community could take it no longer and decided to put a stop to Winnie's antics.

Winnie was put on trial by her peers in the mass democratic movement and in Soweto later that month. The trial was carried out mostly in closed meetings in Soweto and Johannesburg, and included secret memos sent to the ANC leadership in Lusaka. Winnie, who had conducted her own "people's courts" inside her Soweto home, was now to be judged herself in a similar fashion. But she refused to cooperate or accept that she or her football club had done anything wrong. For leaders of the movement and Soweto, it was no easy verdict to reach, namely that the "Mother of the Nation" was guilty and deserved "banishment," politically if not physically, once again. Such a step was certain to become a national scandal and play right into the hands of the authorities, who were always anxious to seize upon the slightest pretext to discredit the entire anti-apartheid movement.

It was a moment of real testing for the movement's leadership. Already, in August 1988, a "Mandela Crisis Committee" had been established to deal with the fire-bombing of the Mandela home on Vilakazi Street by another gang at odds with Winnie's football club. (Reflecting the mood of the district, none of the neighbors had helped put out the blaze.) Now the committee was to serve as the "court" that would pass judgment on Winnie. The jury included some of the movement's heavyweights, people like Cyril Ramaphosa, general secretary of the National Union of Mineworkers; Aubrey Mokoena, leader of the Free Mandela Campaign; Reverend Frank Chikane, general secretary of the South African Council of Churches; and a number of other well-known church leaders. Methodist Bishop Peter Storey, who was not a committee member, later said that he was involved in thirty-five meetings and "encounters" between January 9 and 16 in various attempts to resolve the "Winnie crisis." The committee consulted repeatedly with both the ANC leadership in Lusaka and Nelson himself through his lawyer, Ismail Ayoub. It took Nelson's personal intervention to convince Winnie to finally release Gabriel Mekgwe and Thabiso

Mono, the two remaining kidnapped youths still being held at her home.

A Crisis Committee memo sent to ANC President Tambo in mid-January 1989 reflected the agony of its members as more and more evidence surfaced as to what had happened at Winnie's home. The committee had obtained its first detailed account of the kidnappings from a Mandela football club member, Katiza Cebekhulu, who said that he had actually taken part in the beatings. Recounting his experience before Stompie's fate was known for sure, he told the committee that all four had been "heavily assaulted" and that he believed Stompie was dead. On the basis of his account, the committee called a meeting of all Soweto civic group leaders the night of January 16, after Mekgwe and Mono had been turned over to Bishop Storey. These two confirmed Cebekhulu's account. (A doctor who testified at Winnie's 1991 trial said Mekgwe had received "nineteen blows at least" on his back, hip, chest, face, and eyes from a leather whip. He also found fifteen abrasions from whip lashes on Mono's body.) They also told the committee that Winnie herself had struck the first blows and punches. After recovering from their ordeal, they had been made to clean their own blood off the walls and floor of the interrogation room. Then they had been impressed into the services of the club as guards and cleaners.

All this was being told to the committee only days after the event and more than two years before the same testimony would be formally presented to a Johannesburg court. It was also at this meeting that the proposal was first put forth that Winnie be formally ostracized from black politics. The committee resolved that "all progressive organizations should no longer give her a platform" and that she be ordered immediately to dismantle her football club "lest the community dismantle the club for her." Finally, the committee demanded that Winnie "desist from creating an impression that she speaks on behalf of the people" and advised all "progressive lawyers" to refrain from helping her any longer.

Winnie's first response upon being informed of the meeting's decisions was to reject its authority and demand a list of all those present. "She seems to think that she is above the community. She shows utter contempt for both the Crisis Committee and the community," Oliver Tambo was told. The committee appealed for his guidance to deal with "this new ghastly situation that is developing before our very eyes" and asked whether he saw any way of rehabilitating her. Winnie was threatening to call a press conference and announce her resignation from the ANC, a step that would have inflicted devastating damage on the entire anti-apartheid cause. It was the kind of political blackmail she would come to use again and again in dealing with her opponents in the ANC after Mandela's release.

But movement leaders, with the backing of ANC headquarters in Lusaka and at least Nelson's full knowledge, did not flinch. On February 16, the United Democratic Front and the Congress of South African Trade Unions, the two main legal black political and labor organizations in the country, called a press conference to announce her formal banishment from the movement for having "abused the trust and confidence" of the black community. "In recent years," they said, "Mrs. Mandela's actions have increasingly led her into conflict with various sections of the oppressed people and with the mass democratic movement as a whole." The statement went on virtually to convict her of the kidnapping and beating of the four youths: "We are not prepared to remain silent where those who are violating human rights claim to be doing so in the name of the struggle against apartheid. . . . The mass democratic movement hereby distances itself from Mrs. Mandela and her actions. We call on our people, in particular the Soweto community, to exercise this distancing in a dignified manner." Winnie remained silent, but she would never forget or forgive those UDF leaders responsible for her downfall. She would seek her revenge against them after her husband's release in February 1990.

This was the stormy background to Winnie's formal trial, which began on February 4, 1991, in the Rand Supreme Court in Johannesburg, next door to the main building of the Methodist Church whose authority she had also challenged. Both Winnie and Nelson had insisted she would be proven innocent of all charges if only she could have "her day in court" to tell her side of the story. She finally got it. The trial, stretching out over fourteen weeks to mid-May, became an ordeal for the entire ANC as well as for the

Mandelas. It created a fault line within the National Executive Committee, dividing its members in their loyalties between the Mandelas and the broader interests of ANC, Inc. Nelson at first convinced the old guard to stand by Winnie, and tried to rally the entire Executive Committee to her cause. Winnie's supporters wanted to portray the trial as another example of the apartheid state persecuting her on purely political grounds. The NEC took this line initially but before long changed its tack, overruling the Mandelas and establishing its political distance from Winnie. In the end, it did not even question the legitimacy of a white apartheid institution to sit in judgment on the wife of its own president.

Winnie put together a defense team certain to attract attention. It was led by George Bizos, who had defended her husband in the political trials of the early 1960s and was highly regarded in anti-apartheid circles. The choice of Bizos was not surprising given his history as a long-standing ANC and Mandela advocate. But Winnie wanted to demonstrate that her political support in the black community went beyond the ANC, so she hired Dikgang Moseneke, a prominent leader of the Pan Africanist Congress (and later its vice president), to assist Bizos. She insisted as well that Dali Mpofo be included on the defense team. Then a twenty-nine-year-old novice as a lawyer, Mpofo's only claim to fame was his status as Winnie's not-so-secret lover.

The trial started with much political fanfare and a big show of support for Winnie. Members of the Women's League, dressed in the ANC's black, gold, and green colors, turned out to cheer for her. Some of them took over a row of seats at the back of the trial room and remained, like the chorus in a Greek tragedy. Outside the courtroom, they chanted: "Mother of the Nation, we are with you," "Winnie, we love you," and "Viva the ANC." Winnie also organized the Winnie Mandela Support Ad Hoc Committee, composed of her long-time friends and admirers. The opening session of the trial saw many senior ANC and Communist Party leaders show up, at Nelson's personal request, but before long the crowd of her supporters dwindled to a handful; her support committee melted away after holding one press conference; and senior ANC officials other than Nelson stopped attending her trial.

The turning point in the official ANC attitude came on February

26, the day her support committee held its sole press conference at Johannesburg's City Hall. Neither Winnie nor Nelson showed up, though they had been expected. Instead, top ANC leaders had them closeted in a private meeting in which they informed the Mandelas that the organization would no longer allow itself to be used for Winnie's political purposes. The revolt against Winnie—and indirectly against Nelson himself—had begun. Winnie was put on notice that this was her trial, not the ANC's, even if a white judge was presiding. The stern-faced, Germanic-mannered judge, Michael J. Stegmann, had no reputation as a liberal, either. Under the South African judicial system, since Winnie was not charged with murder (she had been indicted on eight counts of kidnapping and assault), Stegmann alone would hear her case, hand down a verdict, and pronounce sentence. Yet the ANC raised not a word of criticism about Stegmann or the way Winnie was to be tried.

It looked at first as if Winnie and her ANC friends would succeed in sabotaging the whole proceeding. Four of her eight fellow defendants skipped bail and failed to show up. Then one of the prosecution's star witnesses, Mekgwe, disappeared—from the same Methodist Church manse he had been kidnapped from originally—amid rumors that he had been "kidnapped" by ANC operatives. (Only much later was it learned that he had left the manse voluntarily, this time to go into hiding in Zambia. Mekgwe alleged from there that he had been bribed by Winnie not to testify and had been helped by ANC intelligence operatives close to her to get across the border secretly.) Mekgwe's mysterious disappearance so frightened Kgase and Mono, the prosecution's two other chief witnesses, that they told Stegmann they were simply too scared to present their testimony. It looked for a few days as if the trial would simply abort for lack of witnesses. But Stegmann bore down on Kgase and Mono, warning them that they faced prison terms if they refused to testify. They finally did, but not until early March.

Their testimony was horrifying and must have been a torment for Nelson, present for much of it. Kgase and Mono told the court that Winnie, whom they were ordered to address as Mommy, had presided over their interrogation. She had tried to extract "confessions" from them about Verryn's alleged homosexual activities. Winnie at one point supposedly yelled at them, "You are not fit to be alive." Kgase then described how Winnie had led the assault on all four of them, punching him in the eye and hitting him with a leather *sjambok* whip "a lot of times." Mono told the court that Winnie "hit me with open hands and fists on my face." Then, other members of the football club had joined in "trampling on my body. I was lifted up in the air and dropped." Stompie, the supposed police *impimpi*, had come in for special attention, the two witnesses said. After being beaten, he was taken outside, thrown into a bathtub full of water, and his head forced under until he nearly drowned. He finally "confessed" to having given information to the police about other activists, they said, and was so bruised and battered at the end of his ordeal that he could barely walk. Kgase and Mono had subsequently been "rehabilitated" and press-ganged into the football club, but not Stompie. The last they saw of him was the night of January 1 when he was taken away from the backyard room by "Coach" Richardson.

The performance of "Accused No. 8," as Winnie was formally referred to in the court proceeding, was of course the highlight of the trial. On April 16, she finally took the stand, and she remained under examination for three days while both the prosecution and judge sought to extract the truth. The truth according to Winnie was arguably stranger than fiction. Bizos, who had coached her for days before the trial, had decided that Winnie should act as if she had neither done nor seen nor heard anything wrong. It soon became clear that Falati was to serve as Winnie's scapegoat, though Falati's lawyers didn't know that beforehand. Falati, the court was told, was responsible for everything. It was she who had been the bearer of stories about Verryn's alleged homosexual activities, and she who had proposed that the youths be brought to Winnie's home. That had happened the afternoon of December 29, just before Winnie left for a visit to Brandfort and hours before Richardson, Falati, and Winnie's driver, John Morgan, had gone to fetch the four victims. Winnie was all innocence. She had not even been aware that the four victims were living in her backyard, let alone that they had been kidnapped and assaulted, until she read about it in the newspaper days later. She had never met any of them personally and only remembered Stompie as "a child washing his hands at the water tap" out back. As for the infamous Mandela

United Football Club, it had ceased to exist by the time of the incident; she had never had any "bodyguards" and never knew that any of the "boys in the back" had served as nighttime guards around her home. It was a totally unbelievable story, but neither Winnie nor Bizos seemed to care.

Bizos's defense of Winnie rested heavily on Winnie's whereabouts the night of the kidnapping, but he had an embarrassing problem in this regard. Despite her fury over press reports of her involvement in the kidnappings, Winnie had never once told a single reporter, or made any statement, that she had gone to Brandfort that crucial night. "Nobody ever asked me," she stated casually. But she had become so distraught over the press reports that she had decided to give an interview to a Dutch television station "because I could not take the wild allegations and wanted to clear my name." Still, she said nothing even then about her trip to Brandfort, she testified, because the reporter himself had not raised the question.

In fact, it was not until Richardson's trial in May 1990, almost a year and a half after the event, that Winnie chose to disclose her trip to Brandfort. Bizos lined up two witnesses to corroborate her story. Tabo Motau, a student, told the court he had driven her to Brandfort in the early evening of December 29 in place of Morgan, her regular chauffeur. The other witness, Nora Moahloli, was a schoolteacher in Brandfort with whom Winnie had allegedly spent that and the following night before returning to Soweto on December 31. Moahloli, the only Brandfort witness presented to the court, produced as proof a diary and a piece of paper with scribblings on it to substantiate Winnie's presence at a meeting there on December 30. None of the other participants in that meeting were presented as witnesses, and Winnie could not remember any of their names. There were several holes in Moahloli's testimony that also raised considerable doubt about Winnie's alibi. For example, references to her Brandfort visit were out of chronological order in Moahloli's diary, and she had somehow managed to use three pens on the piece of paper that was supposed to prove Winnie had been present for a discussion of items needed to equip a day-care center; the December 30 date at the top had been written in a different ink than the list of items, strongly suggesting that it had been added later.

Winnie managed to make some memorable declarations during her three days on the witness stand. She had, she said, insisted that Richardson "tell the truth" to a reporter who interviewed him on February 19 about the alleged kidnappings and beatings. She had been present during the interview and had insisted he confess that there had indeed been "beatings," not just harmless "clappings," as she alleged Richardson had first told her. "The least he could do was to speak the truth," she told Judge Stegmann. "Men of honor speak the truth, my lord." No one seized upon the occasion to ask her whether "women of honor" had an obligation to speak the truth as well.

Winnie had finally had her day in court. Now it was Judge Stegmann's turn. His judgment of her testimony and character, handed down on May 13, was devastating. Winnie, like her co-defendant Falati, had displayed "a remarkable absence of candor," and had gone out of her way to avoid telling the truth. Her testimony, he said, had been full of "careful vagueness," "equivocation," and "improbabilities."

The key issue, of course, was whether Stegmann, like the movement's court two years earlier, judged Winnie to have been the mastermind behind the kidnappings of the four youths. Stegmann concluded that she must have been, for, as he so eloquently stated it, "To imagine that all this took place without Mrs. Mandela as the moving spirit is like trying to imagine Hamlet without the prince." Only when it came to pronouncing judgment on Winnie's role in the beating of the youths did he show any doubt as to her guilt. The prosecution had failed to prove that her Brandfort alibi was a lie, so there remained a reasonable possibility that, as she had claimed, she had gone there before the assaults began, he said. Still, she must have known about the kidnappings and beatings later, but even when pressed by Soweto leaders to release the youths, she had refused to free them. At the very least, Stegmann concluded, Winnie was guilty as an accessory after the fact to all that had happened. He found both Winnie and Falati guilty of the kidnapping charges and Winnie of being accessory to the assaults.

Just about every reporter in the courtroom that day concurred with Stegmann's assessment of Winnie as a "calm, composed, deliberate, unblushing liar." What shocked everybody, however, was his outspoken indictment of her character, since no white or black official had ever dared to speak out in such unvarnished condemnation of the former "Mother of the Nation." Even Winnie, who had listened impassively to Stegmann's six-hour review of the case, was visibly shaken. About the only words she could find to say in reaction to his findings were that she was happy Stegmann had not pronounced her guilty of assaulting children. "That is all that matters to me," she blurted out. By the time she reached the courthouse doors, Winnie was once again her usual smiling self, but not so Nelson. His confidence had clearly been shaken by Stegmann's verdict and judgment of his wife. For once he could think of no reason to break into his usual radiant smile.

Stegmann sentenced Winnie the following day to a prison term of five years on the kidnapping charges and an additional one year for her role as an accessory to the assaults, but not before he condemned her "complete lack of compassion" for the victims, whom, he noted, she had held for twenty days before yielding to enormous pressure to free them. "There has been no indication that any of you feels the slightest remorse or would not do it again," he said. Falati was also sentenced to six years in prison and Morgan, the driver, to one. George Bizos immediately announced his intention of appealing Stegmann's verdict, but the political and emotional damage done to Winnie and Nelson could never be undone. (On June 2, 1993, the Appeals Court in Bloemfontein upheld Stegmann's verdict on the kidnapping charges but reduced Winnie's sentence to a one-year sentence suspended for two years, plus a fine of approximately $10,000. The court overturned the conviction on the accessory charge.)

The trial shattered Nelson's last illusions about the woman he had so long adored. For the second time in a little more than two years his wife had been found guilty of serious misconduct, first informally by her own peers and now formally by a court. Stegmann had reached the same conclusions about Winnie as her peers had. Nelson could continue professing his faith in her innocence. But he knew better. He could no longer protect Winnie from those in the ANC leadership who wanted to force her out. No one on the National Executive Committee was taking issue with Stegmann's horrendous judgment on his wife's credibility and honor. The silence after the judge's verdict was deafening. Furthermore, the ANC hierarchy had refused to follow Mandela's request that it treat her trial as a political one. It had taken a stand against him as much as against Winnie. Nelson was suddenly faced with the embarrassing prospect of having a wife convicted of kidnapping at his side as he traveled around the world. She would be an enormous political embarrassment to him. Still, the guilt-ridden Nelson was not prepared to let her go or stop defending her. Not yet. It would not be until the fall of 1991 that he turned that corner and for reasons that had nothing to do with her trial.

By mid-1991, Winnie was not only a convicted child snatcher, she had also become a master political schemer capable of endless machinations to promote her political career. When Nelson was first released, she had briefly played the role of subservient wife, allowing him all the limelight. On platforms, she stood demurely at his side or behind him, hardly saying a word to the assembled masses who had come to hear and see their messiah. At the appropriate moment, she would perform the Mandela ritual, the two standing side by side with their conquering smiles and clenched outstretched fists while Winnie bellowed out, "Amandla, Awethu": Power to the People.

This phase of subservience was short-lived. Nelson, initially besotted by Winnie, was only too ready to help promote her political career. He began by helping Winnie win election as head of the ANC branch and the Women's League in Orlando West so that she would have a local power base. He went from door to door, calling on people to vote for her. She was easily elected, giving her a springboard to bigger things at the regional and national levels. With the help of Nelson and his friends in the ANC's old guard, Winnie finagled an appointment as head of the organization's Welfare Department by the fall of 1990. This promotion stirred considerable controversy, but Nelson defended it at a press conference on February 8, 1991, saying that those who opposed her appointment could be counted "on the fingers of one hand." This position gave

Winnie the platform she needed for her innumerable appearances in the townships and squatter camps that allowed her to begin building a following among the most militant ANC supporters.

As Evita Peron had done in Argentina, she projected herself as the hero of the poor and downtrodden. At the same time, Winnie was busy building an alliance with "radicals" and "revolutionaries" in the ANC, particularly those belonging to the South African Communist Party. She and Chris Hani, the chief of staff of Umkhonto, were seen together regularly. Hani was not only a top member of the ANC leadership but he was also a member of the SACP central committee. Winnie flaunted her close friendship with Hani even on the official 1991 Mandela Christmas card, which featured a picture of the two of them on the back. Whether Winnie actually secretly belonged to the Communist Party was a subject of great speculation but no certainty. She occasionally wore a party pin, but she often sported militant dress, and the pin fitted in nicely with her military uniform and cap. She wanted to show that her sympathies lay with the Communists and Umkhonto.

Her other major public ally was Peter Mokaba, former president of the South African Youth Congress, which later became the resuscitated ANC Youth League over which Mokaba continued to preside. Its members served as the ANC's "shock troops" in the townships and were known as the Young Lions. Winnie's militant image made her very popular among this group. Altogether, she had powerful friends and allies, from the squatter camps to the top echelons of both the ANC and the Communist Party.

Winnie's enemies were powerful as well, mainly within the ANC Women's League, but also included many senior and middle-ranking ANC officials. Chief among the latter were former leaders of the United Democratic Front who had taken part in the February 1989 decision to ostracize her from the mass democratic movement. This faction was led by Ramaphosa, the most powerful labor union figure in South Africa. Winnie had succeeded in sidelining Ramaphosa immediately after Nelson's release, but he was too popular to keep down for long. Other ANC officials felt that Winnie was simply too big a political liability for the organization, giving it an unwanted image of reckless militancy and political corruption, particularly after her kidnapping conviction.

In time, Winnie's bulldozer tactics alienated more and more ANC activists. For example, she saw nothing wrong in intimidating people into voting for her, in some instances using Nelson to help achieve this. Several branches of the ANC's regional organization in Johannesburg at one point sought to block her bid for election to the regional executive, complaining about her strong-arm methods. Just as it was time for the vote, Winnie walked into the meeting with Nelson at her side. He proceeded to deliver an impassioned plea that she be elected, after which the vote was immediately taken. Another example came when she was elected chairperson of the Johannesburg regional Women's League. She sent notes to everybody she thought would not support her, threatening to denounce them as government "spies" if they voted against her. But it was Nelson and his personal promotion of Winnie that remained most crucial to her steady accumulation of positions.

In late April 1991, Winnie suffered another serious reverse: Her bid to become president of the Women's League failed miserably. Even Nelson could not help her this time, because the woman who engineered her defeat was Albertina Sisulu, who maintained a simmering rivalry with Winnie. She had suffered almost as much as Winnie from police persecution before 1990, and her husband, Walter, had been imprisoned almost as long as Nelson. But as a quiet, grandmotherly figure with no driving political ambition, she was always overshadowed by the more flamboyant Winnie. Many blacks felt that Albertina was the one who really deserved the title "Mother of the Nation." Their settling of political accounts came in Kimberley, at the League's first national conference inside South Africa since the unbanning.

The two main contenders for the presidency were Winnie and Gertrude Shope, a longtime NEC member who had been head of the ANC's women's division in Lusaka. The conference was consumed by the election issue. Winnie bused in her supporters, and even tried to cheat when it was time for the voting. As one participant recalled, there were different, colored ballots, with no names on them, for each candidate. This was to accommodate the large number of illiterate women attending the conference. Winnie's color was green. Her supporters began cutting the green ballots in half in the hope of doubling Winnie's vote. But the ruse was

quickly discovered and stopped. As it turned out, the really decisive factor in the election was Albertina. She publicly called upon
her supporters to cast their votes for Shope and they did. The
result was a crushing defeat for Winnie, who garnered only 196
votes to Shope's 400. Albertina was then elected unopposed as vice
president, while Winnie had to settle for being elected as one of six
"additional members." Less than two weeks later, Winnie was
found guilty in the kidnapping trial.

Having watched his wife publicly shamed and politically defeated,
Mandela next had to endure a humiliation of another kind—the
eclipse of his old guard allies. The occasion was the ANC's long-
awaited national conference, to be held in Durban July 2–7, 1991.
At this meeting a new slate of ANC leaders was to be chosen.
While Mandela's official installation as president was little more
than a formality, a crucial battle was shaping up over the selection
of a secretary-general, the person who would stand the best chance
of succeeding him as ANC president. The old guard would have
preferred to see Alfred Nzo, the incumbent secretary-general, remain in place. But Nzo was never a serious contender for re-
election. He was widely held to be responsible for the ANC's
internal disorganization and had been reduced to little more than
Mandela's errand boy. Instead, the battle shaping up was between
Thabo Mbeki and Chris Hani. They presented a stark contrast:
Mbeki the moderate versus Hani the radical. At the last moment,
however, they both agreed to withdraw from the race to avoid a
bruising power struggle. Mandela then lobbied for Jacob Zuma, the
ANC intelligence chief and a Zulu, to become the new secretary-
general, explaining that he wanted a balanced "ethnic" leadership,
particularly one with a Zulu to counter Chief Buthelezi's charges
that the ANC was dominated by Xhosas.

Once again, Mandela was not to have his way. Instead, former
UDF officials collaborated with Communist Party militants to lead
a movement to draft the highly popular Cyril Ramaphosa. There
was no way Mandela could control the outcome of the secret
voting by the 2,244 delegates attending the conference, and Ramaphosa trounced Zuma, 1,156 to 490. (Zuma was subsequently chosen to fill the newly created post of deputy secretary-general.) The

thirty-eight-year-old Ramaphosa received a massive ovation as he was hoisted onto the shoulders of a crowd of admiring delegates and carried like a conquering hero from the back of the hall to the podium.

Ramaphosa's election symbolized the passage of power from the old guard to a younger generation of activists, many drawn from the ranks of the UDF, which finally disbanded a month after the ANC national conference. There was also a personal message for Mandela in Ramaphosa's election, for the new secretary-general, as we have seen, was no personal friend of Nelson's or Winnie's. Mandela, moreover, had not forgotten Ramaphosa's offhand comment that Mandela should not expect to just walk out of prison and take over the ANC. The labor union leader had also belittled Mandela's political importance, telling *Leadership* magazine in November 1989 that his standing was "no different from the status of any other member of the ANC," and remarking that Mandela was just "one of those people who may have to be considered for a leadership position."

Though Winnie was elected, despite her conviction, to the Congress's National Executive Committee, this victory was hardly a ringing endorsement of her activities. She had placed twenty-sixth in the election for fifty open seats on the committee, which now numbered sixty-six, and most of her militant allies opposed the path of negotiation that her husband had chosen. Indeed, when the dust settled, Mandela had few allies in the new leadership lineup. Oliver Tambo and Walter Sisulu were given largely honorary positions: national chairperson and vice president, respectively. Thomas Nkobi, another mainstay of the old guard, remained as treasurer. But the trend ran in the other direction: UDF, Communist, and labor union activists came flooding into the new Executive Committee and were clearly a rising force. All the indications were that a rough time lay ahead for Mandela.

It probably came sooner than he had expected. The byzantine intrigues that took place within the ANC leadership were something to see, and many of them seemed aimed solely at curbing Mandela's power and freedom of action, particularly in carrying out negotiations with de Klerk. At issue this time was whether Mandela or Ramaphosa would be in overall charge of contacts with the government. In late July 1991, the new NEC elected from its own ranks a twenty-six-person National Working Committee (NWC) to run the ANC on a day-to-day basis. While Mandela was abroad in early August, the NWC undertook a major internal reorganization of the ANC bureaucracy, replacing Winnie as head of the ANC Welfare Department (a young Communist militant, Cheryl Carolus, was installed in her place) and delegating overall responsibility for negotiations to Ramaphosa's office. The small London-based periodical *Frontline File* compared the reorganization to a coup, and blamed it on a "Communist cabal" that strongly objected to "Mandela's autocratic style of decision-making." However, it wasn't just the Communists who were unhappy with the way Mandela had conducted negotiations with the government since his release; the vast majority of NEC members were infused with the UDF ethos of collective decision-making and wanted to wrest control of the process from him.

Mandela was furious with Ramaphosa's challenge to his authority, and he fought back. He had some success in getting both decisions reversed or modified—at least temporarily. Winnie was reinstated as head of the Welfare Department, and the committee in charge of negotiations was broadened to include Mandela, Sisulu, and Mbeki. Nonetheless, it was a team now, not Mandela conducting negotiations on his own with the government.

With his authority curtailed and his patience exhausted, Mandela would never again interfere with ANC decisions on Winnie's behalf. In fact, between early September and November 1991, Nelson's attitude toward his wife suddenly hardened, as two related events finally jolted him into the realization that Winnie was becoming impossible. Both concerned her increasingly public love affair with Mpofo, the dashing young man who had been part of her defense team. Their affair dated back to before Nelson's release from prison when Dali, as everyone called him, had lived for a time at the Mandela residence. Nelson had learned about this and had written Winnie a letter telling her to get "that boy" out of their home. Dali left, but the affair continued and became more and more public. In June 1991, *City Press*, a weekly, published two stories about the affair with no denials from any quarter.

For some reason, Nelson didn't seem to be that upset about their liaison at first, but Winnie began flaunting her lover too publicly. After her reinstatement at the Welfare Department, she had the audacity to appoint Dali as her chief deputy, an arrangement that gave them a business cover for being together constantly. Winnie then went on a trip to the United States the first week of October, ostensibly to raise money and recruit artists for a "Children of Africa Concert" scheduled to be held in Nigeria later that year. She took Dali with her, and they went first-class, spending what was rumored to be 20,000 rand (about $7,100) just on tickets (the ANC later denied that the money had come from its coffers). The trip was a failure. Winnie and Dali returned from the five-day spree (which took them to the West Coast and Hollywood) with neither funds raised nor artists signed up for the concert. When word of their lavish expenditure reached Nelson, he exploded.

About the same time, reports began reaching diplomatic circles that Nelson had caught Winnie and Dali *in flagrante delicto* in an office at the ANC's Johannesburg headquarters. This affront may have explained his special rage and his actions toward both of them after they returned from America. Nelson unilaterally fired Dali as deputy head of the Welfare Department, a step that caused Winnie to write a twenty-page resignation letter to the ANC Executive Committee defending her behavior and trip to the States. The conflict between the two Mandelas was now an open secret within the ANC leadership, and anti-Winnie ANC members spread the word with considerable glee.

The NEC finally had to intervene to resolve the conflict. At a November 25–26 meeting, it decided—for reasons it never made clear—to reject Winnie's resignation and reinstate Dali as her deputy. (Apparently, the NEC was still hoping that Nelson and Winnie could sort out their differences and avoid an embarrassing separation.) None of this reached the press, however; the only hint that something was amiss between Nelson and Winnie were reports that began appearing in the local press that same month that Winnie and Nelson were no longer living together. The ANC put out a cover story that this was only because of threats being made on their lives and the need to take "security precautions" to protect them. But apparently Nelson turned elsewhere for companionship after these incidents, as Barbara Masekela, former head of the

ANC's department of arts and culture and a sister of the famous trumpet player Hugh Masekela, began appearing at his side on public occasions. In early December, it was Barbara, not Winnie, who accompanied Nelson on his second trip to the United States.

It took the Mandelas until the following April to announce their separation, though everybody in Johannesburg knew that their marriage had disintegrated and that Nelson was coming under increasing pressure from the ANC leadership to distance himself from Winnie for the sake of its reputation.

By this time, the ANC had settled into a new style of bifurcated leadership under Mandela and Ramaphosa. The two men, whether they liked each other or not, seemed to have worked out a modus operandi. The principle of collective leadership that Mandela had touted publicly but had flouted privately had become the general practice. Ramaphosa had asserted his control over the ANC machinery and had even wrested back from Mandela the day-to-day responsibility for negotiations with the government. There were endless reports of a "cabal" led by Ramaphosa plotting to sideline Mandela altogether, but this never happened.

Mandela seemed to be pinned down, seriously restricted in any personal initiative. His former tête-à-tête meetings with de Klerk, arranged through direct telephone calls, were over. Their infrequent encounters became something akin to American-Soviet summits: the subject of elaborate prenegotiations on the agenda, potential agreements, and final communiqués by batteries of senior aides. Mandela still had influence because he was the ANC's elected president, with tremendous national and international prestige. But his authority had undergone steady erosion since February 1990. ANC, Inc., the broad organization and its wider leadership, had seen its own "corporate" interests endangered by Mandela's authoritarian tendencies and personal diplomacy and had reduced Mandela to the first among equals, with his colleagues constantly reminding him that he was part of a collective leadership.

To his enormous credit, Mandela learned to bow to this "collective will" with remarkable grace. When he saw the serious opposition to a change in ANC sanctions or its nationalization policy, he yielded. When he saw the extent of regional opposition to his proposed meeting with Buthelezi, he retreated. He finally even gave in to pressure from his colleagues to separate from Winnie. In the end, Mandela learned to be what he had initially assured us he was: "a good organization man." But he had to be reminded, over and over again, what that meant in practice.

9

ALL FALL DOWN

Around the time of the ANC's July 1991 national conference, Mandela and other moderates were coming to two important realizations: First, at the negotiating table de Klerk was following an agenda quite different from theirs; and second, it was self-defeating to keep postponing talks because of the political violence and de Klerk's failure to meet ANC preconditions. The practical effect of such a hardline stance was to give veto power to those elements around de Klerk opposed altogether to constitutional negotiations. The ultimatum the ANC had issued to the government in April was, from this perspective, counterproductive to the ANC central goal of obtaining a transfer of power as quickly as possible.

Mandela first signaled a shift, at least in his thinking, at the opening of the ANC national conference. His speech was courageous given that the ultimatum had gone unmet, and that there was little support at the time for a return even to talks about talks. The ANC, Mandela said, had to reconsider its attitude toward negotiations, which should be viewed as "a victory" for the ANC and "a defeat" for the white government, not the reverse. The negotiations were just another "theater of struggle" for the movement, and any further delay in entering this battlefield was playing into the hands of the enemy. The political violence was being perpetrated precisely by those forces opposed to the start of negotiations. "It can

162

never be in our interest that we prolong the agony of the apartheid system. It does not serve the interests of the masses we represent and the country as a whole that we delay . . . the achievement of the objective of the transfer of power to the people." In other words, the ANC should drop all its preconditions for renewing talks with the government and get on with planning for a multi-party conference to launch constitutional negotiations. Mandela even propounded for the first time the idea of a "transitional government of national unity" in which power would have to be shared with de Klerk's despised National Party.

The import of Mandela's words largely escaped notice, overshadowed by the first truly democratic elections for a new ANC leadership, but they effectively marked the start of his campaign to coax the ANC back to talks about talks. Aziz Pahad, one of the ANC's negotiators, explained later that after the national conference the entire ANC underwent a "strategic shift" in its thinking along the lines Mandela had spelled out. The ANC's new immediate goal would become the replacement of the de Klerk government by a multi-racial interim government of national unity. Mandela had quietly rearranged ANC priorities and had cleverly converted the perceptions of negotiations from being a "defeat" into a "victory."

Mandela's new strategy was put to the test barely two weeks after the national conference. On July 19, 1991, the *Weekly Mail* published a series of articles about past government funding for Inkatha rallies and the United Workers Union of South Africa (UWUSA), which had been founded by Chief Buthelezi as a rival to the Congress of South African Trade Unions. The whole affair was quickly dubbed Inkathagate. The sums of money involved were relatively small, but the political implications were devastating. The *Mail* had obtained an internal police report from Major Louis Botha, head of Durban's security branch, in which he discussed why he had given Inkatha about $100,000 to help it organize two political rallies, one in November 1989 and another in March 1990. The weekly also published information indicating that UWUSA had received government funding. The allegations created a national sensation, heightened by President de Klerk and several of his top ministers immediately conceding that they were true, though they disputed the amounts of money cited by the *Mail*. Adriaan Vlok later disclosed that UWUSA had received "no more than 1.5 million rand" (about $525,000 in 1991) over a six-year period, not the 5 million rand ($1.75 million) the *Mail* had reported.

Major Botha's report was particularly damaging because he said Buthelezi himself had thanked him profusely for the $100,000 and had signed a receipt for the money. Botha justified giving Inkatha assistance for the March 1990 rally on the grounds that it had been important to demonstrate that Buthelezi had as much support among Zulus in Natal as Mandela, who had drawn a crowd of 100,000 when he visited Durban in late February. The major expressed his concern that Buthelezi might "seriously consider throwing in his lot with the ANC" if he felt he was becoming too weak and at risk for being "removed from the scene." The worst part of the disclosures for Buthelezi was that de Klerk and Vlok never made it altogether clear whether or not the funding had ceased.

The weekend the *Mail*'s stories appeared, I was in Ulundi attending the annual Inkatha conference. The organization was just then converting itself from a "cultural movement" into a political party, in preparation for the coming struggle with the ANC and any forthcoming national elections. It was a stormy conference devoted mostly to lambasting the *Mail* and shoring up support for an embarrassed Buthelezi. Buthelezi insisted that he knew nothing about the funding, and that Major Botha had lied when he reported that he had been profusely thanked for the money. "I have always paddled my own canoe," he said, in building Inkatha into what he described as "a mighty giant."

On Sunday morning, Buthelezi arranged for the articles in the *Mail* and the Sunday *Times* of that week to be read aloud to the 10,000 delegates attending the conference in a massive tent set up outside Ulundi. The *Times* had run a front-page editorial saying that Inkatha was "perhaps mortally" wounded by the disclosures, and that Buthelezi should resign to make way for the election of a new "untainted" leader. Delegates listened for more than two hours to the reading of the *Mail* and *Times* articles (first in English and then in Zulu), becoming increasingly restless and agitated over the insults to their leader. At the end of the session, there was a "spontaneous" massive ovation for Buthelezi and his leadership. Sitting at a press table at the front of the huge conference tent, my fellow reporters and I wondered whether we were going to be physically attacked. As it turned out, nothing happened, but the atmosphere was nasty and the delegates were in a combative mood.

Buthelezi eventually sought to protect himself through the highly implausible excuse that his longtime private secretary, Melchizedec Z. Khumalo, had accepted the money without his knowledge. Khumalo took full responsibility and resigned his post to distance Buthelezi from the scandal. But there Buthelezi could not escape the damage already done to him: The disclosures had helped to confirm the image of Buthelezi that the ANC and its allies had been propagating, namely that of a stooge and surrogate of the government.

Under Mandela's new policy of pursuing negotiations as another "theater of struggle," the Inkathagate scandal played into the ANC's hand. Mandela believed that the revelation of the government's double-dealing would make de Klerk more eager to give ground in the talks about talks, if only to repair his public image. The two leaders had met just once since the ANC had issued its ultimatum, and that was in a single six-hour session on May 6 to discuss what the government planned to do about the escalating violence. Mandela later said that de Klerk had agreed to issue a ban on a long list of "traditional" or "cultural" Zulu weapons at rallies, and had consented to the idea of phasing out the hostels and to putting fences around them in the meantime, but even six hours of talks did not resolve these issues fully, and the two sides were left to haggle over the details for the next two years.

Mandela and the rest of the ANC leadership were determined not to let slip this opportunity to hold the upper hand in their talks, and so they consented to attend a national peace conference sponsored by a group of South African business, church, and civic leaders. The conference, scheduled for September 14, was to be the first face-to-face meeting of Mandela, de Klerk, and Buthelezi, and would include representatives from nearly fifty political, church, civic, and business groups throughout the country. It seemed at first like a giant step forward and a major achievement, finally opening the way to the first real cooperative effort among the warring factions.

The accord that would be signed at the conference was desperately needed, as the violence once again had spun out of control. On September 8, just a week before the conference, gunmen ambushed an Inkatha march in Thokoza, killing twenty-three people and injuring eighteen others in a hail of AK-47 bullets. The culprits were never caught, but the general assumption was that it had been the work of ANC professionals. The retaliation from Inkatha supporters was immediate and terrible: Again gunmen wielding AK-47 rifles went on a rampage, indiscriminately attacking buses, taxis, and trains. Though the government declared the four most affected townships around Johannesburg "unrest areas" and slapped on a nighttime curfew, within three days a hundred more people were dead.

It was in this atmosphere of extreme tension—verging on a full-scale confrontation—that the representatives of all political groups except the white extreme right wing and the most militant blacks assembled on "neutral ground" at the Carlton Hotel in downtown Johannesburg to sign the first national accord of any kind between a wide spectrum of white and black groups. The conference organizers had drawn up "codes of conduct" for the police and political groups to follow, regulating how they dealt with each other to avoid violence. The codes stressed tolerance and committed all groups to stop intimidating, threatening, or killing one another's members. They were all to refrain from making any statement inciting their followers to violence or hatred. The right of neighborhoods to establish "self-protection units" to combat crime was recognized, as was that of individuals to bear "licensed arms" and use them in "lawful self-defense." But the signatories of the National Peace Accord agreed that no political organization would form these units or maintain a "private army." They established a nationwide matrix of regional and local "dispute resolution committees" to arbitrate disputes, and they set up a standing "national peace secretariat" to implement the whole accord.

The national peace conference proved a disaster, though, as the various commitments, codes, and committees could not transform political behavior. Chief Buthelezi seemed to go the extra mile to ruin the whole atmosphere of the conference, having bused in 2,000 Zulu "warriors" armed to the teeth with their "traditional" weapons, who paraded up and down the street in front of the hotel as if they were besieging a Voortrekker *laager* (the circular wagon encampment of the old Afrikaner pioneering times). It was a disgraceful performance that infuriated even Buthelezi's allies in the government and embarrassed Minister of Law and Order Hernus Kriel, who was blamed for allowing the disruption. (Kriel had recently replaced Adriaan Vlok, who transferred to another cabinet post in the wake of Inkathagate.) Buthelezi and King Goodwill finally addressed their supporters from the balcony overlooking the entrance to the hotel and told them to go home. By then, however, the spirit of the accord had been broken even before anyone had signed it.

Buthelezi didn't stop his odd-man-out behavior there, however. At the end of the signing ceremony, he managed once again to ruin the mood. Photographers wanted to etch the first meeting of the three main peacemakers in the history books with a three-way handshake. It was a tableau tailor-made for Buthelezi, who had positioned himself on the dais next to President de Klerk and Mandela, in image if not in reality the equal of the other two. But as de Klerk and Mandela extended their hands toward Buthelezi, he deliberately spurned the gesture of reconciliation and kept his hands tightly gripping his ceremonial fly whisk. The result was a picture that underlined just how unstatesmanlike Buthelezi could be. When several photographers implored him to cooperate, the chief snapped back that he was not going to "perform like a clown" for them. Either the symbolism of the three-way handshake had somehow eluded him, or he was deliberately rejecting the gesture of national peace and reconciliation.

Though the static tension building up among the three leaders inside the conference hall was palpable, the explosion did not come until the press conference held after the signing ceremony. As it happened, I caused it by asking de Klerk whether the government had authorized the Inkatha demonstration outside. Instead of condemning it, the state president sought to play down the incident, saying "no crime" had been committed and that it was permissible since it had taken place outside any officially declared unrest area.

De Klerk insisted that the police had no authority to strip the demonstrators of their weapons unless they were threatening violence. "The people carrying shields and sticks," he said, had "apparently enjoyed themselves" and "at no stage posed a threat to anyone."

Mandela was understandably livid at de Klerk's flippant attitude. He jumped from his seat and grabbed the microphone to comment that "what the state president has said would not have applied if those people outside were members of the ANC. The police would have used force, firearms, if they refused to move away." He noted that just the day before, 1,200 police and soldiers had cordoned off the ANC stronghold at Phola Park outside Johannesburg and had carried out a house-by-house search, seizing every weapon they found. De Klerk, suddenly thrown on the defensive, assured the reporters that he had issued specific instructions that should any ANC supporters turn up to demonstrate outside the hotel, they should be given adequate space to do so and should be treated equally by the police. Still furious, Mandela shouted from his chair that the ANC had forbidden any such display by its supporters precisely to prevent any trouble from marring the "peace" conference. Buthelezi, for his part, insisted that his followers had every right to parade and display their "cultural weapons" because this was the "traditional" way of honoring King Goodwill, who was attending the conference. As a parting shot at his peace partners, Mandela insisted that the ANC's Umkhonto we Sizwe was no "private army" and therefore under no circumstances would it be disbanded under the peace accord. Nor would the ANC forgo the option of "mass action." Altogether, it was an unbelievably bitter public exchange reflecting not only the widening gap in goodwill that had opened up among the three peacemakers, but the seeming hopelessness of the peace endeavor as well.

Whatever "peace spirit" it was hoped the National Peace Accord would give rise to had evaporated as the signatories passed through the revolving doors of the Carlton Hotel. Despite all the pledges to avoid inflammatory words, Mandela could no longer rein in his fury with de Klerk. Quite unexpectedly, he aired his pent-up frustrations five weeks later during a meeting of leaders from the Commonwealth nations in the Zimbabwean capital, Harare. In an interview published in the Sunday *Mail* there on October 20, Mandela confessed that he had been totally wrong in his assessment of de Klerk. He had at first truly believed the state president to be "a man of integrity." But events had proven that "perhaps we were hasty and that there was a little bit of naiveté on our part." De Klerk, he said, "turned out to be a totally different man from what he was initially."

That same week, de Klerk was taking off his own gloves at the National Party conference in Cape Town and was lambasting Mandela and the ANC for their belligerency. Yet despite their personal estrangement, the two leaders held numerous private meetings throughout September and October 1991 to overcome the last remaining hurdles to the constitutional negotiations that would come to be known as the Convention for a Democratic South Africa (CODESA). Mandela, hewing to his new line that negotiations were the only path to power, spent much of the fall working out the ground rules with the state president.

De Klerk, too, was busy getting his party and government ready for constitutional talks. At a special National Party federal congress held in Bloemfontein on September 4, he outlined in considerable detail his government's terms for a settlement. Though the proposals were carefully honed to be in tune with the best Western constitutional ideals, their central thrust was nonetheless aimed at protecting the white minority and forcing the black majority to share power. Suddenly, de Klerk's constitutionalists were propounding with righteous moral vengeance all the checks and balances associated with Western democracies to prevent the abuse of central government power such as had been enjoyed by the National Party since 1948. The constitutionalists had cleverly combined various elements of the American, Swiss, German, and Yugoslav political systems to keep the black majority from ever ruling in the same way the white minority had for more than three centuries. The key concept was "power-sharing," which had emerged in the late 1970s in white South African academic thinking as an alternative—and more respectable—form of governance to minority white rule. The concept was introduced in South Africa by Arend Lijphart, an American political scientist from the University of California, San Diego. Lijphart's rejection of "majoritarian democracy," in which the majority party rules supreme, was music to the Afrikaner ears as the prospect of handing over power to blacks came closer. Lijphart argued that South Africa was too deeply divided along ethnic and racial lines for its government to function if powerful minorities were excluded. Only a system of joint decision-making among the major ethnically based parties (what he termed *consociation*) would assure effective government and political stability.

The other major innovation in Afrikaner thinking reflected in these proposals was the notion of "constitutional rule," meaning that a written constitution, along with a charter of fundamental rights, should stand as the highest authority in weighing the validity of laws. These were, of course, new concepts for the National Party, which for more than four decades had been making and unmaking constitutions to push through its apartheid legislation. But in its acceptance of the rule of law (protected by an independent judiciary, no less) de Klerk's party did not have merely the protection of individual rights in mind; the proposals also highlighted the need to protect "the interests of groups and communities" and to recognize "the reality of the existence of a multiplicity of groups." What this meant, in essence, was protection of the white minority. The guarantees were not to stop with a bill of rights, either. The National Party's vision of federalism also called for vast autonomous powers for local and regional governments to protect the country from centralized authoritarian rule.

The checks and balances devised by de Klerk's constitutional visionaries to avoid "black domination" included as well a two-chamber Parliament in which both houses would have roughly equal powers, with the upper chamber consisting of members representing the regions. Like the states in the U.S. Senate, each region would have equal representation. In addition, any legislation of special importance, such as changes in the constitution or the federal system, would require a "weighted majority" of two-thirds for approval. The Nationalist key to assuring power-sharing under this arrangement was that each party would get the same percentage of seats in Parliament as its percentage of the vote, and that there would be a collective presidency (such as Yugoslavia had once had) composed of the leaders of the three to five largest parties in Parliament. The chairman of this presidency would rotate yearly, and all decisions would be taken by consensus. In other words, if the National Party did not agree to changes in the status quo advocated by the ANC, it could simply veto them. The principles of collective rule and power-sharing were also to be embodied in a multi-party, coalition cabinet.

Mandela immediately denounced the proposals, rightly, as a recipe for governmental paralysis and the entrenchment of a white minority veto. The ANC, he said, understood *democracy* to mean that the party winning the majority of votes had the right to form a government and make policy of its own choosing. It might choose to invite other parties to form a coalition, but no constitution should dictate that it had to do this. "It's quite clear the National Party is against majority rule," he said bluntly. If de Klerk had his way, he pointed out, a black majority government would never be able to redress the social and economic inequities of the old apartheid order. But de Klerk was equally adamant: "A party that wins 51 percent of the vote should not get 100 percent of the power."

Despite their substantive disagreements, Mandela and de Klerk were able to work out the format for constitutional talks and agree on who should be invited. It was not easy in the absence of elections to determine which black political groups held any standing in the country, but they decided to be all-inclusive and invite just about every white, black, Indian, and Coloured party in the country, including several hastily organized by shaky homeland governments just for the purpose of attending the talks. The only holdout was the Pan Africanist Congress, which had refused to sit down at the same table with de Klerk. The PAC insisted that the talks be held outside South Africa and under neutral African or international mediation.

At the opening of a privately sponsored conference on democracy held in Johannesburg in November, Mandela totally rejected the approach suggested by the PAC. For the first time in months, he was full of praise for the state of ANC–National Party relations and was upbeat about his own success in dealing with de Klerk directly. It would be a "waste of time for us to meet outside of the country," he said. "We have created a sufficient climate to guarantee the success of the negotiations." The ANC and the government had made "tremendous progress" at Groote Schuur and Pretoria. "From our own experience, it has been possible for us—that is, both the government and the ANC—to take command of our discussions without any problems." All the obstacles to negotiations had been successfully removed through their joint efforts, he proclaimed proudly. Never before had Mandela expressed such satisfaction with the way the peace process was proceeding.

At the end of November, twenty parties and other political entities gathered at the Holiday Inn next to Johannesburg's international airport to lay down their own ground rules for the talks. The delegates quickly came up with the idea that all their decisions should be based on the principle of "sufficient consensus," a term left deliberately undefined because of the need to finesse a thorny issue. On the second day, however, the Pan Africanists—who did attend this preparatory meeting—walked out after they realized they could not halt the momentum toward negotiations, denouncing what they saw as a "decision-making pattern" of the government and the ANC systematically first reaching agreement between themselves on every issue and then expecting all others to follow their lead. "The only substantive debates on virtually all issues before the meeting were those introduced by the PAC," huffed the PAC vice president Dikgang Moseneke at an incongruous poolside press conference surrounded by hotel guests in bathing suits. None of the PAC's proposals for holding negotiations abroad had been accepted. Instead, the other parties had agreed that an Afrikaner judge, Petrus J. Schabort, and an Indian one, Ismail Mohamed, should preside over the proceedings and that CODESA would convene on December 20 at the World Trade Center just down the road from the Holiday Inn.

Except for the Pan Africanists, most delegates hailed the final preparatory meeting as a "watershed event." The first attempt to gather together the country's white, black, Indian, and Coloured leaders in the same room had miraculously succeeded. Gerrit Viljoen, de Klerk's chief negotiator, said that he was sure that all South Africans had made "a definite, clear, and irreversible break with the past." After twenty-two months of prenegotiations and talks about talks, the country was on the verge of "real talks, the real McCoy." ANC secretary-general Cyril Ramaphosa agreed wholeheartedly. "More than ever before we are convinced we are walking the last mile," he said. Not to be outdone in praise, Inkatha's chief delegate, Frank Mdlalose, called the meeting a "healing event in our divided society" that showed South Africans had the ability to overcome "all the difficulties and divisions that apartheid and a violent society had created."

Sadly, these comments were far too optimistic, for the approach of constitutional talks actually created new rifts within both the black and white communities. De Klerk had to contend with attacks from conservative and white supremacist groups, while Mandela found himself the brunt of sharp criticism from the militant black nationalists. The ANC leader at first dismissed the Pan Africanist walkout as little more than "a classic storm in a teacup" over which he was "not prepared to spend sleepless nights." He confidently predicted the PAC would show up for the opening session of CODESA. He was wrong. The PAC held a special conference in Cape Town four days before the constitutional talks to decide whether to drop out of the whole negotiating process. The decision was overwhelming. Two thousand foot-stomping, CODESA-bashing delegates, shouting "One settler, one bullet," voted unanimously to boycott. The Azanian People's Organization, which had refused even to attend the preparatory meeting, felt totally vindicated by the PAC decision. It called for the formation of a "patriotic front" among all black groups opposed to the negotiations to relaunch the struggle to force de Klerk to surrender power.

The lines were hardening in mirror fashion among whites. The Conservative Party; the Herstigte Nasionale Party (HNP), founded in 1969 by dissident members of the NP; the neo-Nazi Afrikaner Weerstandsbeweging (AWB, or Afrikaner Resistance Movement), which had emerged as the largest nationwide white supremacist organization; and smaller groups such as the Boerestaat Party all decried the advent of negotiations, seeing them as the start of the slide toward white abdication of power. They readily believed PAC accusations that the ANC and the National Party were conspiring to set up a multi-racial interim government in which they would rule together. HNP leader Jaap Marais denounced the "ugly political intrigue" under way against the white community, and accused

de Klerk of a "betrayal of every principle of democratic government." Andries Beyers, general secretary of the Conservative
Party, was slightly more honest about what was on the minds of all
white supremacists. The only purpose of the constitutional convention, he said, was the surrender of "our right to freedom and
self-rule in our own fatherland." This "right," he insisted, was
"nonnegotiable." This may have been the majority Conservative
view, but the party was in fact split over whether to attend. One
faction, led by the "liberal" Koos van der Merwe, was clearly
tempted. He had even dared to show up at the Holiday Inn on the
pretext of having breakfast there with three black Angolan businessmen. He then let it be known that he might consider attending
CODESA if the right to white, as well as black, self-determination
was put on the agenda. His comments sparked a sharp rebuke from
his leader, Andries Treurnicht. "The Conservative Party does not
negotiate on the basis of power-sharing between all the nations in
an undivided South Africa," Treurnicht said.

But the sharpest blow came from Chief Buthelezi, who chose to
make an issue this time of his representation in the constitutional
talks. He demanded, in effect, three delegations and three voices he
would be able to control: one for Inkatha, a second for his homeland government, and a third for King Goodwill. He argued that
Inkatha was a multi-ethnic, national party, not just a Zulu one, and
represented a national constituency, while the king was the spokesman for the whole "Zulu nation" with the right to a separate
delegation. KwaZulu, on the other hand, was the equal of the four
nominally independent homeland states, which had been given
their own delegations at the convention. He noted that both de
Klerk's National Party and his government had been allowed separate representation and argued that Inkatha and KwaZulu deserved
similar treatment.

Buthelezi, however, found no support in any quarter for his
convoluted argument for three delegations. The ANC pointed out
that the king was supposed to remain above politics, arguing that
his presence would lead to every other ethnic group in the country
sending its "king" or paramount chief. The National Party and the
government several times perfunctorily voiced their backing for

the king's presence, but refused to allow the convention to be derailed at the outset over the issue. The absence of the king, Buthelezi warned, had "serious implications for the Zulu nation and for CODESA." Buthelezi didn't say what the consequences might be. But he had already issued a warning at a rally of his followers outside Durban on December 15. The Zulus should not be left aggrieved, he said, "lest what happens in this country emerges as so terrible and so destructive that the civil wars [in Angola and Mozambique] are child's play by comparison." When it became clear that he was not going to get his way, Buthelezi had to decide whether to accept the humiliation of defeat or boycott the convention. In the end, he chose the latter course but sent a high-ranking Inkatha delegation to represent his interests.

Buthelezi may have thought initially that his absence at the opening session of the convention would be so regretted that it would convince the eighteen other delegations to change their minds in the name of national unity. If that was his calculation, he was badly mistaken. Not a single delegation was willing to follow his boycott. The convention went forward without him and without any great sense of loss at his absence. For his trouble, Buthelezi had managed to sideline himself politically. The outcome was totally contrary to his original intention; in September 1990 he had pledged to his followers, "I personally will be at the negotiating table as president of Inkatha." The convention set up a special subcommittee to examine his request that King Goodwill be invited to attend, but the ANC and its allies kept it buried there without resolution. This, in turn, kept Buthelezi from attending and out of the national limelight he craved, and established a new, bilateral dynamic centered exclusively around the ANC and the government. But even without the KwaZulu leader to stir things up, CODESA's first session would have more than its share of drama.

The World Trade Center outside Johannesburg was a far cry from its namesake in New York City. An unprepossessing white warehouse-style building down the road from the airport, the center had been built to house international exhibitions, which were never held because of sanctions. The huge barnlike structure had mostly sat empty since its construction over a decade earlier, but it hummed to life in December 1991 in anticipation of the first session of CODESA.

The atmosphere was electric as the eighteen delegations, plus the government, settled into their seats on the morning of December 20. Here were yesterday's bitter racial and ideological enemies sitting down at the same table, without intermediaries, to talk about a peaceful transition of power from a white minority to the black majority. It had taken the British to broker an agreement to the Rhodesian conflict; the Americans, Soviets, and Portuguese to end the civil war in Angola; the United Nations and the Americans to pry Namibia away from South Africa; and the Italians, Portuguese, and Americans to bring peace to Mozambique. But the South Africans were on their own, for better or worse, in the search for a settlement. Also there, to give an air of international blessing to the convention, were observers from the United Nations, the Commonwealth, the European Community, and the Organization for African Unity.

Unlike the Middle East peace talks, which had begun in Madrid on October 31, a general conviviality prevailed among the delegates, who mingled and drank tea or coffee together in the lobby outside the octagonal main conference room. The atmosphere was even friendlier than the first ANC–government ice-breaking encounter at Groote Schuur, since by now many of the delegates had already met and dealt with each other. For most blacks, it was a seemingly impossible dream come true; even Mandela, who had long carefully avoided using the word *irreversible* to describe the reform process, was moved to say that "with CODESA the situation in our land is irreversible." De Klerk, in his opening speech, described the convention as "the single most important event" to have occurred since the government had agreed on the necessity for negotiations.

In fact, it was arguably the most historic occasion in the life of South Africa since the National Convention of 1909, when the four former British colonies of Transvaal, Natal, the Orange Free State, and the Cape had agreed to establish a single union. Not a single black person had participated in that convention. This time, there were far more blacks than whites in the conference hall. Furthermore, the need for consensus, or at least "sufficient consensus," on any new constitution assured blacks as much power as whites. The National Party's chief delegate, Dawie de Villiers, moved by the spirit of the occasion, did his best to offer an apology for the horrors of apartheid. His party had hoped that "a policy of separation" would bring peace to the country. Not only had this not happened, but apartheid had produced "greater conflict and increasing injustice." It had not been the whites' intention to deprive other people of their rights or add to their misery, he said, "but eventually it led to just that. Insofar as that occurred, we deeply regret it." This was a significant initial gesture of repentance from a top National Party leader.

It was not long before the first storm clouds began gathering over the conference hall. Louis Mangope, president of the Bophuthatswana homeland, steadfastly refused to sign the Declaration of Intent, a statement of general negotiating principles and goals. He claimed he was not "legally competent" to enter into any agreement that might result in the reincorporation of his homeland into South Africa. This, of course, remained one of the primary goals of the negotiation process. Mangope insisted that only Bophuthatswana's national assembly could change the homeland's status. But he said he was otherwise prepared to participate in the convention and would accept decision-making on the basis of "sufficient consensus."

But the real shocker came at the close of the first session. De Klerk, leading the government delegation, had asked to speak last to the convention, though Mandela had originally been scheduled to do so. He began his speech by citing the historic significance of the gathering and the need to overcome the mutual distrust and suspicion, which he noted "exists over a wide front." In this regard, the government wanted to assure the convention that it was not against the formation of an interim multi-racial government. In fact, it favored a "power-sharing model" with a government "broadly representative of the total population." This could be achieved by changing the composition of the white-dominated tricameral Parliament to include "the total population in an equitable manner." These were code words that meant blacks would be included. His government stood ready to amend the constitution to achieve this and to hold a referendum to win national approval. "All South Africans must participate in such a referendum," he said, but the white, black, Indian, and Coloured populations would still have their votes counted separately. This sounded like a perpetuation of apartheid, but in light of de Klerk's long-standing opposition to a general election for a constituent assembly, his proposal for a general referendum—even if on separate voters' rolls—constituted a major step forward. De Klerk seemed to be searching for a way simultaneously to meet his commitment to whites to seek their approval on any fundamental changes in the constitution and black demands for a new interim government to replace his own.

Unfortunately, the import of de Klerk's concessions was immediately lost in the unexpected broadside he delivered against the ANC toward the end of his speech. Charging that the ANC had not honored its agreements under the D. F. Malan Accord to disclose the whereabouts of its secret arms caches, and was also violating the September 14 National Peace Accord by maintaining a "private army," de Klerk questioned the ANC's right to participate in the constitutional convention at all. He went on to question whether the ANC's commitment to agreements reached at the convention would be worth the paper they were written on if it did not abandon its armed struggle. It was imperative, therefore, that the ANC terminate its commitment to the armed struggle once and for all.

Mandela, who had become increasingly fidgety in his chair, exploded, insisting upon the right of reply. He strode to the podium, visibly seething at what he said was a totally unjustified and ill-timed attack on the ANC. He then launched into what all observers agreed was the most vitriolic attack on a South African president ever delivered by a black man at a public forum. Making matters worse for de Klerk, it was carried live by the SABC for all whites to see and hear. De Klerk, Mandela said, had been "less than frank" in his criticism of the ANC. "Even the head of an illegitimate, discredited, minority regime such as his has certain moral standards to uphold," he charged. Mandela said he was particularly furious because he had been talking to de Klerk until after eight o'clock the night before, and the state president had not even hinted that he was planning to raise the issue of the ANC's private arms caches. De Klerk had asked him as a special favor to be allowed to speak to the convention last. "It is now clear why," he said. De Klerk had plotted to have the last word, assuming Mandela wouldn't reply. Well, he had made a serious miscalculation.

Mandela went on to accuse de Klerk of pursuing a double agenda toward the ANC, simultaneously talking peace and cooperation while "conducting a war" against it. It was all well and good for de Klerk to pretend, as he had at the time of the Inkathagate scandal, that he didn't know about the large sums of money being channeled through the police to the ANC's chief rival. But, he added, "if a head of state doesn't know when as much as seven million rand is spent, then he's not fit to be a head of the government." He had warned de Klerk on countless occasions that no useful purpose would be served by continually attacking the ANC, yet, "he continues to do exactly that and we're going to stop it."

The whole convention was shocked into silence by Mandela's biting words. Mandela's charge that de Klerk was "not fit to be a head of government" would have been sufficient grounds for a treason trial and years of imprisonment only a few years before. There was an immediate sense of deep crisis, a feeling that things could never be the same again between the two peacemakers the nation was counting on to resolve its bitter racial conflict.

Of course, Mandela's explosion at de Klerk had actually been building since the ANC's April ultimatum, and he had already begun to question in public whether the state president was the "man of integrity" he had earlier thought he was. But Mandela told me later that much of his fury with de Klerk stemmed from the fact that he had gone out on a limb with his own National Executive Committee to urge that the state president be allowed to speak last at the opening session, out of the original order. The NEC had opposed granting the favor, but Mandela had intervened to insist on it. Thus, when he had heard the president begin to attack the ANC, he had felt betrayed, he said, and "I feared all the ANC would turn on me." Mandela was truly puzzled as to why de Klerk could not understand his own predicament, and that of the whole ANC, in insisting on the end to armed struggle. How could the ANC demobilize its military wing when the government was not demanding that white right-wing groups dissolve their commando forces? He had already explained to the president in private that what he was asking the ANC to do was to commit suicide. The ANC simply wasn't prepared for that. "What political organization could hand over its weapons to the same man who is regarded by the people as killing innocent people?" he asked the whole convention.

As soon as Mandela sat down, de Klerk insisted upon speaking again, telling the delegates the two leaders had tried repeatedly but in vain to resolve the issue. The two sides had met innumerable times over the previous ten months without ever reaching an understanding. De Klerk and Mandela had then intervened personally to try to break the deadlock; just before the national peace convention, they had held a meeting lasting many hours, as de Klerk described it, where he had pressed Mandela to begin implementing the terms of the D. F. Malan Accord. He had warned Mandela then that he was ready to raise the issue publicly at the signing ceremony of the National Peace Accord, but the ANC leader had assured him the ANC would give "serious attention" to implementing the accord immediately. So he had not spoken out then. But he had decided that the dispute had to be resolved before the start of formal constitutional talks. He had raised it at another meeting with Mandela on December 12, and they had agreed to hold high-level consultations immediately to resolve it. These had taken place just the night before CODESA began. "The friendly exchanges that went on over the past few days resulted in absolute stalemate," de Klerk told the convention as an explanation for his decision to make his comments publicly. It was a matter that had to be solved before other agreements could be reached. Otherwise, de Klerk said, the National Party would be faced with an ANC carrying "a pen in one hand and claiming the right to still have arms in the other hand."

The convention broke up its first session not knowing what lay ahead. The next morning, the embittered leaders sought lamely to patch up their quarrel for the public by greeting each other and shaking hands on the convention floor for all to see. But they didn't fool anybody.

This public blowup complicated enormously the search for a settlement. After all, if the two leading peacemakers could no longer deal with each other and had lost all mutual respect, how could their respective organizations be expected to behave differently? The truth was that each had become frustrated and disillusioned with the other. De Klerk believed that Mandela did not have either the authority or the political will to make the ANC live up to its agreements with the government; Mandela was convinced that de Klerk was making no attempt to curb the violence and was bent on destroying the ANC. Both were under heavy pressure from their respective constituencies not to yield on the ANC's armed struggle, which had taken on major symbolic importance. So they had stumbled into a public showdown, staging verbal fisticuffs on national radio and television that had only served to undermine each other's stature. De Klerk's image as a strong leader was tainted for many whites, the last thing Mandela himself needed; he was already worried about whether de Klerk was strong enough politically to bring his white constituency into a new order. And de Klerk had seriously miscalculated his timing. The ceremony marking the start of the nation's search for a new constitutional order was hardly the appropriate moment to embarrass the ANC and Mandela personally. Furthermore, de Klerk had done so by cunningly maneuvering on a false pretext to be the last speaker, thinking Mandela would then have no chance to reply. This was hardly the mark of a great statesman. No benefit could possibly accrue to the peace process by making Mandela look the fool in front of his own followers.

But for white supremacists, who wished there were no such thing as a peace process—and even for white liberals, who were becoming jittery about black rule—the unprecedented dressing-down of a state president by a *kaffir*, a black man, was an eye-opening experience. The AWB and other right-wing groups seized upon it as an illustration of what whites could expect living under black rule. Liberals remained silent in public, but they, too, were badly shaken in their faith that blacks and whites could cooperate and share power in a constructive manner.

10

THUNDER
ON THE RIGHT

Pieter Botha, the short, sturdy Afrikaner deputy mayor of the far-northern farming town of Louis Trichardt, believes that his people have a new, God-given mission. It is to save the "New South Africa," indeed all of black Africa, from a slow slide into political anarchy and economic disaster. He also strongly believes that the white man, specifically the Afrikaner, has played the role of "savior" in the history of South Africa, indeed of the entire continent. His hero is Joao Albasini, the mid-nineteenth-century Portuguese trader who made himself "chief" of the Shangaan people and "saved" them from annihilation in the civil wars sparked by the expansion of the Zulus under its warrior-king, Shaka. Albasini is a white folk legend in the northern Transvaal, a symbol of the Afrikaner's image of himself as the bearer of Western civilization to the African barbarians. His grave, just outside Louis Trichardt and below the Albasini Dam, is well cared for these days, treated almost as a holy shrine. On the western edge of Kruger National Park, there is also a site called the Albasini ruins, where the remains of a trading post he managed in the mid-1880s have been carefully preserved. "One white man saved the Shangaan. Maybe one white nation can save Africa," Botha told me in December 1991. "South Africa could become the catalyst, the locomotive for a dying continent. We've got to do something for our African brothers north of the border."

Botha wasn't the only Afrikaner talking and thinking this way. So was another Botha, Foreign Minister Pik Botha, whom I accompanied on his trip with President de Klerk to Abuja, Nigeria, in early April 1992. Pik called it "the most important visit we have undertaken in the post-apartheid era." This was because the most populous black African nation was at last opening its arms to welcome white South Africans into the African fold. At a press conference in Abuja, Pik spelled out his vision of South Africa's future role on the continent. South Africa, he said, was destined to become one of the four regional "locomotives" that would pull the rest of the continent out of its economic morass, debt, and political chaos. The other three were Nigeria, Kenya, and Egypt. South Africa wanted to establish a four-way partnership that would work to reverse the marginalization of Africa in President Bush's "new world order."

But it was South Africa he was thinking about primarily, more precisely his own Afrikaner people, and black Africa's acceptance of them as brothers despite their white skin. So Pik was deeply moved when Nigeria's foreign minister, Ike Nwachukwu, said at the opening of their bilateral meeting: "The Boers are one of several tribes that make up Africa. We see no difference whatsoever." The words of Nigerian President Ibrahim Babangida at the April 9 state dinner for de Klerk were even sweeter to Afrikaner ears. The Nigerian leader heaped praise on de Klerk as "the man who closed the book on apartheid" and ranked among South Africa's black anti-apartheid "stalwarts." He compared de Klerk to Chief Albert Luthuli and Archbishop Desmond Tutu, both of whom had won the Nobel Peace Prize; the murdered black consciousness leader Steve Biko; and ANC leader Nelson Mandela. For Afrikaner officialdom it was a highly emotional trip into the heart of black Africa. On the way home, Pik donned the Nigerian dashiki and hat he had acquired in Abuja, got down on his knees at the back of the plane, and called reporters accompanying him to sit down around a Nigerian vase Marike de Klerk had been given. He stretched out his arms over the vase, closed his eyes, and began reciting incantations and prayers that his Afrikaner people would find a new home and role in a black-ruled South Africa.

The two and a half million white descendants of the Dutch, French Huguenot, and German pioneers who settled South Africa in the mid-seventeenth century have reached their long-awaited rendezvous with African nationalism. They are losing power after nearly 350 years of struggle for survival against enormous odds, first against the Zulus and Xhosas, and then against the British Empire. Their struggle has been a long, lonely one filled with hardships, reverses, and the death of 27,000 of their women and children in British concentration camps during the Second Boer War at the turn of this century.

Nonetheless, they succeeded not only in creating their own language and culture out of the mix of Malay, African, and European influences that coexisted in the early years of colonization, but also in seizing power from the economically more powerful English in 1948. For over forty years, the Afrikaners had ensconced themselves in the institutions of the state—the security forces, civil service, education system, and government—to assure their survival for what they hoped would be forever. They built a modern infrastructure of roads, airports, and harbors second to none on the continent; found their way around international economic sanctions to acquire nuclear and missile technology; and spawned the most powerful economy on the continent.

In addition, they created a strong mythology about themselves and their place in Africa—the one "white tribe" among hundreds of black ones, there because God had ordained that, like the Jews, they had been awarded a "promised land." They even had a Covenant with God, one celebrated every December 16 on the anniversary of their spectacular victory over the Zulu hordes at Blood River in 1838. Only a religious miracle could account for the fact that 530 Afrikaners had held off an attacking Zulu force of 12,000 to 15,000 without suffering a single death. Surely it was a sign that the Afrikaners were God's Chosen People. A massive granite Voortrekker Monument outside Pretoria celebrates their saga.

One of the most difficult tasks for any outsider is to assess the meaning of the many historical and cultural myths Afrikaners have spun around, and about, themselves and their role in history. These were de Klerk's own people, and he was leading them on a trek into a totally different kind of wilderness. His promise this time was not their own separate nation but minority status in a black-ruled one. De Klerk was even courting the extinction of the special Afrikaner identity in the New South Africa, not an easy responsibility to shoulder as a member of that community's political elite. While he faced no serious challenge to his leadership from within the NP, de Klerk headed a party that represented only a minority of white voters after the 1989 elections and was aware that the threat to his reform program would come mainly from right-wing forces outside his party, forces that grew stronger as the peace process began to falter toward the end of 1991.

One of the most striking features of the white political debate in South Africa is the absence of any frank discussion about apartheid. Afrikaner political leaders tend to discuss the future of whites in the "New South Africa" with practically no reference to the moral issues involved, even though they were the architects, builders, and defenders of the most hideous system of racial segregation in contemporary times. Afrikaners on the whole seem to feel themselves morally blameless. They steadfastly turn a deaf ear to the agonizing of their own theologians in the Dutch Reformed Church—indeed, in the entire white religious community—over whether whites might owe something to blacks after the devastation wrought upon African society by three centuries of colonization and apartheid.

In November 1990, this agonizing reached a climax at a five-day religious conference, held in Rustenburg, west of Pretoria. More than three hundred church leaders from eighty denominations gathered to discuss whether apartheid was a "sin," maybe even a "heresy," and if so, what the consequences were for whites. It turned out to be a dramatic affair with highly emotional "confessions" offered by white elders of the Dutch Reformed Church; these were immediately rejected as insincere or insufficient by black ministers. At the end, however, the conference produced the "Rustenburg Declaration," a document of enormous importance for all the churches, but especially for the Dutch Reformed Church, which had for decades given its moral blessings to apartheid.

The document said, in part: "We confess our own sin and acknowledge our heretical part in the policy of apartheid which has led to such extreme suffering for so many in our land. We denounce apartheid, in its intention, its implementation and its consequences, as an evil policy. The practice and defence of apartheid as though it were biblically and theologically legitimated is an act of disobedience to God, a denial of the Gospel of Jesus Christ and a sin against our unity in the Holy Spirit." The declaration went on to admonish whites that there had to be genuine repentance and "practical restitution" to obtain God's forgiveness. "Without justice true reconciliation between people is impossible." The church leaders conceded that some of them had "actively misused the Bible to justify apartheid, leading many to believe that it had the sanction of God." They had even "insisted that its motives were good even though its effects were evil." Their failure to denounce apartheid as a sin, they confessed, had encouraged the government to retain it.

This remarkable declaration represented a watershed in Dutch Reformed Church thinking, even though de Klerk's own Dopper Church did not approve it. Unfortunately, it had absolutely no impact on the debate over the future of the Afrikaner community in the New South Africa. Neither de Klerk nor any other Afrikaner political leader ever referred to it. In fact, as discussed in chapter 3, de Klerk once told me that he did not agree that apartheid was "a sin" or that the intentions of its practitioners had ever been "evil." It simply had not worked out the way its National Party architects had intended. So the debate over the Afrikaner future, such as it was, centered on whether to accept black majority rule or to fight for some kind of white homeland, either a separate state or one in federation with other black-ruled ones. Those in favor of an independent white nation kept on evoking the same old biblical mythology the original architects of apartheid had created. They were deaf to the new thinking contained in the Rustenburg Declaration.

◆ ◆ ◆

The history of the Afrikaners and of their legendary Great Trek into the interior, starting in 1835, in search of the promised land has created the myth perpetuated to this day that whites have a passionate attachment to the soil and their farms. In reality, the whole early history of the Afrikaners is about the progressive takeover of the land from the Africans through treaties, fraud, battles, and outright seizures. A feud over land forms the centerpiece of what Afrikaners regard as their greatest tragedy, etched in a long frieze across the walls inside the Voortrekker Monument depicting the story of Piet Retief and his men, massacred by King Dingaan in February 1838 before they could sign a "treaty" that would give the Boers a vast tract of land in Natal. Whether Dingaan actually ever agreed to give away the land is still a subject of considerable historical dispute. Jay Naidoo, author of *Tracking Down Historical Myths*, has raised serious questions about the authenticity of what is said to have been a copy of the original treaty, which has mysteriously disappeared. In any case, Dingaan's purported treachery led to the undoing of the Zulu kingdom after the Afrikaners' miraculous victory at the Battle of Blood River on December 13, 1838, and the Voortrekkers' seizure of Natal, where they established another of their short-lived republics. The Afrikaners' insatiable appetite for land and cheap labor led to the current incredibly unjust partition of the country, in which 4.5 million whites own 87 percent of the land and 33 million Africans the remainder.

One hundred fifty years after Blood River, it is clear that the Afrikaner mythology about the land is today mostly just that—myth. The vast majority of Afrikaners have lost all contact with the land and retain no direct interest in it. After the National Party took power in 1948, the Afrikaners moved en masse into the state bureaucracy, trading in their plows for pencils and their land for public office. The result is that Afrikaners today are mostly urban dwellers and bureaucrats working in the civil service, the post offices, schools, railways, and other state-run companies. According to Hermann Giliomee, a political science professor at the University of Cape Town, by 1977 two-thirds of Afrikaners held white-collar jobs. In white schools, Afrikaans-speaking teachers are by far in the majority—72,711 to only 32,087 English speakers—and the police and military are similarly dominated by Afrikaners. It is rare to run into an English speaker in the post offices or in any of the government ministries; the senior civil service is almost 100 percent Afrikaner, and in 1992 there were just two ministers out of twenty-two—Trade and Industry Minister Derek Keys and Energy Minister George Bartlett—who were English speakers. The extent to which Afrikaners had lost touch with the land was perhaps best reflected in the declining farm population. By 1992, there were somewhere between 50,000 and 60,000 white farmers, the majority of them Afrikaners. Even if all of them were Afrikaners, the total white rural population would amount to somewhere between 200,-000 and 300,000, roughly 10 percent of the total Afrikaner population of 2.7 million. Moreover, many of the Afrikaner farmers were absentee landlords. The Afrikaners' attachment to their pioneering past seemed to have been largely reduced to holding weekend *brais*, or barbecues, drinking mampour fruit brandy, and holiday camping.

The keepers of Afrikaner mythology have yet to redefine formally the meaning of Afrikaner culture to take into account the urbanization of their own people. Pieter de Lange, a former head of the secretive Broederbond, said in 1990 that the Afrikaner had to find a new definition of himself and his role in Africa because of his new urban setting. Instead of thinking of the *volk* as a separate people, the Afrikaner would have to adopt a new "inclusive" view of himself as an African rather than a European. "The circumstances of the Afrikaners have changed as they became urbanized," he said. "But they haven't realized it yet and are still thinking of themselves in exclusive terms," referring to the Afrikaners' notion of themselves as a special "Chosen People." De Lange felt that urbanization would make it easier to redefine the Afrikaner, and what was important to him. His own redefinition was the following: "An Afrikaner is a man who wants to make his future in Africa." He would still have his own culture but would henceforth think of it, and himself, as African. However, de Lange seemed far ahead of the prevailing view among Afrikaners, who in 1990 still clung desperately to an "exclusive" notion of their European origins and own separate identity.

The urbanization of Afrikaners has presented serious problems for right-wing political movements espousing a *volkstaat*, or separate Afrikaner and white homeland. In fact, it has seriously undermined their appeals for a new "trek" into the wilderness. This has not deterred some from trying, however. What will no doubt be the last failed attempt to establish a white homeland was led by Carel Boshoff, a gentle, bearded professor and former missionary turned theologian, who heads a small cultural movement known as the Afrikaner Volkswag. Boshoff has been at the center of Afrikaner intellectual ferment throughout most of his career. He was chairman of the South African Bureau for Racial Affairs, the Afrikaner intellectual elite's answer to the liberal South African Institute of Race Relations, in the mid- and late-1970s. He was for three years chairman of the Broederbond, resigning in 1983, a year after the Nationalist-Conservative schism. Boshoff defected from the Broederbond, and with twenty other like-minded intellectuals established his Afrikaner Volkswag. Afrikaner purists like Boshoff saw the implications of "power-sharing" with nonwhites, Coloureds, and Indians as too ghastly to contemplate—the start of the slippery slope toward black majority rule. Boshoff and his followers favored partition to maintain an independent Afrikaner nation.

Boshoff remained a professor at the University of Pretoria's Divinity School until he resigned in early 1988 to pursue his dream of creating an all-white *volkstaat*. He was not the first dreamer. An earlier attempt to tilt at this Afrikaner windmill had been undertaken by the eponymous son of Hendrik F. Verwoerd. Starting in the late 1970s, the younger Verwoerd tried to establish a kind of Afrikaner pilot commune at Morgenzon in the southeastern Transvaal, 125 miles east of Johannesburg. His goal was to create "Oranjeland," an all-white nation, and his supporters were called Oranjewerkers, or Orange Workers. By the mid-1980s, young Verwoerd had attracted 2,000 to 2,500 whites to his Society of Orange Workers in Morgenzon. But he soon discovered a fatal flaw in his project: his followers preferred to rely on black labor rather than their own. So Oranjeland had become diluted with black bodies and sweat, and Morgenzon had spawned its own black township, providing laborers to get the embryonic white homeland going. By 1990 the experiment was largely a failure and was scarcely mentioned even by Afrikaner fanatics.

Boshoff set out in early 1991 with the same objective but a different strategy. He had come to the conclusion that the only way the Afrikaner could build his own nation was by looking for a thinly populated area where whites, if not a majority, could hope to become one eventually. The Afrikaners constituted only 6.25 percent of the total population in the early 1990s, so Prime Minister Verwoerd's original idea of removing millions of blacks living in existing white areas was simply not practical. "You may resettle one million but in the time it takes to resettle them, three million more are born," he remarked. The younger Verwoerd's idea of trying to establish a white nation in the midst of an industrial area where blacks were the overwhelming majority was just as impractical.

So Boshoff had selected a region in the Orange River–Karoo Desert basin in northwest Cape Province that was already populated by 120,000 whites and contained relatively few nonwhites. There was rich farming land, lots of water, and an outlet to the sea, as well as a magnificent dam assuring a steady supply of power. Whites could make a go of it on their own, developing light and high-tech industries and farming. Above all, he would not make Verwoerd, Jr.'s mistake of bringing in blacks to do the work. It would all be done by whites this time. "I think it's possible. I think it's reasonable. I think it's fair," Boshoff said of his proposed homeland, which he called Orandia. In his vision it would eventually cover 20 to 30 percent of present-day South Africa and would stretch from the Atlantic Ocean to Graaff Reinet and Aliwal North in the east, much of it semidesert land in the Karoo region. Would Afrikaners already living in the cities and suburbs be ready to uproot themselves and make another trek into the austere conditions of a semidesert? "That is the question," he conceded. "That has to be put to the test." But Boshoff insisted that his separatist solution was no crazier than what de Klerk was proposing at the time, some kind of ethnically based federation in which whites risked ultimately losing their separate identity.

The real-life village of Orania, the nucleus for Boshoff's Orandia, is located about 70 miles southwest of Kimberley, on the road between two tiny *dorps*, Hopetown and Petrusville. Built in 1968, it was originally a temporary village for the families of eighty engineers and technicians working on the construction of the nearby P. K. le Roux Dam, but was then abandoned when the work was finished in 1990. Orania was fairly well endowed with facilities when Boshoff and twenty-nine like-minded separatists purchased it in September 1990 for 1.6 million rand ($567,000). It had a large reservoir with a recycling system for garden water; a school; a big recreation center; a post office; a swimming pool; tennis courts; and eighty flimsily constructed homes laid out along tree-shaded streets.

My first visit to the village coincided with the arrival of the first six families in February 1991. Orania seemed more like a rundown ghost town than anything else. Sixty-eight of the homes were in good enough condition to be used immediately, but the other twelve needed to be restored before they could be inhabited. The biggest problem initially for the new Afrikaner pioneers was expelling sixty Coloured families still living behind the town in semi-slum conditions. That these Afrikaners were determined to keep Orania pure white was made clear by the reception given by the village supervisor, Thys Fick, who initially refused to shake a black reporter's hand and would not address him directly.

By March 1992, the village had taken on considerable life, even if it was still not a going concern economically. There were 360 residents and a lot of work being done on many of the homes by white carpenters and masons. The houses were selling for about 35,000 rand, the equivalent then of $12,400. The pride and joy of the village was its "multi-media center," a system of education where each student used computers to learn at his or her own speed. According to Danie van Rensberg, a retired civil servant and member of the town council, Orania welcomed anyone who was an Afrikaner, accepted Christian schooling in Afrikaans, supported the idea of a *volkstaat*, and was willing to do his own work. No Coloureds were welcome, even if they did speak Afrikaans as their mother language and might even accept the *volkstaat* ideology. Van Rensberg asserted that in this new White Jerusalem there would be no internal apartheid because, as he put it, "it will be a country belonging to only the Afrikaner people." Van Rensberg was also fixated on the idea that whites had to be self-reliant and not depend on black labor of any kind. "If a nation does not do its own work,

192 / C H A I N E D T O G E T H E R

it cannot last," he said. The downfall of white-ruled South Africa had been that it had come to depend on nonwhites "without giving equal rights to blacks. You can't maintain that sort of situation forever." The Achilles' heel of the Morgenzon settlement, he argued, had been the acceptance of black labor: "If you use black or Coloured labor, then you commit suicide."

Still, Boshoff faced the problem of finding whites willing to work in conditions such as those at Orania. The village council was employing twelve to fifteen white workers in March 1992 and paying them only 200 rand ($70) a week plus housing. But the "housing" offered was the tiny houses previously occupied by the Coloureds, over the hill behind Orania where conditions were terrible. Two white workers fled Orania in May 1992, telling the media they couldn't stand it anymore. They complained that they had been treated "like slaves." Nothing had prepared them for the hardships they found there, which included tearing down house doors to make beds for themselves. They had been ostracized socially and had been treated like lepers by the town's residents. Orania seemed to have sown the seeds for class conflict as it tried to replace Coloured with white workers. One wondered how long it would be before the residents were once again calling upon the Coloureds to do their work.

Even sympathetic Afrikaner farmers around Orania, van Rensberg had to admit, questioned its viability. The village had no industries, even light ones, and only a handful of shops and a restaurant. The town, he said, was basically living on the pensions and savings of its residents, and subsidies from the holding company that had founded it. Orania's first formal budget (for maintenance, the waterworks, electricity, and administration) was set at 460,000 rand per year, with residents paying 300,000 of the total and the company, or rather Boshoff's Volkswag, the rest. But the potential for growth was enormous, van Rensberg insisted. "For whites, things are going to become difficult in Azania," he remarked, using the black nationalist name for South Africa. There were already lots of unemployed whites who would be seeking refuge here before long. The town council was busy preparing for "thousands" of newcomers and for sheep, ostrich, and fish farming. The first farm adjacent to Orania had already been bought. By the year 2000, Orania expected to have 4,000 to 7,000 residents. "We have the water, the land, and the will," boasted van Rensberg.

For the one American couple living in Orania, Tim and Brenda Vaughan from Calaveras County in California, "will" was the key, and in their view the Afrikaners had plenty of resources. Before he immigrated to South Africa in 1988, Tim had always admired "this one little [white] nation in the middle of Africa." After first farming in the eastern Transvaal, he had been attracted to Orania by its "Calvinistic spirit," he said. He was convinced Orania would make it because "the Afrikaners are tough. They'll get a homeland or be dead. They are going to *laager* [circle] around the Bible and their religion." The Afrikaners were like the Jews, he reasoned, and if the Jews could have their Israel, why couldn't the Afrikaners have theirs? "What makes a Jew better than an Afrikaner? Why can't we have a little piece of desert and be left alone?"

In June 1990, amidst ominous warnings from groups under and above ground that the "resistance" was starting, bombs went off across Pretoria—in garbage bins, black taxi stands, a museum, several National Party offices, and a school designated for the four hundred children of returning ANC exiles. Between April and mid-July 1990, two blacks were killed and forty-eight others injured in a dozen bombings around Johannesburg. Arms were also being stolen out of armories and police stations. The liberal Afrikaans-language weekly *Vrye Weekblad* infiltrated an informer into right-wing extremist ranks in mid-June and came out blazing with a story that plans were afoot to assassinate both de Klerk and Mandela. The informer, Jan Johannes Smith, was too scared to attend a press conference on June 22, but editor Max du Preez handed out the bloodcurdling affidavit Smith had given the police, detailing how Mandela was to be assassinated with a .303 rifle at Jan Smuts International Airport upon returning from a trip to the United States.

It all sounded exceedingly serious. Police had already arrested twenty-eight white supremacists and were holding them incommunicado under the Internal Security Act, which they had so ruthlessly employed against anti-apartheid activists over the years. It seemed fitting justice. White liberals like Frederik van Zyl Slabbert, director of the Institute for a Democratic Alternative for South Africa (Idasa), were taking the white terrorist danger deadly seriously. According to Slabbert, many right wingers were "strategically placed" in the police and army, or their reserves, with access to arms on an immediate basis. "You only need twelve people to decide to put bombs in twenty-four spots over thirty days to cause a lot of trouble," he warned during a luncheon with foreign correspondents in July 1990. It was a frightening time because initially it was not known whether the police, many of whose officers harbored right-wing sympathies and strong anti-ANC antipathies, would crack down on its own brethren.

For all their bombast and bombs, there was a buffoonlike quality to many right-wing leaders, who seemed to think they were the romantic heroes in some kind of "freedom struggle" stage play. Take, for instance, Piet "Skiet" Rudolph, the right wing's premier "freedom fighter" in 1990. He stole arms from the Air Force Headquarters in Pretoria and took responsibility for the Easter bombing of Melrose House, where the treaty of the Boer surrender to the British in 1902 was on display. He also set off bombs at two National Party offices as well as outside a black labor union building and the Afrikaans-language newspaper die Beeld. In March 1990 he went underground and managed to avoid arrest for 185 days until he was finally caught on September 17. In the meantime, he made various telephone calls proudly defending his various actions on behalf of the whites' new "freedom struggle." He also made a video recording, which he sent to local newspapers and radio stations, declaring "open war" on de Klerk's government. "If ever it was necessary to follow a scorched-earth policy, it is now," he intoned.

Rudolph became the self-styled commander of the ultra-right-wing terrorist group Orde Boerevolk, and for a short time he was the main symbol of the new white resistance. After his arrest, he went on several hunger strikes to win sympathy for his demand to be treated as a "political prisoner" and be freed, since many imprisoned ANC members were being released at that time. Rudolph fasted for thirty days with five other right-wing detainees before he finally gave up his much-publicized protest on March 30, having lost twenty-six pounds. Through his lawyer, he had sworn that he was "ready for death," only to give up his hunger strike when the going got tough. Clearly, he was not ready to become a martyr for his cause after all.

Yet not all white supremacists were play-acting and bluffing like Rudolph. A number of white extremists carried out hideous and gratuitous acts of revenge on blacks after Mandela's release. There was the case, for example, of two men from Richard's Bay in northern Natal, David "Piet" Botha and Adrian Smuts, who belonged to the Orde Boerevolk and the neo-Nazi Afrikaner Resistance Movement (AWB). They were also members of the "Israel Vision Church," which believed blacks to be "wild animals without souls." They became furious when, in early October 1990, a group of blacks went on a rampage in the streets of downtown Durban and stabbed a number of whites. So, on October 9 they drove down to Durban to take revenge in the same kind of crazy way as the blacks, but to much more devastating effect. They opened fire randomly on a bus taking blacks home from work, killing seven and wounding twenty-seven others. In September 1991, Botha and Smuts were sentenced to death for what their judge described as a "cold-blooded, gruesome and cruel" attack on the bus riders.

Another example was the case of Henry Martin, Adrian Maritz, and Lood van Schalkwyk, members of the same terrorist Orde Boerevolk, who planted a bomb at a taxi stand in Pretoria in August 1990, injuring fifteen people. Miraculously, none were killed. But the three also sent a parcel bomb in October 1990 to Nick Cruise, a computer technician at a Durban firm doing work for the ANC. He was less lucky, dying instantly when he opened what he thought was a computer sent in for repairs.

Martin, Maritz, and van Schalkwyk were caught in November of that year, and early the next July went on a hunger strike to gain sympathy for their demand that their crimes be labeled "political" and they be granted amnesty. Like Rudolph, they were repeatedly reported by their lawyer to be "nearly comatose" and ready to die for their cause. The local media followed their deteriorating condition day by day with dramatic reports, particularly after Martin went beyond sixty-three days of fasting. This meant that in theory he was on death's door, since the ten Irish hunger strikers who had died from fasting in 1981 expired after anywhere from fifty-nine to seventy-one days. The government made the decision on August 28 to let them die rather than release them. Mandela himself then went to see the three on their "death beds" in a Pretoria hospital in a show of misguided sympathy and support for their demand to be considered "political prisoners." Again, the hunger strike turned out to be mostly a hoax; the three had secretly been taking enough food to stay alive. They finally ended their protest at the end of the first week of September, and Martin and Maritz were granted bail on September 13. The two terrorists never stood trial. They fled the country on forged passports in October and turned up shortly afterward in London, claiming they were turning over information to the ANC about the "dirty tricks" of the security forces.

There was no shortage of semi-demented right wingers like Martin and Maritz, many of them dangerous killers and some of them even members of the Conservative Party, holding respectable positions. Koos Botha, a Conservative deputy in Parliament from the Pretoria area, wrote an article for the Afrikaans weekly *Rapport* in May 1992 in which he admitted having placed the bomb at Hillview High School, the one intended for the children of ANC returnees from exile, in 1990. To blow up the school, he had obtained fifteen kilograms of explosives from the white Mine Workers Union. He also admitted in the article that he had placed bombs at post offices in Ventersdorp and Verwoerdburg and at the headquarters of the Congress of South African Trade Unions. It was "the climate" within the Conservative Party that had led him to commit such acts of terrorism, he explained, but he had changed his mind about resorting to such tactics and now favored negotiations for a white *volkstaat*. Botha said that party leader Andries Treurnicht had known all about his activities for some time.

Even crazier than Botha's antics were those of Koos van der Merwe and Andries du Toit, two Conservative Party town councilors from the Johannesburg suburb Boksburg, who, in April 1992, put a limpet mine in front of a garbage can at the Rand Show. This was the biggest annual exhibition-cum-fair of the year, attended almost entirely by whites because of the relatively expensive ten rand entrance fee. Nine whites, including three women, were injured in the blast. The bombers had left a note attributing the blast to the White Wolves, a well-known white terrorist group. The note said: "Black terror was a huge headache [but] terror by whites will make it look like a picnic." Apartheid might be dead, but "long live apartheid." Why they targeted the whites attending the Rand Show remained a mystery; perhaps they thought they would get better publicity there. Among the nine people arrested six weeks later for involvement in this and other bombings, which took place over the 1991 Christmas and New Year holidays, were the two Conservative councilors.

By early 1992, the right-wing movement was fragmented into close to two hundred cells and small groups, partly by design to avoid police detection and partly because Afrikaners are notoriously quarrelsome and divisive. New names were springing up with every bomb blast, a tactic Islamic fundamentalist groups had used in Beirut and elsewhere, but many of the factions were actually part of the AWB. Wim Booyce, one of the best South African analysts of right-wing politics, estimated that "at a push" there were perhaps twenty-four or twenty-five groups that were really active.

The AWB's proud emblem was an arrangement of three sevens, the religious symbol for Christ, made to look like the Nazi swastika. Their members wore brown and black uniforms, also copied from the Nazis, and their leader, Eugene Terre'Blanche, was addressed as "My Leader" just as Hitler had been. One of the worst examples of their neo-Nazi tactics occurred in Louis Trichardt on November 24, 1990, when fifteen AWB supporters attacked a group of Sunday school children with whips and clubs as they were about to have a picnic on the lawn of the civic center. The police did nothing to stop them. Though it took until June 1992 before the attackers were brought to trial, five of the fifteen were eventually found guilty. They were given eighteen-month suspended jail sentences and fined 3,000 rands each.

Neo-Nazi in its paraphernalia, colors, and tactics, the AWB in its goals was purely Afrikaner. It wanted the land making up the old Boer republics of the nineteenth century—the Orange Free State, the Transvaal, and those short-lived republics in northern Natal— to remain in white hands and under white rule. That this was no longer even a remote possibility only made its members more fanatical in their demands and attacks on de Klerk as a "traitor" to his people. The AWB seemed at times to have the makings of a real threat to de Klerk's authority. By 1992, it boasted somewhere between 5,000 and 10,000 members scattered around the country, but concentrated primarily in the Transvaal and Natal. Its paramilitary wing may have consisted of as many as 5,000 men and women, though the public displays of their forces rarely exceeded 500. Terre'Blanche liked to portray himself as an old-style Boer commando chief, riding a horse on every public occasion and outfitting himself in jodhpurs, brown paramilitary uniform, and a pioneer's hat. Often drunk, and with a well-known penchant for extramarital affairs, he was easy to dismiss as the greatest right-wing buffoon in the country.

Despite his antics, however, he was by far the best orator the right wing had. He spoke like an Old Testament prophet, with a deep, thundering voice. He also loved talking in apocalyptic terms of the coming Boer uprising against an ANC "Communist government." He promised a "revolution" when the right moment came, calling it "the Third Boer War" for liberation after the two fought against the British in the nineteenth century. "All we want is the Boer republics—the Transvaal, Free State and the northern part of Natal with Richard's Bay as our harbor," he said. "That land is our land."

Moreover, Terre'Blanche did not shy away from confrontation with de Klerk's police. On the night of August 9, 1991, the AWB was determined to stop the president from speaking at Kommondo Hall in Ventersdorp. Terre'Blanche organized 2,000 men from all over Transvaal who came armed with tear gas canisters, knives, pistols, rifles, and, to fend off the police dogs, metal arm guards or arms covered in plaster of Paris and spikes. They faced 1,500 heavily armed policemen who had orders to "shoot to kill" if things got out of hand. The Battle of Ventersdorp, as it was later called, erupted from spontaneous combustion rather than careful calculation, as AWB commandoes marching down Voortrekker Street encountered a formidable police line. For thirty minutes, there was a pitched hand-to-hand battle and total mayhem in the main street. When the tear gas and smoke cleared, three AWB men lay dead and thirty-six others injured, the first victims of the "Third Boer War." Seven policemen were also wounded, several by gunfire. Skiet Rudolph, then the AWB's secretary-general, who had led the march with Terre'Blanche, professed that "the battle" had marked an irreversible turning point in white politics.

Despite the Ventersdorp confrontation, the right-wing backlash to de Klerk's reforms was felt first and foremost at the ballot box. On February 19, 1992, only six weeks after the less than auspicious opening session of CODESA, his National Party suffered a stunning defeat in a by-election held in the Afrikaner university town of Potchefstroom. The results of the election shocked de Klerk, for it meant that his white followers were abandoning him. But the Conservative candidate, party general secretary Andries Beyers, won 56 percent of the vote, a surprisingly large margin. When de Klerk heard about the results that night, he decided to take one more enormous political gamble: He would call a nationwide referendum on his reforms and negotiations with the ANC. He would even put his own political future on the line, announcing that he would resign if the referendum was defeated. By midday the next day, de Klerk had won the approval for his gamble from both his cabinet and the party caucus.

De Klerk proved to be in his element. He savored high risks and high stakes, despite his avowed preference for bridge over poker. The campaign leading up to the March 17 referendum brought out in de Klerk a masterful display of his political acumen when it came to dealing with the electorate of nearly three million white voters. De Klerk conducted an all-out, American-style, meet-the-people campaign wrapped in a blitz of TV and newspaper ads, street posters, bumper stickers, and bunting. He got the white community's most popular singers, actors, artists, and athletes to endorse him and appear with him in public. He appealed to the whites' adoration of sports, warning that if he lost, it was certain that the upcoming rugby tours by Australian and New Zealand teams—the first in more than a decade—would be canceled. South Africa would again be the pariah of the world. He kept up a strenuous schedule of visits to the white community. He addressed innumerable public rallies but also went to places like old-age and retirement villages, shopping and civic centers, business luncheons, university campuses, and small *dorps*. His whirlwind trips sometimes involved a dozen stops in one day. Perhaps the most colorful was his arrival in a motorboat decorated in party colors at a lakeside shopping center in the military town of Verwoerdburg. After a short speech, with a local blond Afrikaner mother-with-child beauty at his side, de Klerk strolled from store to store pumping hands. Any doubts that he was a consummate politician were laid to rest during that referendum campaign.

The National Party also demonstrated that it had learned its lessons from the American tactics of negative advertising by launching an all-out attack on the Conservatives, painting them as the party of racial hatred, backwardness, violence, and certain civil war. The Conservative alternative was simply "too ghastly to contemplate," as one of de Klerk's predecessors, John Vorster, had said when seeking to nudge whites toward reform. The Nats seized upon the Conservatives' campaign alliance with the AWB to brand their opponents as promoters of "terrorism." As so often tends to be true in American campaigns, there was never any real discussion of the issues as de Klerk appealed to the loftier hopes of whites for peace and reconciliation and the Conservatives to their fears of life under black majority rule.

The referendum proved a spectacular victory for de Klerk and his party: His policies were approved by 68.6 percent of the nearly 2.8 million participating voters in a turnout of 85 percent of all those registered—one of the highest voter turnouts ever. The results showed what effective campaigners the Nats could be once mobilized by the Conservative challenge. De Klerk was ecstatic, taking the outcome as a massive endorsement of his leadership. This was "the real birthday of the real New South Africa," he declared, speaking from the garden steps behind the presidential offices in Cape Town. "Today," he proclaimed, "we have closed the book on apartheid. It doesn't often happen that in one generation a nation gets an opportunity to rise above itself." ANC officials, on the other hand, were terrified by the whole referendum spectacle. They saw for the first time just how masterful de Klerk and his party could be in campaigning. Suddenly they realized what they were likely to face when it became time to compete with the National Party in the New South Africa.

De Klerk's referendum victory forced the Conservative Party into a full-scale retreat from the political arena and a reconsideration of their whole agenda. On June 27, it convened a "special general congress" in Pretoria that marked a watershed in the party's rearguard battle to defend white supremacy. First, the Conservatives gave up pretending that they were any longer defending the interests of all whites and reduced their self-defined constituency to only Afrikaners. (Most of the English speakers, they felt, had cast their votes in the referendum in favor of an eventual black-dominated unitary state.) The other major shift was the abandonment of Verwoerd's Grand Apartheid scheme for hiving off the entire black population into ten tiny homelands so that whites could keep 87 percent of the country's land mass. Clearly, two thirds of the white voters no longer bought such nonsense.

In its ideological and geographic attempt to replace the old apartheid dream, the Conservative leadership came up with the highly impractical idea of basing a new *volkstaat* on the thirty-nine districts in which the party had won a majority of the white votes in the referendum. The problem, though, was that these districts were not contiguous and almost all were rural, creating a leopard-spot vision of a white nation. This Conservative plan sounded like the photographic negative of the disastrous fragmented black homelands, like Bophuthatswana, whose seven pieces stretch from the Botswana border in the north to ThabaNchu, sixty miles east of Bloemfontein. How the proposed white homeland would ever become viable economically was not clear.

Andries Treurnicht told me after the congress that the thirty-nine constituencies should be considered just "core areas" around which other white land could be added to enlarge them. He also assured an Afrikaner reporter that white support for such a homeland was "much larger than these thirty-nine constituencies" and included many of de Klerk's National Party supporters. His vision apparently involved a loose confederation, or commonwealth, between the white *volkstaat* and other ethnically based black "nations." There would be no central government or legislative body, but these ministates would all be economically interdependent. While admitting that the "old South Africa" was a lost cause, the Conservatives were still clinging to the Afrikaner mythology that the *volk* was the creation of Divine Providence and therefore had a right to a separate existence. Even the international community agreed that "only ethnic communities are acknowledged as a 'people' and have a claim to self-determination," the party said.

Criticism of the Conservative Party's new dream for a white homeland came from all sides, but most important, from within its own ranks. At the congress, five senior delegates, led by Andries Beyers, distributed a document proposing a slightly more realistic scheme for a white homeland. Known as "the New Right," Beyers and his group proposed that the country be divided into nine or ten regions, or states. The Afrikaners would be given the northern Transvaal, the one district the Conservative Party had won in the referendum, and Pretoria would be its capital. Afrikaners and Coloureds together might constitute a second state around Cape Town and north to Upington in the far northern Cape Province, the New Right proposal said. Other states would be similarly ethnically defined except for a "cosmopolitan state" in the center, with Johannesburg as its capital.

Beyers, who had been stripped at the start of the congress of his party post for bucking the leadership's archaic views on apartheid, had marshaled enough support for his plan that Treurnicht, a stodgy hardline conservative, decided to avoid a showdown at the special congress and put off a vote on the executive committee's own proposal. But on August 13, 1992, the internal split Treurnicht had hoped to avoid finally took place. Beyers walked out with his four colleagues to found his own Volksunie Party (United People's Party), which was willing to enter into negotiations with the ANC and other black political groups for a white enclave within a black-ruled South Africa. No right-wing group had ever before agreed to hold talks with the ANC. Furthermore, Beyers was the first Conservative to accept the fact that a white-dominated region or state might begin as part of a larger black-ruled federation and then have to negotiate for its own sovereignty at a later time, if ever. Equally startling, Beyers stated later in 1992 that his party had abandoned a racial definition of Afrikaners. An Afrikaner, he said, was not a white person but a member of a "cultural group to which quite a number of English-speaking and Coloured people have assimilated." What defined an Afrikaner was whether he or she felt a belonging, a "togetherness," on the basis of language, culture, and history. For an erstwhile Conservative, Beyers was certainly charting new territory for whites. While his Volksunie was only a small splinter group, it nonetheless constituted an opening to the Conservative world that both de Klerk and the ANC could use to begin a dialogue. Beyers met Mandela on November 19 for a largely symbolic meeting that marked a new direction in the Conservative search for the white man's salvation.

By mid-1992, then, the strengths and weaknesses of the right-wing threat to de Klerk seemed pretty apparent. It was not all bluster, but neither was it cause for serious alarm. The main threat posed by the AWB and its like-minded allies was one of terrorism, not full-blooded counterrevolution. The AWB was a pale image of the Irish Republican Army; even its ability to avoid the detection and arrest of its bomb-throwing members remained questionable. There was no overall command structure anymore, as a whole new list of right-wing groups came to light under exotic names like the "Afrikaner Volkstaat Beweging" (Afrikaner Nationhood Movement) and the Boere Republikeinse Leer (Boer Republican Army). Moreover, in the aftermath of the March 1992 referendum, neither the AWB nor the Conservative Party could pretend to have a moral mandate to speak or act on behalf of the majority of whites. The results totally undermined any sense of moral legitimacy for the armed resistance the right-wing might have thought it enjoyed among whites. Just like those advocating a separate white homeland, those clamoring for a resistance struggle seemed to have seriously misjudged the mood of the white community. They could not escape the fact that nearly 69 percent of whites had come out in favor of de Klerk's reforms and negotiations with the ANC.

For a long time after the referendum, the AWB fell silent. This silence was due partly to continuing effective police infiltration of white right-wing terrorist circles. Wim Booyce said he knew of no Western country where the police had done such a good job of infiltrating and smashing right-wing terrorism. According to his calculations, the police had an 83 percent success rate in catching those responsible for acts of terrorism. At a special congress of right-wing groups held in Klerksdorp the weekend of May 29 and 30, 1992, Eugene Terre'Blanche sought to rally his dispirited followers with statistics. Almost 900,000 whites had voted against the referendum, he reminded them, and that was more than the ANC's 700,000 members and the Communist Party's 25,000 combined. "We are prepared to offer our lives on the altar to fight for a white homeland," he said. But his revolutionary bravado rang exceedingly hollow. Terre'Blanche might still be alive to fight another day, but his dream of restoring the old Boer republics was just that, pure fantasy and nothing more. Booyce himself came to the conclusion that right-wing terrorism would only become a problem if black terrorism surfaced in the white suburbs. Then, he said, the "Beirut scenario" of a country carved up into areas under the control of various different militia might come into play. He was referring, of course, only to South Africa's white cities, towns, and suburbs that would become embattled enclaves surrounded by the majority black population.

The most serious attempt by white supremacists to halt the march of history came on April 10, 1993. That day, a Polish immigrant and AWB member, Janusz Walus, walked up to Communist Party leader Chris Hani outside his home in the predominantly white Johannesburg suburb of Boksburg and shot him dead. Hani, a former top Umkhonto commander, was the hero of the township youth, and his death was apparently intended to spark such an upheaval of black outrage that the negotiations would be drowned in a sea of blood. But it didn't happen. Walus was apprehended within hours of Hani's assassination, and police also soon arrested a prominent member of the Conservative Party, Clive Derby-Lewis, and his wife, Gaye Derby-Lewis, a well-known campaigner for right-wing causes, as the suspected masterminds. Tens of thousands of blacks did take to the streets in protest over Hani's killing. But Mandela and de Klerk made repeated impassioned pleas for calm, and the ANC and the government, working on parallel lines if not exactly together, managed to keep the negotiations—only recently resumed—back on track. Hani's assassination served as a horrible reminder to all South Africans of the genuine danger individuals like Walus and the Derby-Lewises also posed to the personal security of national leaders like de Klerk and Mandela. Plots to assassinate either, or both, of them seemed even likelier as the day approached for the effective handover of power to blacks. After all, Prime Minister Verwoerd had been shot through the neck by one would-be assassin in 1960, and knifed to death in Parliament by a successful one in 1966. There was thus already a terrible precedent for such political tragedies in South Africa. One could only hope it would be spared another.

11

A STEP TOO FAR

I n May 1992, just as the CODESA talks were to resume after a four-month hiatus, two scandals broke that weakened de Klerk's negotiating hand. The first scandal involved massive corruption, theft, bribery, and misspending in the Department of Development Aid, responsible for improving the dismal lot of blacks in the homelands. The scandal, which was taken to reflect the general government attitude toward black poverty, came to light through an official investigation that was made public in Parliament on May 7, just a week before CODESA II was to begin sitting. The report had, in fact, been kept secret since the previous September 13 to allow time for criminal proceedings against eleven officials brought to court on various charges; none had been found guilty as of May 1992, and nine of them had been cleared after internal hearings.

The presiding judge in the investigation had reached a devastating conclusion about the attitude of civil servants in that particular department: "There was good reason for officials to believe that if you stole and were caught, you merely paid back and nothing further happened. But if you were not caught that was your good luck." On the basis of several earlier investigations, there was also good reason to suspect that this described the prevailing ethos throughout much of the Afrikaner-dominated civil service. The judge had been unable to quantify how much money had been pilfered and misspent altogether, but concluded that it was likely a question of "millions, if not billions," of rands. The department was "so terminally ill . . . that the time has now arrived to turn off the life-support system," concluded the judge. De Klerk had at least done that; in October, a month after he was handed the report, he had abolished the entire department.

The extent of the corruption was highlighted by television pictures showing hundreds of portable toilets sitting in an empty field near Letsitele, in the northeastern Transvaal, without any houses around them; this was the result of a scam by two development aid employees who had designed the toilets themselves and had then sold 15 million rands' worth to the department. Not to be outdone by television, the Sunday *Times* of May 10 ran a front-page picture of scores of the toilets lost in an empty field under the banner headline: "Toilet Town: A Famous Landmark of Nationalist Misrule."

The report was particularly damaging to the government because all the corruption and embezzlement of funds had taken place under two of de Klerk's senior negotiators: Gerrit Viljoen, constitutional affairs minister, who had been the minister in charge from 1985 to 1989, and Stoffel van der Merwe, who had headed development aid from 1989 to 1991 and was the National Party's general secretary at the time the scandal broke. Viljoen, as it turned out, had rejected an independent outside investigation of the corruption within his department and had only fired, according to a Viljoen aide, "about ten" officials implicated in the misappropriation of funds. On May 4, three days before the scandal broke, de Klerk announced that Viljoen was being replaced as constitutional affairs minister by his assistant, Roelof Meyer, as of June 1. Viljoen went off on doctor's orders for a month-long rest. He had suffered a minor heart attack, it was said, brought on by total exhaustion from the negotiations. There was, however, no question of his being relieved of his post because of the corruption findings. Instead, he was named "minister of state affairs," with no specific duties assigned except that of assisting de Klerk with the negotiations. Peter Soal, a Democratic Party member of Parliament, summed up the feeling of many South Africans when he said during a parliamentary debate on May 11 that de Klerk's ministers were "like barnacles clinging to office for dear life." Asked about governmental corruption at a press conference during CODESA II, de Klerk shrugged it off. Every government in the world had scandals, even the American administration, he said. Still, the state president was setting a disturbing precedent by absolving ministers of all misdeeds committed within their departments. What would whites say when similar large-scale corruption took place under black ministers in the future?

The other scandal involved one more horrible skeleton from apartheid's closet—the killing of four popular anti-apartheid activists from Cradock on June 23, 1985. The four were returning at night from nearby Port Elizabeth when their car was stopped at a police roadblock. They were never seen alive again, their bodies found alongside the road a couple of days later. Their assassination had touched off nationwide protests and demonstrations that had led to the declaration of a state of emergency. The Botha government never took any action to discover who was responsible, nor did de Klerk's. But on May 8, 1992, the *New Nation*, a pro-ANC weekly, published a photocopy of a message sent on June 7, 1985, by the State Security Council (the equivalent of the U.S. government's National Security Council, only with more police powers) from its office in Port Elizabeth to its headquarters in Pretoria. It purported to be the summary of a telephone discussion between Brigadier Christoffel van der Westhuizen, then head of the council's Eastern Province Command, and a General van Rensberg, a member of its secretariat in Pretoria. The "signal message," as the document was called, named three Cradock activists—Matthew Goniwe, Mbulelo Goniwe, and Fort Calata—and proposed that they be "permanently removed from society as a matter of urgency," despite the widespread reaction that could be expected "locally as well as nationally." Two of the three—Matthew Goniwe and Calata—were among the four found dead just two weeks later.

The document was subsequently traced to the pro-ANC Transkei homeland leader, Brigadier Bantu Holomisa, who disclosed that he had received it anonymously in his mail. The signal message confirmed the black community's worst suspicions about the activities of the security services and their long-presumed responsibility for the murder of more than sixty other activists between 1981 and

1989. The greatest embarrassment for de Klerk, however, was that van der Westhuizen was at that very time serving as the chief of staff of Military Intelligence (MI). Since the authenticity of the document was never questioned by the military, the revelation immediately raised questions about the role of many other senior officers and ministers who had served on the State Security Council in the mid- and late-1980s and were still in office, including no less than the president himself.

Once again de Klerk did his best to contain the new political damage inflicted on his government. The same day as the *New Nation*'s disclosure—and after Holomisa sent him a copy of the message—de Klerk ordered a judicial probe into the allegations. He also issued a statement saying that "the government has no knowledge whatsoever of the alleged actions and at no stage was this case, or similar cases, discussed or considered by the cabinet or the State Security Council." Any suggestion that either body had "planned or approved murder" was "devoid of all truth," he said.

But the damage to de Klerk's reformist image had already been inflicted; the two scandals gave the ANC and its allies the perfect springboard from which to launch a campaign aimed at discrediting and weakening de Klerk. On May 13, two days before CODESA II was due to open, the "tripartite alliance" of the ANC, the Communist Party, and the Congress of South African Trade Unions held a summit in which they issued a statement declaring that the rash of scandals constituted the "symptoms of a regime in terminal moral decay." De Klerk was no longer fit to rule. The only solution, the ANC insisted in another statement, was for the entire de Klerk government to resign and make way for the installation of an interim government of national unity.

In the midst of this propaganda war, government and ANC negotiators were scrambling to cobble together a package settlement deal that could be approved at CODESA II. Despite the clash between de Klerk and Mandela at CODESA I, their aides and the body's numerous working committees were back at work by early February 1992. The government's constitutional proposals of the previous September formed the basis of much of the proposed compromise, but strangely, de Klerk had become far less anxious than the

ANC to reach an agreement. The package involved a set of inter-locking parts that was supposed to take the country through a two-phase transitional period to a new political order. In the first phase, a nineteen-member multi-party "transitional executive council" would be appointed from the CODESA delegations to "level the playing field" for all political parties. The council would be given the "powers necessary" to prepare for elections as well as to make policy in four sensitive areas—regional and local govern-ment, finance, law and order, and defense. Decision-making would be by consensus whenever possible, but in case of deadlocks a vote in which 80 percent of the council's members agreed to a given decision would suffice. An independent election commission was also to be set up to oversee "free and fair elections," as well as a special media commission to assure fair coverage for all parties by the state-run SABC. In the second stage, general elections would be held for an interim Parliament in which all political parties winning at least a small percentage (3 to 5 percent) of the vote would participate. This Parliament would be empowered both to write a new constitution and to pass normal legislation. Half the members would be elected on a national basis and half on a regional one to assure that smaller local parties were included. All this presup-posed some kind of "interim constitution" to govern the country during this transitional period, to be achieved either by amending the existing constitution or by writing an entirely new one.

This constitutional package proved so complicated that its au-thors had extreme difficulty explaining to reporters, let alone the general public, how it would work. The ANC's Thabo Mbeki, one of its chief negotiators, said on the eve of CODESA II that there might have to be two interim constitutions, one for each of the two phases envisaged during the transitional period, but he wasn't sure. No one else was certain, either. Clearly, confusion reigned, and it was bound to mean trouble later. As it turned out, both the govern-ment and the ANC continued making changes in their negotiating positions right through the first hours of the convention. Little wonder, then, that CODESA II stood an excellent chance of ending in "breaklock," an expression coined by political writer Shaun Johnson of the *Star* to describe the constantly changing status of the negotiations in the last week as they wobbled between "breakthrough" and "deadlock." The night before CODESA II opened, Mbeki described the "weather" hanging over the convention as only "fair to mild—with storms threatening." His forecast was to prove all too correct.

Not surprisingly, an air of crisis hung over the convention on the morning of May 15 when the 228 delegates once again gathered at the World Trade Center. Among other outstanding issues, the government and the ANC had been unable to come to any agreement on the size of "special majority" that would be required for the constituent assembly to approve certain fundamental issues such as changes in the constitution or the powers of future regional bodies. The ANC had been insisting on 66 percent, the government on 75 percent. The latter was the same percentage all parties, including the ANC, had agreed would be required for adoption of a Bill of Rights. The liberal Democratic Party proposed the obvious compromise—70 percent across the board for approval of all major constitutional issues. The bargaining also involved a new government proposal, introduced only two days before CODESA II, to establish a second body, or Senate, as part of the interim Parliament that would also have to approve the country's final constitution. Government negotiators frankly admitted that they were using the Senate as a bargaining chip to wring another concession from the ANC, namely a 75 percent "special majority" for the adoption of all important sections of the constitution.

The attempt to turn this deadlock into a breakthrough continued just before the start of CODESA II. The tension was enormous and tempers badly frayed by the long days of negotiations over the preceding week. Tertius Delport, Viljoen's deputy at one point, who together with Meyer led de Klerk's negotiating team in mid-1992, was in an especially foul mood; he had been battling the flu, laryngitis, and lack of sleep for a week. ANC officials charged that he had become irrational, irascible, and impossible to work with in the negotiations. National Party negotiator Stoffel van der Merwe sought to put the best face on the situation at a 9:00 A.M. press conference, noting that everyone was "living days of high drama" but that was "the stuff negotiations are made of." Van der Merwe disclosed the de Klerk government's demands: that the convention agree first upon a full-blown interim constitution; that a 75 percent special majority be required to approve all issues concerning regional government; and that a second chamber be constituted in the interim Parliament and given the authority to ratify the final constitution. Furthermore, he thought it was likely to take "quite a number of months" to negotiate an interim constitution. "I can assure you we will not have an interim constitution by July," he said. July had been the ANC's self-declared deadline for starting the whole process of transferring power by putting in place the proposed "transitional executive council."

Van der Merwe offered the ANC what purported to be a concession: The government was willing to get legislation through Parliament by the ANC's July deadline, amending the current constitution to allow the transitional executive council to begin functioning. But the ANC saw van der Merwe's "concession" mostly as a trap; it feared that unless the council were part of an overall package deal, the government would just stall the whole transition once it had some blacks sitting in Pretoria. The ANC and its allies went into caucus while the other CODESA delegates waited impatiently in their seats to begin the proceedings. At one point, a clearly irritated Delport stormed into the press room to announce that he "failed to see what further negotiations there could be" at that stage. "I'm going back to get an answer from the ANC," he said dramatically, "and if the answer is no, then I state categorically they do not want CODESA to succeed." A couple of hours later, Cyril Ramaphosa emerged from the caucus room to present a final ANC counterproposal: It would agree to the 75 percent special majority, but only if the government would agree to hold a referendum on all outstanding issues if, within six months, no agreement was reached on the constitution. Furthermore, the referendum would only have to be approved by a two-thirds majority. De Klerk, in turn, saw this as a trap. All the ANC would have to do would be to wait six months and then hold a referendum it was sure to win, approving its own constitution. It was deadlock again.

CODESA II finally began five hours late, with the cold prospect of failure staring all the delegates in the face. There was a collective holding of breath to see how Mandela and de Klerk, after their bitter exchange at CODESA I, would handle the deadlock. The two judges presiding over the convention had artfully devised a plan to prevent another ugly confrontation: They deliberately postponed speeches by the two leaders until the next morning, and asked them to get together that night to look for a way out of the impasse. So, after listening to a plea from Democratic Party leader Colin Eglin for the two men to put their heads together, the convention adjourned with neither de Klerk nor Mandela having said a word. "I don't believe that the differences are so great that the de Klerks and Mandelas here can't resolve them," pleaded Eglin. De Klerk canceled a scheduled press conference, and Mandela was unexpectedly conciliatory at his own that afternoon.

What happened that night showed the wisdom of these two men, as well as the limits of their ability to cut a deal on behalf of their respective organizations. The issues at stake were too complicated, the interests and parties too diverse, for such a style of personal wheeling and dealing to work. About all they could do, they both realized, was to keep the negotiations from being derailed completely. After consulting with their respective delegations, Mandela and de Klerk met over coffee late that night to discuss a way forward. It was their first tête-à-tête since before CODESA I, and they talked for about an hour before bringing in Delport, Meyer, and Ramaphosa to hear what they had discussed. They had been unable to find a compromise to the constitutional deadlock, but they had agreed on the need to keep up appearances and avoid a public confrontation. There would be no personal attacks on each other, but each would state his position clearly. They agreed to speak the first thing the next morning in reverse order from CODESA I, meaning Mandela would go last this time.

De Klerk seemed eager to counter the recurrent charges that his government was seeking by all means to maintain a minority veto during the transitional period and even afterward. "It is simply not true. When we say that the book on apartheid has been closed we mean it," he insisted, using the same formulation he had used after the March referendum. But then, speaking in Afrikaans, he went on to explain that the Afrikaner people wanted to be "assured that the space in which they live will be safe and protected, that one form of repression will never be replaced by another form of repression." The government, National Party, and "many other delegations" would insist on "proper checks and balances" just as the Founding Fathers in America had done to assure that "no majority should ever be able to misuse its power . . . to dominate or to damage the interests of minorities." De Klerk's bottom line was that Afrikaners were not going to allow South Africa's black majority to engage in the "simple majoritarianism" of a "winner-takes-all" electoral system. Even an interim constitution could not be "a slapdash, rickety affair" because this might lead to "mistakes" that would cost "us," by which he obviously meant primarily the whites, dearly later on.

Mandela's address was measured and more statesmanlike. He sought to dissipate the gloom hanging over the convention by highlighting all the issues on which a measure of agreement had been reached. Using a debater's technique, he mentioned them one by one and then asked, "Who here is opposed to this?" The ensuing silence gave the false impression that there was a lot more agreement than everyone knew there actually was. Nonetheless, Mandela closed with a word of warning to de Klerk: "The time has come that you truly cross the Rubicon. You must understand clearly that the days of white minority domination are over." CODESA II ended shortly thereafter in a constitutional and political haze. Nobody knew what would happen next.

The illusion of a quickly negotiated settlement had been shattered, and the two sides were really farther apart than most people had realized. It was not clear how many pieces remained to be assembled for a settlement that de Klerk commented had begun to look "rather like a jigsaw puzzle." When asked whether he was ready to cross the Rubicon, he joked, "If I look back, I can't even see the Rubicon any more." But few believed him, certainly not within the ANC camp and certainly not the ever critical *Sunday Times* editor Ken Owen. In his weekly column the following day, Owen asked, "If they will not accept a two-thirds majority in a referendum as representing the overriding will of the people, what will they accept? The answer, apparently, is a blocking mechanism. . . . If the whites (or the Afrikaners) perceive a mortal threat, they must retain the means to block it. They will not, in the end, submit their fate to the will of the majority." Owen warned the government that it was demonstrating "appalling politics" and that with its insistence on a veto it would "make war certain."

De Klerk's view on the nature of the impasse was, of course, somewhat different. The parties were down to the bottom-line issues now, like federalism and the checks and balances necessary to assure a real democracy, he said. There was "a fairly broad division" within CODESA, he felt, on whether federalism should prevail as the underlying structure of the New South Africa. De Klerk also spoke about another "basic issue" facing the negotiations—the lack of trust: "There is definitely still a wide lack of trust between many, many parties. There is not a position of full trust between the National Party and the ANC. Likewise, I would say I don't think there is complete trust between leaders," he added pointedly. "You build trust through cooperation," de Klerk suggested. "As we succeed, trust will grow. Mutual trust is really in the final analysis the prerequisite for final and full success."

In retrospect, CODESA II should never have taken place when it did. It was an attempt to give birth to a premature constitutional settlement, and miscarriage was the inevitable result. It had raised false expectations of an early breakthrough and had then failed to deliver the goods. De Klerk had warned beforehand through his aides that he felt the ANC was pushing too hard for an agreement. The government had only wanted to use CODESA II to deliver "progressive reports" on the various issues under discussion. De Klerk's reaction to the ANC's steamroller tactics was to bring up more conditions, like his last-minute proposal for a Senate in the interim Parliament, in order to stonewall the ANC onslaught. The Afrikaner government had formed a *laager* around its power base and had held off the attacking African majority once again. In the process, it had shown the ANC that it could put together a sizable opposition block inside CODESA, as seven of the nineteen delegations had taken the government's side at CODESA II, enough to ensure that there would be no "sufficient consensus" to its disliking. True, most of its allies were lightweight homeland leaders or the declining Coloured and Indian parties, but they represented other minority communities that were skeptical about black rule holding anything better for them than had apartheid. The Inkatha Freedom Party and Bophuthatswana—more serious counterweights to the ANC bloc—were among those who were siding with de Klerk in demanding a strong federal system of government. The split allowed de Klerk to argue that South Africans were sharply divided on the question of federalism, and that agreement had to be reached on this fundamental building block of a constitution before elections for an interim Parliament could be held. De Klerk was slowly twisting the negotiations around to his advantage: the issues of federalism and other checks and balances he wanted decided first—and which the ANC wanted to postpone until after a constituent assembly was elected—were coming to the top of the agenda. He had even won his argument that an interim constitution should be in place during the transition to assure unbroken constitutional rule.

But the ANC had wrung important concessions from de Klerk, most notably, agreement on an elected constituent assembly and an interim Parliament. And its approach to the transitional phase of transferring power had also prevailed with de Klerk's acceptance of a "transitional executive council" to prepare elections and assure their fairness. The ANC's biggest mistake had been to try to overwhelm the Afrikaner lines by discrediting de Klerk's government before CODESA II. Mandela seemed to realize this error in his closing speech. There, he talked about the need to dissipate "the tensions" surrounding the talks and to create a more relaxed atmosphere that would be conducive to a settlement. Mandela now realized that the ANC was in for a long, tough slog before it saw a real transfer of power, particularly if it stuck to its original plan to negotiate an overall package deal. The alternative was to go step-by-step, perhaps gaining a foothold in government through the proposed transitional council first, and then negotiating the details of an interim constitution, Parliament, and government later.

The rumor had circulated at CODESA II that de Klerk and Mandela had agreed at their nighttime summit on a piecemeal approach. De Klerk spoke at his final press conference there of "simultaneously" going ahead with the installation of the transitional council while the debate continued over an interim constitution. Mandela felt moved to set the record straight. "Nothing could be further from the truth" than the report that he and de Klerk had agreed on a piecemeal way forward. "Linkage forms the central part of our strategy," he said. There would be no start to the transfer of power until agreement had been reached on all the parts and mechanisms of the transitional process.

Within days of CODESA II, ANC officials began speaking of the need to rethink their whole negotiating strategy and objectives. It was slowly dawning on them that the government was maneuvering them into a trap, for they could not be certain that a supposedly interim constitution would not become permanent, or at least would not last for years and years. As Albie Sachs, one of the ANC's constitutional experts, said on the last day of CODESA II, the ANC needed to "go back to the drawing board, if not to square one" in the negotiating process. Even so, CODESA II brought into sharp focus all outstanding differences over the shape of a settlement, and that was badly needed. The ANC clearly had to rethink its visceral opposition to any form of federalism and power-sharing. Even the representative of the Organization of African Unity, Nigerian Foreign Minister Ike Nwachuku, had taken de Klerk's side. He had noted upon leaving South Africa on May 18 that his country was divided into thirty states, each "autonomous yet subordinate to the federal government." His departing advice to the ANC: "I believe that a country as diverse as South Africa must have a system that makes diversity its strength. I would say adopt a federal system and give everyone in South Africa the opportunity to decide what is best for their groups."

But before Mandela could regroup the ANC and devise a new approach at the negotiating table, he found that the South African Communist Party had seized the initiative in directing the next phase of the struggle. It was primarily the Communists who, throughout the year 1992, took the lead in devising an effective strategy to propel the ANC into power as quickly as possible, through either negotiations or insurrection. The internal debate under way inside the party over the "correct path to power" pitted the radicals against the realists, with their respective influence rising and ebbing with the tide of negotiations. The radicals were led by Ronnie Kasrils, a white Communist and romantic revolutionary who seemed sincerely to believe that the alliance could generate a big enough head of steam through "rolling mass action" to overthrow de Klerk's black homeland allies like dominoes and then force the National Party to surrender power. On the other side of the debate were the realists, headed by party chairman Joe Slovo. They believed that the heights of the white power bastion would have to be scaled in small steps through negotiations, compromises, and power-sharing. The two factions vied constantly for influence within the ANC alliance, taking turns in holding sway.

After the deadlock in constitutional talks at CODESA II, the radicals held full sway for the next four months. Kasrils, a member of both the party Central Committee and the NEC, was put in charge of organizing the ANC's "rolling mass action" campaign, which began on June 16, the anniversary of the 1976 Soweto student uprising. With his boyish enthusiasm and flair for revolutionary rhetoric, Kasrils dubbed the campaign Operation Exit, meaning the exit of the de Klerk government. The party served as a galvanizing force for the campaign. General Secretary Chris Hani traveled across the country rallying support for the campaign, which consisted of marches, the occupation of state buildings and city centers, and finally a two-day national strike on August 3 and 4. The ANC set up "action councils" to mobilize local civic, church, labor, and political groups in which SACP cadres often proved to be the core activists.

Throughout July, there was constant agitation in the streets, as various public places—everything from supermarkets to post offices—were occupied. The national strike more or less brought the economy to a standstill, and an August 4 march through Pretoria to the symbolic bastion of white power at the Union Buildings presidential complex was probably the largest that city had ever seen, with 60,000 or more demonstrating in the streets. But the overall results were a disappointment, falling far short of generating enough pressure on the government for it even to flinch, let alone abdicate power. Clearly, it was going to take a lot more "mass action" to breach the thick walls of Afrikaner power.

Arguing that the ANC ought to be a "liberation movement" in deed as well as in spirit, the radical Communists had dreams of carrying out a real uprising, such as they had not been able to

achieve over the previous thirty years, against the white government. They proposed adopting the Leipzig Option, a reference to
the mass demonstrations in that former East German city starting
in early autumn 1989 that accelerated the collapse of that country's
Communist regime. They argued that the ANC could weaken the
de Klerk government indirectly by undermining its allies in the
black homelands, namely Brigadier Oupa Gqozo of the Ciskei,
President Louis Mangope of Bophuthatswana, and Chief Buthelezi
in KwaZulu. The Communist radicals, in alliance with equally
radical non-Communist elements in the ANC, promoted the idea
of physically occupying the seats of power in the three homeland
capitals of Bisho, Mmabatho, and Ulundi.

A first attempt to march on Bisho took place on August 4, the
same day as the march in Pretoria. The August march, led by Chris
Hani, ended with the Ciskei troops almost opening fire on 20,000
ANC activists gathered at the homeland's border just outside King
William's Town. Undeterred by the danger signals, the ANC militants planned a second march for September 7. This time they
engaged other ANC national leaders, including Ramaphosa, who,
in a show of support, sent several National Executive Committee
members to help organize the march. The NEC even endorsed a
proposal by its Communist radicals to take the march right into the
center of Bisho and occupy government buildings.

As could well have been predicted, the march ended in disaster.
The 70,000 marchers reached the Ciskei border just outside Bisho's
Independence Stadium, where they were met by multiple lines of
heavily armed Ciskei troops and police. Carried away by the occasion, Ronnie Kasrils sought to lead several hundred activists in a
dash through a gap in the stadium fence in a bid to reach downtown
Bisho. He was overheard to say, "It's going to be a cinch. It's going
to be a cinch." But Ciskei troops were waiting for them as if an
ambush had been deliberately planned. They opened fire both at
Kasrils's group and then at those gathered along the barbed wire
who were being led by Cyril Ramaphosa. Within minutes, at least
29 marchers had been shot to death and more than 200 others
injured. Lying flat on the ground for nearly fifteen minutes, Ramaphosa and other senior ANC and SACP officials miraculously
escaped injury. But at least four of the dead fell within a couple of

hundred feet of Ramaphosa, who had been protected from the bullets by colleagues who jumped on top of him. It was later determined that Ciskei troops had fired a total of 425 rounds of ammunition into the crowd.

Bisho was a traumatic experience not just for Ramaphosa and Kasrils but for the entire ANC-SACP leadership. For the radicals, the massacre was a political disaster that assumed the dimensions of their own Waterloo rather than another Leipzig. It called into question their whole strategy, even their sanity, in leading tens of thousands of people into a situation so clearly fraught with danger. De Klerk had even written Mandela three letters warning of a bloody confrontation and pleading with him to call off the march.

The September 7 march was an incredibly irresponsible miscalculation on the part of the ANC's national leadership, given its experience with Brigadier Gqozo in early August. Gqozo, an unpopular and weak leader kept in power only by the military might of the South African government, was the epitome of the apartheid puppet. He was so besieged and insecure that military force was about all he had left to contain the ANC challenge to his shrinking authority. Mandela took no part in the march, and there was no evidence that he even supported this confrontational approach toward Gqozo. But neither did he actively oppose it, even though he clearly saw the risks involved after the aborted August march. When confronted with a wave of militancy that periodically swept through the ANC, he always chose to ride it out rather than stand against it. The demand for mass action to unseat Gqozo was too strong within the border region, and finally even within the National Executive Committee, for him to oppose the movement.

The Bisho massacre was symptomatic of a much larger problem setting in for both ANC and SACP leaders by mid-1992, namely the progressive loss of control over their followers as the radicals' revolutionary doctrines and tactics were progressively tried out on the ground. Another example of this phenomenon was the township "self-defense units," many of which had run amok in the convulsions of township violence. Once again, the Communists had been in the forefront of promoting a revolutionary policy that had led to sour consequences. Radicals within the SACP like Kasrils, and in this case even Hani, were strong advocates of the organs of "people's power" like community civic associations, "people's tribunals," and above all "self-defense units." The SDUs, as they were called, started appearing in the townships in early 1991 after the ANC's consultative conference in December of the previous year came out in support of them. But ANC supporters were slow at first to organize them because they lacked arms and organization, and Umkhonto, lacking clear instructions from the top ANC leadership, initially failed to come to their aid.

The SDUs were supposed to be the prime example of the "people in arms" defending themselves and "their liberated zones" within the townships from police raids and Inkatha attacks. In theory, community neighborhoods were to choose members to form the units, and Umkhonto was to provide instructors, paramilitary training, and arms. Their assigned tasks were to patrol ANC–controlled townships and squatter camps, particularly at night, to raise the alarm if there was an attack, and to lead the defense. Kasrils, a former Umkhonto intelligence chief, began agitating for the formation of SDUs in 1990, while he was still a fugitive from the police. The ANC leadership was then under heavy criticism for not defending its supporters in the bloody conflict with Inkatha, and so the idea suited them. Radical Communists like Kasrils, and even relative moderates like Jeremy Cronin, romanticized the SDUs as the correct revolutionary response to the Inkatha challenge. If Inkatha members had the right to bear "traditional weapons" and white right-wing groups could form paramilitary forces with impunity, then surely ANC communities had the right to organize their own self-defense units. Cronin, a member of the party's Central Committee, first presented the project at a seminar at the University of the Witwatersrand in April 1991, suggesting that the SDUs could merge with Umkhonto and become "the basis for a people's army and police force in the liberated, democratic, nonracial South Africa we are struggling for." At its national conference in July 1991, the ANC again called for the establishment of SDUs.

The results, however, were often unpredictable, as many SDUs spun completely out of ANC control and were taken over by delinquents, warlords, and gangsters. The police, who estimated that there were eighty-five SDUs in operation by June 1992, denounced them for undermining not only their own authority but law and order generally in the townships. At first, the ANC and SACP naturally rejected these claims. But by mid-1992, Hani was publicly conceding that many SDUs had become a real problem, often turning their guns on the very communities they were supposed to be protecting. In the July issue of the party publication *Umsebenzi,* Hani called for a reassessment of their performance and purpose. There was insufficient political control and no clear line of command over the SDUs, whose existence had led to "an alarming revival of kangaroo courts and kangaroo justice," he said. Worse yet, they often served as fronts and shelters for criminals. Some were being infiltrated by police and army intelligence agents who were deliberately stirring up trouble in order to discredit the whole idea, while others had fallen victim to the wayward behavior of returning Umkhonto guerrillas who had found themselves without jobs and had become township warlords or gangsters to earn a living.

One of the worst examples of an SDU gone awry was in the Phola Park squatter camp on the edge of Thokoza township south of Johannesburg. Phola Park was initially held up by the ANC to foreign guests as a showcase of township poverty and popular resistance. The SDU there had established a "liberated zone" that the police and even the army had failed to crush. In March 1992, however, the camp's SDU staged a successful coup against the elected residents' association. Then, in May, the police carried out a major operation in an attempt to eliminate the SDU, arresting twelve people they described as "dissident" Umkhonto members who had used the SDU to commit robberies and murders all around Johannesburg, with a total of 338 violent crimes. The ANC regional chairman, Tokyo Sexwale, confirmed privately in June that gangsters had indeed taken over the Phola Park SDU, but he insisted they were no longer Umkhonto members. However, the police crackdown failed to achieve its objective, as the gangsters continued to operate and eventually took their revenge against Prince Mhlambi, the leader of the resident's association, whom they suspected had helped the police; he was gunned down in

Thokoza on October 11, the third member of the residents' association to be assassinated.

The worst mayhem caused by the SDUs occurred in the Vaal Triangle, the industrial heartland of the country about 25 miles south of Johannesburg. On September 14, 1992, an SDU member in Sebokeng township shot and almost killed Bavumile Vilikazi, the deputy ANC chairman for the Johannesburg region. Later, the SDU member turned himself in, saying he thought Vilikazi was a policeman. In early November, six members of the Ephraim Zwane family were gunned down by members of another SDU in Sebokeng. Perhaps the most infamous example was Ernst Sotsu, an ex-Umkhonto member turned township warlord who controlled a number of SDUs in both Sebokeng and nearby Boipatong. By the end of 1992, Sotsu's "Top 20" gang was held responsible for the deaths of no less than eight pro-ANC union officials who were challenging his authority.

The mounting disillusionment with the various attempts at insurrection and revolutionary tactics was a major factor in triggering a reconsideration of tactics by the Communist and ANC leadership in late 1992. The voice for compromise this time came from no less than the bête noire of the de Klerk government—Joe Slovo. If anyone had the political credentials to trim the ANC's sails, it was Slovo, just like Nixon going to China. Writing in the party's quarterly, the *African Communist*, Slovo vigorously defended the need for the ANC to make some serious compromises in its negotiating position. The movement had not won the war against the apartheid government, he reminded his readers, and it was not by any stretch of the imagination engaged in "armistice talks" with a defeated enemy. Slovo went so far as to propose that the new constitution the ANC was bargaining over include a "sunset clause" providing for a fixed period of "compulsory power-sharing" with de Klerk's National Party. In the context of the ANC's thinking at that point, such a proposal constituted a major concession to the whites, for power-sharing had always been equated with the white demand for a minority veto.

Slovo's ideas almost immediately found their way into a policy document called "Strategic Perspectives," which the ANC National Working Committee was called upon to debate in the last week of October 1992. The document again reminded the ANC that it was not in a position to "enforce a surrender" on the de Klerk government, and said "the objective reality" called for cooperation with the National Party to move the peace process forward. The ANC had to adjust to the fact that it would have to cooperate with the National Party in pursuit of some common goals, even while pursuing others that were divergent. Even after adopting a new constitution, the country would need a government of national unity led jointly by the ANC and the National Party. One possible solution would be a set of binding bilateral agreements to formalize this cooperation for the foreseeable future—for example, offering "job security, pensions and a general amnesty" to the defense forces, police, and civil service to avert the danger of undermining the transfer of power to the black majority. The document set off the most wide-ranging and divisive debate within the ANC alliance over what the negotiations were intended to achieve, and Slovo had placed himself right in the middle of the controversy.

In late 1992, the Communist Party seemed to be rethinking strategy, tactics, and past mistakes of judgment. For example, the same issue of the *African Communist* contained an in-depth critique of the alliance's attempt to implement the Leipzig Option. "How realistic is this option?" asked Jeremy Cronin, editor of the quarterly. "We must be careful not to fetishize mass insurrection or see it as the only possible revolutionary way." The issue also included a devastating critique of the march on Bisho. Raymond Suttner, another Central Committee member and one of the organizers, reported that the march had been held without clarity of purpose and had been ill-timed and a mistake tactically, particularly in its failure to take into account the likely reaction of the Ciskei government. Taken together, the two articles constituted a powerful call for a new realism on the part of both the Communist Party and the ANC.

Mikhail Gorbachev had clearly had a decisive impact on Slovo, if not on the entire South African Communist Party leadership. Slovo admired the Soviet leader's political courage, viewing him as a kind of liberator of "the truth" and miracle doctor. He had taken it upon himself to play the same role within the SACP, having set forth his analysis of the crisis shaking the communist world in a document entitled "Has Socialism Failed?" Published in January 1990, on the eve of the unbanning of the ANC and the SACP, it caused an earthquake inside his own party. His main conclusion was that the communist regimes of the East had gone bankrupt because they had become totally detached from the people they ruled and had made a parody of socialism. The root causes in Slovo's mind were Stalin and the stultifying phenomenon of Stalinism that had lived on long after the Soviet dictator's death. "So many communists [had] allowed themselves to become so blinded for so long" to the evils of Stalinism, he wrote, because there was a total absence of real democracy or debate within ruling communist parties. They had failed to grasp what Rosa Luxemburg had understood in 1917 when she had argued with Lenin that "freedom only for the supporters of the government . . . is not freedom at all." "Real democracy under a one-party system," Slovo concluded, "is not just difficult but in the long run impossible." Included in his exegesis was a mea culpa for the role the SACP had played in the spread of Stalinism. It had engaged in "a mechanical embrace of Soviet domestic and foreign policies" and had promoted "the Stalin cult" without question. As Slovo saw it, the road to the party's salvation lay in its embrace of what Communists used to deride as "bourgeois democracy," namely multi-party democracy. However, Slovo preferred to call it democratic socialism.

Slovo's reformism did not generate much enthusiasm among his comrades. Though Slovo had the backing of Chris Hani and many other senior party leaders, a proposal at the party's December 1991 congress to substitute democratic socialism for the traditional Marxist-Leninist ideology was soundly defeated. Leading the charge against the reformers were Stalinists like Harry Gwala, who had already humbled Mandela in his attempt to meet with Buthelezi in 1990. Gwala proudly wore a Stalin pin on his lapel and delighted in posing as the number-one public defender of Stalinism. He also did not hide his preference for total confrontation with Inkatha in Natal. Gwala wanted to organize a mass march on Ulundi, an idea the ANC national leadership strongly rejected in the wake of the Bisho massacre. "It's a white man's outlook to say you cannot march," he remarked. "The white man says, 'Why are you struggling?' just because people get killed." Gwala also had nothing but disdain for what he called Slovo's "bourgeois reformism." The problem, he asserted, was that "some of our leaders are getting tired of fighting. They want an easy path to socialism. . . . They are getting old physically and in their ideas, too."

Among Stalinists like Gwala, Slovo now found himself viewed as a traitor to the ANC's long-standing goal of an effective transfer of power to the black majority. Gwala came close to accusing Slovo of racism. If authentic democracy in Western Europe meant the winning party formed the government, he wrote in a position paper sent to the *African Communist* in November 1992, why should the same principle not hold in South Africa? "The answer here," he said, "is that it is because the majority in this country are Africans who under the leadership of the Liberation Movement would win the elections. Therefore, power must not slip from white hands." These sentiments were shared by some non-Communists in the ANC's leadership, such as the head of its information department, Pallo Jordan. He produced his own paper for the same publication, attacking Slovo as being "charmingly ignorant of the history of the twentieth century" and advocating a total "capitulation" to the white government. The Slovo scenario aimed at nothing less, said Jordan, than enabling "the liberation movement and the regime to ride blissfully into the sunset together."

On the other end of the spectrum, Slovo got no public support for his power-sharing proposals from Chris Hani, even though Hani agreed with his analysis of the dilemma facing the ANC alliance. Hani was often depicted as a "black populist" because of his super-militant statements calling for things like the formation of self-defense units and confrontation with the security forces. But he had also had a classical education in Latin and owned a home in Dawn Park, a section of the once whites-only suburb of Boksburg outside Johannesburg. He had moved there in 1991 in an attempt to break down the old system of racial segregation, and other black political and labor union officials had followed his lead. Hani was highly popular within the whole ANC movement because of his honesty, militancy, and record as a guerrilla commander who had actually seen battle in the field. Before Ramaphosa's election as the new ANC secretary-general in July 1991, Hani and Mbeki were seen as the leading candidates to follow Mandela as its next president.

Hani was aware of his reputation for being "a demagogue" and "incapable of profound thinking," but he told reporters after his election as SACP general secretary in December 1991 that he wanted to "give expression to the aspirations of the populace." Though obviously a committed Marxist, he steered carefully away from using Marxist-Leninist jargon or analysis in his speeches. Hani told me during a long interview in November 1992 that he was neither a Stalinist (Stalin had "deformed" socialism and democracy) nor a Leninist (Lenin had totally misjudged the resiliency of capitalism and was out of date). "I would love to say that I'm a socialist who . . . must begin to shape his views influenced by what has happened objectively and subjectively to socialism in the Soviet Union and Eastern Europe," he said. What did that mean? First and foremost, he was "a socialist who realized you cannot have socialism without democracy." In other words, like Slovo, he was a "democratic socialist," but since his own rank and file had rejected the term, he could not officially use it.

Though the issue remained unresolved, Slovo and his allies in the Communist Party had opened an important debate on the limitations of the alliance's power and the realistic options available to it. As Slovo explained during a November 1992 interview, the alliance faced a central dilemma: "The ANC is going to win the elections, whether by 55 percent or 65 percent I don't know. It is going to take 'office' the day after the elections, but it is not going to take power, not as we understand that term." Taking effective control of the government, the Communists had come to realize, might take years to achieve and could only come about in phases. As Jeremy Cronin put it, "We need to begin to invest ourselves in state power, whether it's the Parliament, the repressive apparatus, or the bureaucracy. But it's going to be a long, uphill battle. It's their bureaucracy, not ours; it's their terrain, not ours."

It seemed somewhat incongruous that the same party that had promoted with such vigor an insurrectionary strategy had suddenly turned around to become the advocate of a "half-loaf solution" of sharing power with the enemy. The conversion naturally raised questions once again about the true character and future intentions of an organization that was, after all, exercising considerable influence over the whole ANC alliance. Was the SACP really undergoing serious reform or was this just a tactical retreat? No one could deny, however, that there was clearly a lot more open debate and that extremely divergent views were being freely expressed over policies. The party had accepted that multi-party democracy was not just a "bourgeois" luxury, and had come out strongly for the independence of trade unions.

Slovo would eventually win the argument for power-sharing within the ANC's leadership, setting the scene for Mandela to lead his organization back to the CODESA negotiating table in April 1993. But it was only made possible by the discrediting after the Bisho massacre of the would-be revolutionary strategy promoted by the ANC and Communist Jacobins. De Klerk, too, had been discredited and weakened by the new scandals that had hit his administration in late 1992. Altogether, it had been a sobering fall season that had produced a maturing of attitudes on all sides about the pressing need for compromise and a settlement before South Africa slipped into total anarchy.

12

NOWHERE TO HIDE

I t would take until April 1993 before CODESA would be reconvened. Throughout 1992, the political violence, which reached
a peak with the Bisho massacre in September, had slowly been
destroying everything: viable township life, government authority,
constitutional negotiations, and the last shreds of trust and mutual
respect among Mandela, de Klerk, and Buthelezi. Yet nobody
wanted to take responsibility for it; each leader blamed the other
and tried to distance himself from his followers' excesses—funeral
and other massacres, terrorist attacks on commuters on the trains,
and necklacings even of women. In an interview in July, Mandela
refused to believe that the head of the South African government,
with all the old repressive powers of the state at his command,
could not do a better job of curbing the violence. These were the
only two possibilities in Mandela's mind: either the security forces
were out of control, or de Klerk, as Mandela had repeatedly suggested, was conniving with them. Surely de Klerk's National Intelligence Service would know who was behind the violence and would
have agents inside the hostels passing on information about when
and where Inkatha was planning to strike next. The police could,
and should, be intervening to stop these attacks. "In my view, he
might not be aware of every attack. But generally speaking, the fact
that the police and security services are involved, he would know
very well," he said. "A head of state who does not know about the
things that are happening is not fit to be head of state."

If his hands were clean, Mandela continued, echoing sentiments expressed for some time, he would have disciplined those police and army officers involved in passing secret state funds on to Inkatha after their actions became public. He would have removed Christoffel van der Westhuizen as head of Military Intelligence once written evidence of his central role in ordering the assassination of the four Cradock activists had been disclosed in the press. He would never have allowed Inkatha to hold a demonstration outside the Carlton Hotel in the midst of the signing of the National Peace Accord. And he would have offered a different response to Mandela when the ANC leader informed him that Inkatha members were attacking peaceful church protesters outside the grounds of the World Trade Center during CODESA II. The ANC leader found the state president's response "very disgusting" when he replied, "Mr. Mandela, when you join me, you will realize I don't have the power you think I have." Mandela brushed aside a suggestion that perhaps there were indeed elements within the security forces beyond de Klerk's control. "You could say that," he replied. "But what would be the explanation for him changing the [Natal Zulu] law when these weapons were banned?" He pointed out that de Klerk had authorized the change that allowed Zulus to carry dangerous weapons in the name of Zulu "culture" and "tradition" after 6,000 people had already been killed in the country. "These weapons are being used to kill people," Mandela said. "Do you prefer to respect what you call a 'custom' or do you want to protect the lives of people? Which is more important? That is what I said to him. But he just had no explanation."

It was hard not to sympathize with Mandela's puzzlement over de Klerk's attitude toward the violence and his own security forces. There were just too many incidents of inexplicable police behavior in which officers had aided Inkatha against the ANC. In Alexandra in March 1992, for example, Inkatha marked the first anniversary of its takeover of the Madala Hostel by launching another outward push to grab more territory. Madala inmates terrorized more township residents into leaving their homes pell-mell, creating a whole new zone of burned, trashed, or vandalized houses popularly known as Beirut. The comparison to the Lebanon capital was perhaps a bit hyperbolic, but the devastation within that area was evident, and more than 3,000 longtime Alexandra residents, 685 families, were forced to flee and find refuge in churches, the town council's premises, and other nearby locations. The whole district around Madala Hostel remained deserted; not a car or person—except police and army patrols in armored vehicles—dared to pass under the hostel's windows for fear of sniper fire. Scores of passersby were in fact shot at, many of them killed outright. Between March 7 and 28, the Alexandra clinic treated 341 people for wounds and registered eleven deaths from the anniversary fighting.

The attitude of the security forces throughout the conflict remained incomprehensible to residents and reporters alike. The police would mount periodic searches of Madala Hostel, looking for guns, but they never cracked down hard enough to end the random sniping. The South African Police (SAP) seemed to be only marginally less fearful of the Zulu hostel dwellers than local residents. Captain Eugene Opperman, an SAP spokesman, explained why the police were not taking firmer action to end the sniping. "Have you seen that place? It's like a fort. We have to think about the safety of our men." For Opperman, the problem of Madala Hostel was one for the politicians to resolve, not his men, or so he explained to me. Incredibly, the SAP were offering Alexandra residents only one form of protection from Inkatha's wrath: safe passage to other makeshift refugee centers when they decided to flee their homes. "Instead of stopping the whole thing, the police escort people out of their homes," remarked a bitter Marcus Paile, an official from the committee dealing with several hundred refugees who were packed into the Alexandra town council's offices. "They do nothing to the people who are killing, robbing, and raping."

How could the SAP expect residents, or reporters, to believe their spokesmen when they insisted time and again they were acting with "impartiality"? The SAP had done nothing to stop Inkatha from "cleansing" the Madala Hostel of non-Inkatha residents. It had made only half-hearted efforts to stop sniper fire from the hostel's windows. It had provided no protection for the residents living in the streets around the hostel. The police had also not helped any of them to reclaim their homes, and had even allowed Inkatha supporters to occupy the houses. That July, the symbol of the emptiness of their law-and-order mission in Alexandra was summed up in one unforgettable sight: armored police vehicles patrolling the litter-strewn streets of "Beirut" lined with abandoned and gutted homes on the pretext of demonstrating their commitment to providing "law and order" for township residents. After fifteen months of allowing chaos to reign, in June the SAP had finally sent in a special 800-man task force, backed up by army patrols, to reestablish a measure of normality. Although the combined police-army operation succeeded in lowering the political temperature and reducing casualties, the police still did not offer any help to the refugees so that they might reclaim their Inkatha-occupied homes. "The police cannot go around from home to home trying to decide who is the rightful owner," police spokesman Colonel David Bruce explained. He added that there was no way that the police could offer Beirut residents twenty-four-hour protection from the sniper fire of hostel inmates or the assurance that "their kiddies are going to be safe playing in the garden." As Mandela asked on many occasions, "Would the police act the same way if whites were the victims?"

Compounding the problem was the fact that de Klerk often showed an astounding lack of sensitivity when he made one of his infrequent visits to a black township. In the wake of the June 17 massacre of forty-six people in the township of Boipatong by an Inkatha raiding party from a nearby hostel, de Klerk wanted to make some gesture to show his sorrow. So, three days later, he went to express his condolences to some of the victims' families. The situation was still exceedingly tense, as residents were convinced that the police had helped the Inkatha attackers. The mood among the residents that Saturday morning was ugly. Nobody wanted de Klerk to come anywhere near the township. As one resident, Meshak Dekelidi, told me, "We don't want to see de Klerk here. It's his government killing most black people."

At the sight of de Klerk's convoy of cars and armored police vehicles, the township youth exploded. It was as if he had stumbled into a beehive and was being attacked by a swarm of angry bees. His motorcade halted alongside the Joe Slovo squatter camp, where many of the killings had taken place. Within seconds, however, his limousine was surrounded by angry residents shouting, "Go away, go away" and even "Shoot, shoot." None had arms so far as I could see, but some had rocks in their hands. De Klerk's bodyguards hurriedly formed a protective circle around his car, pistols and rifles at the ready. It became so tense at one point that I ran inside the circle, thinking his bodyguards were going to open fire at any moment. De Klerk was two feet from me, sitting behind a bullet-proof window in the back seat of his car, staring glumly at the screaming black mob around him. He never got out. After a minute or two, the motorcade sped off, with young people chasing it down the dusty township roads. It was a humiliating visit and departure for de Klerk that spoke volumes about the state of his relations with the black community, at least that part of it favorable to the ANC. De Klerk was furious, accusing the ANC of sabotaging his visit. Instead of a gesture of sympathy for the massacre's victims, his trip had been turned into a symbol of his unpopularity in the townships.

The fallout from the Boipatong massacre was not just the damage done to de Klerk's personal prestige. The ANC, outraged by the performance of the police, immediately suspended all contacts with his government, putting on ice the already stalemated CODESA process for the rest of the year.

De Klerk, however, had far more than a simple political dilemma on his hands. He proved to be no reformer or promoter of affirmative action when it came to the SAP and the South African Defence Force (SADF). Not having been a part of former President Botha's securocrat establishment, de Klerk had no close allies in the senior command of either the SAP or the SADF. This was widely acknowledged to be a major weakness in his power base, and he seemed extremely reluctant to purge any of the old securocrats. In mid-1992, the same coterie of senior officers involved in the counterinsurgency struggle against the anti-apartheid movement was still commanding the SADF and its network of shadowy special forces, commando groups, and intelligence services. De Klerk had even promoted some of those with the worst reputations for past involvement in operations to eliminate ANC activists, including General A. J. "Kat" Liebenberg, who became the head of the SADF, and Christoffel van der Westhuizen, who took over the Military Intelligence Department. About the only change de Klerk made in the overall security establishment was to promote the National Intelligence Service, under Niel Barnard until early 1992, to preeminence among the various competing intelligence groups. The NIS was directly responsible to de Klerk and became his personal eyes and ears on the rest of the security apparatus.

But a broader, more troubling pattern of appointments had emerged, as de Klerk showed no inclination to remove any of the old politicians, technocrats, and power-brokers of the long Botha era. The secretary-general of de Klerk's office until mid-1992 was Johannes "Jannie" Roux, the same person who had served as President Botha's right-hand man in that position since 1984. Roux had a terrible reputation among anti-apartheid activists as one of Botha's most brutal henchmen. Nor upon taking office did de Klerk fire the two ministers viewed as the most hated symbols of the old repressive apartheid machinery, Law and Order Minister Adriaan Vlok and Defense Minister Magnus Malan. Even after the political heat on him became too intense over the Inkathagate scandal, the president shuffled Malan and Vlok into lesser ministerial posts rather than dismiss them. Not until late August 1992 did de Klerk carry out even a symbolic purge of the police force, retiring thirteen generals, or about one quarter of the top command.

De Klerk's attitude seemed to be summed up in his terse comment after the November 1990 inquiry by Judge Louis Harms into the activities of the so-called death squads, the mysterious assassins responsible for the killing of more than seventy anti-apartheid activists before 1990. Though the evidence was lacking, these assassinations were widely assumed to be the work of the government's secret police and army branches. "Let bygones be bygones," de Klerk had said. It made no difference to him that the Harms Commission had been stymied in its investigation into the secretive Civil Cooperation Bureau (a security branch of the army probably responsible for the death squads) by the destruction or disappearance of key documents, and he ordered no investigation to determine who had been responsible or what had happened to the missing files. Clearly, de Klerk was not anxious to risk a scandal that would have exposed the role of those police and army officers, and probably even serving senior ministers, in the old repressive apartheid machinery.

De Klerk's reforms of the security apparatus thus remained largely restricted to finding better ways of fighting the soaring crime wave and to launching a start on the integration of blacks into the SAP. The police force was expanded by 10,000, and Vlok announced in March 1991 that he intended to create "a kinder, gentler force" through a new training program. Police colleges began to be integrated in 1992, though whites were assured that there would be no "forced integration." This was particularly true at the command level, where whites continued to hold 95 percent of the posts even though nonwhites made up 60 percent of the rank and file in the 115,000-person force. Just four nonwhites were brigadiers in mid-1992, and there were then no nonwhite generals.

Not surprisingly, the ugly apartheid impulses within the SAP kept reasserting themselves. Many units of the force, like those in Pietermaritzburg and Carletonville, continued in their old ways and methods. In April 1992 a courageous judge in Pietermaritzburg sentenced to death a white police officer, Captain Brian Mitchell, who had masterminded the massacre of eleven people at Trust Feed, a nearby mountain village, in December 1988. He had ordered four *kitskonstabels*, half-trained auxiliary policemen who were under his command, to wipe out a hut filled with people he suspected of being ANC supporters but who turned out to be Inkatha sympathizers. At the time of Mitchell's trial, there were a total of thirteen policemen in the dock in three different rooms of the courthouse. The verdict handed down in the Mitchell trial was as much an indictment of the entire SAP command as of Mitchell himself. Judge Andrew Wilson said he was convinced by the testimony of several SAP officers that there had been an extensive attempt among senior officers all the way up to SAP headquarters in Pretoria to cover up Mitchell's misdeed and derail his trial.

There were numerous other examples of police misconduct. In Carletonville, a mining town west of Johannesburg, an entire police unit ran amok: All nineteen members of the Welverdiend Unrest Unit were suspended in early 1992 on charges of involvement in the death of seventeen township activists. *New Nation*, an enterprising black weekly, had obtained evidence on tape that members of the unit had tried to hire a township hitman to kill a local ANC activist. In the Natal town of Mooi River, another police station commander, Lieutenant George Nichaus, went on trial in September 1992 on two counts of murder and two others of the attempted murder of ANC demonstrators.

It was not until Judge Richard Goldstone came on the scene in early 1992 that a neutral, sane voice began to be heard in South Africa. Goldstone was remarkably open with reporters, a trait I had never encountered in dealing with any other South African judge. Maybe it was the result of his exposure to the American media; he had spent the 1989–90 academic year as a guest scholar at Harvard University. In any case, the judge was not afraid to speak his mind and did so with the canniness of an astute politician. He knew full well that he was dealing with the most explosive political issue in the country, yet he felt no fear.

De Klerk had empowered Goldstone to hold hearings on the allegations of security force involvement in the violence, following the terms of his agreement with Mandela and Buthelezi at the National Peace Conference in September 1991. Goldstone began his inquiry in February 1992, supervising the work of various subcommittees attached to what was formally known as the Commission of Inquiry Regarding the Prevention of Public Violence and Intimidation, which held hearings into the worst incidents of violence around the country. Goldstone, widely considered a liberal, was the first credible independent authority to tell the ANC publicly that it was part of the problem. On May 28, Goldstone released to Parliament an interim report on his initial findings that at first infuriated the ANC. Based on the commission's investigations into the violence in three areas of Natal and three townships around Johannesburg, the report said that "the commission has no doubt that the primary cause of the violence in all these areas is the political battle between supporters of the African National Congress and of the Inkatha Freedom Party. Both sides resort to violence and intimidation in their attempts to gain control over geographic areas." There would be no lessening of the violence "unless and until the leaders and supporters" of the two factions agreed to disarm and "abandon violence and intimidation as political weapons." Goldstone also said that at that point his commission had still not received any credible evidence of "a third force" at work in the violence, though it was still investigating the allegations, as well as charges of direct security force involvement. Even if these charges proved true, Goldstone said, such meddling would not have been possible except for the "ongoing ANC–Inkatha battle." Mandela at first bristled at Judge Goldstone's assessment of the ANC's co-responsibility for the violence. But eventually the whole ANC leadership would grow to respect the judge because he was to prove so instrumental in bringing to light the misconduct of the South African security forces.

The ANC did not have long to wait. Judge Goldstone had requested outside evaluations of the SAP's procedures and methods, and the first panel, under Harvard Law School professor Philip Heymann, published its findings on July 10. The panel sharply criticized the police for resorting too quickly to the use of live ammunition in dealing with unruly crowds. Heymann recognized that the police leadership had encouraged such an outcome by failing to provide riot equipment to protect policemen from stones and other objects thrown at them. They carried no shields, no helmets, and were not equipped with water cannons or sneeze machines. "There is no excuse for using lethal force when adequate sub-lethal substitutes could be made available," the Heymann report said, adding that the SAP should "reduce the paramilitary quality of [its] present thinking and training" and adopt methods being used widely in Europe, the United States, and Australia. The report also criticized the SAP's specially trained Internal Stability Division, an anti-riot force of 5,600 that had been formed in early 1992, as too paramilitary and too far removed from the community. "There is no more important resource for the police than their relations with the local community. There is no resource that is more in doubt in South Africa," Heymann noted.

The Heymann report did not cover police mishandling of the horrendous Boipatong massacre. But a second report, issued on July 22, was devoted entirely to this incident. After the June 17 massacre, Judge Goldstone brought in a British criminal justice professor, P. A. J. Waddington, and two British police officers, to study the police reaction to the massacre. Their report was a scorching indictment of the whole SAP modus operandi in crisis situations, finding serious faults in its intelligence capability and contingency planning, a woefully inadequate command and control system, and a total absence of any community-relations program. Words like *serious incompetence* kept cropping up throughout the Waddington report. Police had reacted in a totally "ad hoc" manner the night of the massacre. The whole SAP response had been "bedeviled by a failure of leadership at all levels." The SAP seemed to be "an unaccountable police force" with no procedures in place to determine who had done what and when. The only consolation for the SAP was that Waddington had found no sign of direct police complicity with the Inkatha attackers, as had been alleged by the ANC and many Boipatong residents. "Omissions arose, not from deliberation, but incompetence," the report concluded.

Waddington particularly criticized the SAP's heavy reliance on torture to obtain confessions. The SAP investigative style, he observed, seemed to be based on solving cases by torturing one suspect so that he would incriminate others. Any doubts about the veracity of this allegation were laid to rest by the "confession" of Jonathan Gluckman, one of the country's top pathologists, published in the July 26 issue of the *Sunday Times*. Gluckman showed the newspaper a stack of two hundred autopsies he had performed on detainees who had died in prison. "Ninety percent of the people in these files, I am convinced, were killed by the police," he told the paper, calling it "murder, straightforward murder by the police." He added that prison deaths were still continuing at an average rate of about one a week, and even though he had written to de Klerk about his concerns (as well as to various ministers and police commanders), he had received no reply. Frustrated and disgusted, Gluckman told the newspaper, "I can't stand it any longer." The final straw had been the death of a nineteen-year-old boy from Sebokeng whose body had been found in a field, badly beaten, only twelve hours after the police had arrested him. Gluckman's charges of widespread police criminality seemed amply supported by the SAP's own published statistics. In 1990, 1,871 policemen were found guilty of criminal offenses, 11 of them of murder and 35 of culpable homicide.

For all these damning indictments, the SAP was dealing with a difficult situation that provided some extenuating circumstances. There could be no doubt that the ANC and Inkatha were seriously at war with each other. The Peace Accord of September 1991 had not made one iota of difference; a year later, Buthelezi would claim that 503 Inkatha members had been killed since the signing of that accord. Yet the majority of the more than 3,000 killed in the political violence during that period were probably ANC members, as they were constantly either on the attack or under attack in their war with Inkatha.

President de Klerk managed to ignore, stonewall, or dismiss the growing evidence of security force involvement in the violence until November 1992. In that month, an avalanche of embarrassing disclosures made it obvious to all that the infamous covert military services were indeed still active in various projects to discredit the ANC and Umkhonto. This time, it was all happening on de Klerk's watch, and he could no longer say, "Let bygones be bygones," for his own credibility was at stake.

The first disclosures came from a disgruntled Pretoria businessman, Abel Rudman, who gave documents to the *Weekly Mail* that substantiated his claims that he had been responsible for running a Military Intelligence project code-named Crist. He had spent twelve million rand (about $4.2 million) on establishing a newspaper, *Newslink*, in Gabarone, the capital of Botswana. Its mission had been to spread disinformation about the ANC and Umkhonto in Africa and to portray them in as unfavorable a light as possible. While MI had closed down *Newslink* following the Inkathagate scandal, the newspaper had been launched on August 30, 1990, long after de Klerk had taken office. Rudman claimed MI had also budgeted five million rand to set up a front company in Washington, D.C., called International Network Information, for the same anti-ANC propaganda purposes. Rudman was "singing" because he had failed to recover from MI six million rand he claimed he had spent on Project Crist. The SADF confirmed virtually all his allegations.

Coincidental to the Rudman disclosures were others that month relating to another Military Intelligence operation, Project Echoes, whose goal was to disseminate false information linking Umkhonto to the Irish Republican Army. The British anti-terrorist police had intercepted two South African operatives sent to London in April 1992 to carry out the project when one of them took it upon his own initiative to try to arrange for the assassination of a dissident South African police officer, Dirk Coetzee, then living in London. Project Echoes came to light during judicial inquests under way in November into the assassination of two anti-apartheid activists, the black lawyer Godfrey Mlangeni and the white professor David Webster.

But it was Judge Goldstone who exposed the de Klerk government's worst embarrassment. On November 16, he called a press conference to announce that his commission had just carried out a spectacular raid on a secret MI operations center in Pretoria and had seized documents revealing that the military had contracted a twice-convicted murderer, Ferdi Barnard, to run an undercover operation against the ANC. Barnard had been employed from May to December 1991, and was only one of forty-eight secret agents working for MI. Another had been William Flores, the operative who had been caught in London and implicated in a plot to kill Coetzee. The files had also disclosed the existence of a Directorate of Covert Collections (DCC), a mysterious MI body never heard of before, that was in charge of the whole anti-ANC operation.

Goldstone had uncovered the operations center of the military's "dirty tricks" department. Particularly devastating to persistent government denials of all involvement in the violence, the source who had led the Goldstone commission to the DCC building in Pretoria was an ex-Mozambican Army soldier, Joao Cuna; he told the commission that he had been hired by the DCC to assassinate ANC activists in Natal. On the basis of these findings, the commission said that it had "no doubt that political violence and intimidation in South Africa will not be effectively curbed until there has been a thorough investigation of all South African public and private security forces," and Goldstone boldly asked de Klerk for additional powers to investigate all the activities of his security forces.

The Goldstone raid in itself was an extraordinary event for which there was no precedent in South African history. It was the equivalent of a U.S. special prosecutor conducting a surprise search of a Pentagon secret operations center. The raid caused panic inside the military and outright anger from de Klerk that Goldstone had gone public with his findings before informing him about them. Even his chief constitutional negotiator at that point, Roelof Meyer, was implicated because the seized files said that when he was defense minister he had personally ordered Barnard's firing in December 1991. Meyer heatedly denied that he knew anything about Barnard or the MI operations. But the same files implicated the former MI chief of staff, Lieutenant General Rudolph Badenhorst, and the entire MI command.

De Klerk, who in the wake of Inkathagate had pledged to end all "dirty tricks" political operations, could no longer discount these various anti-ANC projects as the work of a "few rogue individuals" acting on their own. Most embarrassing to him was that the most outspoken propagandist against Umkhonto since September 1992 had been the army's chief, Lieutenant General Georg Meiring, hardly a "rogue." In addition, only hours before Goldstone's revelations, the president had assured the British Broadcasting Corporation while on a visit to London that, "There is no third force. There is no sinister cabal within the security forces working against the government." He was in "firm control" of those forces, he had insisted. Goldstone had, in effect, disclosed that the emperor wore no clothes, and de Klerk was furious. Furthermore, Goldstone's demand for wider powers to investigate the security forces posed a real threat to his entire government. The president realized that he had to act to take the initiative away from the judge and at least give the appearance of intending to clear up what had become a month of unending disclosures and scandals about his own security establishment.

Two days after Goldstone's press conference, de Klerk announced that he intended to conduct his own investigation, appointing Lieutenant General Pierre Steyn, the SADF chief of staff, and police Lieutenant General Alwayn Conradie to lead the probe. Steyn was also put in overall charge of the many independent Military Intelligence services and was asked to draw up recommendations for their restructuring. In addition, de Klerk ordered him to scrutinize all of the documents Goldstone had seized at the Directorate of Covert Collections center "to ascertain whether any activities have taken place which might be in contravention of the law or government policy." In effect, de Klerk had ordered another private in-house investigation to stonewall Goldstone's proposal for a public inquiry that might lead to more embarrassing disclosures. Once again, he was reacting to contain the political damage.

One month later, de Klerk announced that he was suspending or retiring early twenty-three unnamed officers, including two generals and four brigadiers, and held out the possibility of criminal prosecution of some of them. He declared that Steyn's preliminary investigation had found evidence of "activities which could lead to the conclusion that political murders had occurred." He absolved all cabinet ministers and claimed that only a "limited" number of military officers, who had systematically misled their civilian superiors, had been involved. "I'm shocked and disappointed, but I'm always resolute," he said at a press conference. On December 29, the names of nine of those involved were published, all of them senior army military intelligence officers, including all the top officers in charge of the Directorate of Covert Collections. But a number of senior officers whose names had been very much in the public eye were not included on the list: Lieutenant General van der Westhuizen, the current MI head; army chief Lieutenant General Meiring; and SADF chief General Liebenberg, who had been MI head when some of the anti-ANC projects had been launched.

The Goldstone inquiry also exposed a vast network of past and continuing ties between the South African Army and police and Inkatha. Taking testimony about the activities of the Black Cat gang in Wesselton township outside the white city of Ermelo, Goldstone was able to confirm, in large part, the reports (first printed in the *Weekly Mail*) of numerous forms of cooperation between the SAP and the KwaZulu police. The Black Cats became a branch of Inkatha, and some of its members had been given paramilitary and political training in KwaZulu. The Ermelo police allowed their KwaZulu colleagues to operate freely in Wesselton and even furnished arms to the Black Cats. When several guns used by Black Cat members to kill a Wesselton ANC activist were seized, the SAP quietly returned them to the KwaZulu police.

Another focus of the Goldstone probe centered on the whereabouts and activities of 190 specially chosen Zulus from KwaZulu who had been secretly trained for six months by the South African military in 1986. These Zulu youths had been given military instruction in Namibia before its independence, and many of them became involved in the violence as either South African auxiliary policemen or Inkatha bodyguards. A number of them were known, or suspected, of involvement in murdering ANC activists. Many had served as *kitskonstabels* in the SAP and were sent to bolster police posts in and around Pietermaritzburg, where the ANC–Inkatha fighting was heavy. Afterward, they were integrated into the KwaZulu police force.

Ample evidence also emerged that the SAP and KwaZulu police continued the close cooperation they had established prior to 1990 during their common struggle against the pro-ANC United Democratic Front. Brigadier Jacques Buchner, who headed the SAP in the Pietermaritzburg region in 1987–88, a particularly intense period of repression of the UDF, had subsequently become commander of the KwaZulu police under Buthelezi, who remained the homeland's overall police chief. Buchner was still serving there in late 1992, though awaiting retirement.

One consequence of the Goldstone revelations was that they soured even further the relationship between Mandela and Buthelezi. Mandela placed himself more and more at a distance from Buthelezi and, like other ANC leaders, began referring to him as a puppet and surrogate of the government. The final straw for Buthelezi was Mandela's attack upon him before the United Nations Security Council, which had convened a special session on South Africa on July 16–17 that both leaders attended. There, Mandela castigated Buthelezi, saying "the fact of the matter" was that he had become "the extension of the Pretoria regime, its instrument and its surrogate." Upon returning from the U.N. session, Buthelezi was livid. "Enough is enough," he told the annual conference of Inkatha at Ulundi on July 18. Mandela had gone to the United Nations "to destroy" him as a legitimate negotiating partner. He no longer had any intention to "sit next to Dr. Mandela to talk peace and cooperation."

Whether the open rift between Mandela and Buthelezi made the political violence even worse was difficult to determine. The degree of Buthelezi's personal responsibility for the violence will probably never be known, but his professions of total innocence and self-absolution of all responsibility appeared increasingly disingenuous as the conflict took on the character of planned warfare involving professional hit squads. Buthelezi was, after all, also the chief of the KwaZulu police and had defended vigorously his followers' right to carry "traditional weapons" at rallies and in marches.

There was at least strong circumstantial evidence that he fully approved of, if he did not order himself, the activities of his senior aides involved in expanding by force of arms Inkatha's presence in the townships around Johannesburg. Melchizedec Z. Khumalo, his former private secretary, was called before the Goldstone commission to testify about the activities of the 190 Inkatha youths who had been secretly trained by the South African military. Khumalo had shared direct responsibility for their activities with the deputy commissioner of the KwaZulu police, Brigadier Sipho Moses Mbatha. In testimony before the commission in March 1992, Khumalo disclosed that both he and Buthelezi had initially co-signed the monthly paychecks of the trainees. Clearly, Buthelezi knew all about the training program. But Khumalo insisted that he alone had known that the two companies providing the training and paying the salaries of the men for three years were actually fronts for the South African Defense Force. Judge Goldstone remarked upon hearing Khumalo's testimony that Buthelezi's "lack of inquisitiveness boggles the imagination."

Brigadier Mbatha was also called upon to testify and gave such a shoddy performance that Goldstone essentially accused him of outright lying. The commission also exposed multiple links between the KwaZulu police force and the Inkatha Youth Brigade operating in Wesselton. Inkatha members in the Black Cat gang had obtained guns from the KwaZulu police and had been trained in KwaZulu. They had also engaged in various battles with ANC supporters, several of whom were killed.

Buthelezi was never directly implicated in the Wesselton investigation or the other "support" activities of his police force in Inkatha's battles with the ANC. Still, the idea that his private secretary and deputy police commissioner could have been involved without his knowledge or approval was simply not believable, particularly given his authoritarian style of rule. Nonetheless, Buthelezi continued to strike the pose of a leader who knew nothing and deplored all resort to violence.

❖   ❖   ❖

In the aftermath of the embarrassments each had suffered (and would suffer) in the fall of 1992, de Klerk and Mandela came to understand ever more clearly that—even if South Africa risked becoming a Greek tragedy writ in modern script—they had no long-term choice but to pursue a compromise settlement and re-launch the pursuit of their constitutional talks. As Western diplomats kept saying loudly in public, "There is no other show in town." They were obliged to negotiate just as they were obliged to reach some kind of compromise settlement and rule together. But this time, they realized that the government and the ANC had to reach a bilateral understanding between themselves before any multi-party talks could possibly meet again.

So the two leaders met on September 26 to get the peace process back on track. Their summit at least achieved this goal, for the ANC National Executive Committee formally approved the resumption of talks with the government at a meeting a few days later. But Buthelezi's self-assumed pose as the odd man out became formalized with the agreements reached at the summit. Not only was the Inkatha leader marginalized, but the accords sought to dictate conditions to him and his followers without consultation or approval. It seemed to a paranoid Buthelezi that Mandela and de Klerk were in league to eliminate him permanently from the political scene.

The Record of Understanding, as the document that came out of the summit was called, locked de Klerk into accepting an elected constitutional assembly to draft and adopt a new constitution and serve as a transitional parliament. Buthelezi totally opposed such a body because of the near certainty that Inkatha would emerge from the elections a minor party. Just as humiliating to Buthelezi was seeing Mandela and de Klerk decide on their own that his followers should be prohibited from carrying "traditional weapons" in public, and that Inkatha-dominated hostels around Johannesburg should be fenced in and placed under police supervision.

Predictably, Buthelezi went berserk. If he couldn't be at the center of the process, he was determined to wreck it. Buthelezi warned de Klerk and Mandela that his followers would tear down the fences "with their bare hands." His reaction to the announcement by de Klerk and Mandela that "dangerous weapons" would henceforth be completely banned in public was equally belligerent: "I will never ever under any circumstances ever ask anybody for permission to carry a Zulu cultural weapon." A Zulu without his weapon, he declared, was "like a man without his shadow." He promptly organized marches through Johannesburg and Durban in which his followers defiantly carried these weapons without the police intervening to disarm them. De Klerk turned a blind eye to the marches.

So what did the September summit accomplish? The Record of Understanding immediately became another "Record of Misunderstanding," with the usual imprecisions, conflicting interpretations, and this time the bitter opposition of Buthelezi. How could it be otherwise? The Record made certain that the KwaZulu chief would remain the odd man out, the determined spoiler. In addition to the agreements that related to Inkatha, the government also agreed to release by November 15 more than 300 political prisoners still locked away (and de Klerk kept that part of the bargain). Pure political necessity had inspired the two principal peacemakers to sign such an agreement; de Klerk wanted to get the negotiations going again, and Mandela had to satisfy at least some of the ANC militants' demands for measures against Inkatha's worst excesses.

But the Record at least served to revive negotiations. In early December, the government and ANC began the first of a series of bilateral meetings at an unprecedented five-day *bosberaad*. By early 1993, four private bilateral meetings had produced the rough outlines of a potential settlement. On February 12, the two sides announced that they had reached agreement in principle on a five-year transition during which a multi-party cabinet, government, and Parliament would share power on the basis of the outcome of a general election to be held probably in early 1994. Each party would be represented in this first government of national unity according to the percentage of the vote it won. Any party that gained at least 5 percent in the elections would have a right to be included in the transitional government. An interim Transitional Executive Council (originally proposed prior to CODESA II), representing all parties accepting the process, would oversee preparations for the elections and would assure a "level playing field" for all the contestants.

Basically, de Klerk had given up many of his initial negotiating aims. He would get his power-sharing for the first five years under a black majority, but after that he would have to accept the "simple majoritarianism" he had once decried as totally unworkable in a deeply divided society like South Africa's. He had also backed down from his whimsical proposal for a collective presidency of three to five party leaders who would rotate as chairman, as well as on his demand for all decision-making by consensus; both had been mechanisms for assuring a white minority veto. But it seemed a compromise of sorts was slowly in the making, as the ANC was softening on its insistence that all power reside with the central government. De Klerk was also relenting on his demand that the powers and borders of the country's new regions (or provinces or states) be determined before the constituent assembly even met to discuss this issue.

On March 6, 1993, the CODESA process formally resumed, after a ten-month break, with the holding of a preparatory meeting to organize a new session. The expanded number of participating delegations—twenty-six instead of nineteen—augured well for efforts to gain a broader consensus, but poorly for any quick success with such a wide variety of views now present. The Conservative Party and the Pan Africanist Congress, both of whom had vehemently opposed CODESA previously, were present. CODESA formally resumed its work at the beginning of April, and this time not even Hani's assassination on April 10 stopped it.

After much palaver and fierce argument, on June 3 a date was set for the country's first national election in which the black majority would be allowed to participate and 342 years of white minority rule would finally come to an end—April 27, 1994. Voters would be called upon to elect 400 representatives to a constituent assembly, both to write a new constitution and to serve as a Parliament. Much remained to be hammered out, not the least of which was the powers and composition of the new president and presidency, as well as the nature of some kind of federal government. And there was still strong opposition from the extreme white right and black left to the whole concept of power-sharing between whites and blacks. But after more than three years of talks, a date for the end of white minority rule had been set. The biggest stepping-stone in the nation's history had been laid. It remained for de Klerk and the whites to make the irreversible leap, finally, into the New South Africa.

CONCLUSION

After three years of sickening violence and deadlocked negotiations, de Klerk and Mandela resembled two exhausted heavyweight boxers at the end of a long title bout, both bloodied and badly bruised. The vision of two heroic leaders working together to lead their long-divided communities toward the promised land of racial cooperation had become blurred by the tragedy of their own bitter personal falling-out and mutual public recriminations. They had diminished each other in stature, whittled down to very mortal size by having proven incapable of controlling the events and centrifugal forces set loose by de Klerk's reforms; these had served as well to steadily grind down their authority and leadership.

Mandela's role had undergone a noticeable metamorphosis within the ANC. He had been elevated to a new, lofty status, above the day-to-day administrative concerns and internal squabbles of the National Executive Committee. He was now the distinguished elder statesman of the movement, who met foreign heads of state and important visitors and led delegations on formal occasions. His ANC colleagues had taken to affectionately calling him "the old man" as often as Madiba, his clan name. There were signs that his health was fading, and much attention was paid to his bouts of exhaustion that became much more frequent starting in late 1992. Mandela nonetheless remained a powerful voice for moderation within the ANC hierarchy. After the ANC–Communist Party radicals had discredited their own Leipzig Option and "rolling mass action" at the Bisho barricades in early September, Mandela had suddenly reasserted his authority in a bid to rehabilitate both the strategy of negotiations and the reputation of ANC moderates. He ended his own personal attacks on de Klerk, and succeeded in toning down the whole ANC campaign to discredit him. When the ANC finally met de Klerk again on September 26, Mandela was at the head of its delegation and speaking confidently on its behalf; several participants, however, reported that his physical stamina faded noticeably toward the end of a long day of discussions. Despite his waning authority and physical strength, Mandela had prevailed in his efforts to get the peace process under way again, as the agreement announced on February 12 to resume negotiations witnessed.

If Mandela's day-to-day leadership of the ANC was in eclipse, his national and international stature as the movement's "grand old man" remained unblemished. De Klerk, on the other hand, had suffered enormous damage to his initial stature as one of the world's great reformers. In the three years since Mandela's release, it had become clear that de Klerk was making the same mistakes that Ian Smith, the former Rhodesian prime minister, and Mikhail Gorbachev, the fallen Soviet leader, had committed before him. The damning parallel to Smith was particularly ironic, since upon embarking on his reform program back in 1990, de Klerk had specifically criticized Smith for his shortsightedness, his failure to seize the optimal historical moment to strike the best deal possible with his black nationalist foes. De Klerk had said that he wasn't going to let events back him into a corner or wait until he was forced by political and military weaknesses to surrender power. That was why he had seized the initiative to unban and negotiate with the ANC, acting while Afrikaner power was still intact. Still, like Smith, de Klerk had ended by dragging the negotiations out for more than three years, far longer than was necessary, while his strategists were busy devising constitutional proposals to perpetuate white power and his security men sought to weaken the ANC. He had proven just as reluctant as Smith to yield power to the blacks, and just as convinced that time could somehow play in the whites' favor.

The comparison so easily drawn between de Klerk and Gorbachev, on the other hand, had changed in meaning over time. At first, it was meant in praise of de Klerk's bold initiatives, imaginative style of governance, and sheer political guts. After Gorbachev's messy political demise at the end of 1991, however, the parallel took on a far less flattering connotation: that of an indecisive leader who was overwhelmed, and finally swept aside, by the very avalanche of changes his well-intended reforms had set rolling. In an interview in August 1992, de Klerk was adamant that he was not about to become "another Gorbachev" in this sense. Gorbachev's cardinal error, he said, had been to try to reform an unacceptable and unworkable ideology, namely communism, rather than make a total and complete break with it. He had obviously given some thought to the causes of Gorbachev's demise and clearly believed he was avoiding the Soviet leader's indecisiveness in making a clean break with the old order: "I have parted fully and finally in all respects with the old policy of apartheid, separate development, call it what you will . . . I have been ready to go all the way all the time. I'm going to go the full mile."

So he said. Yet after three years of reformism, de Klerk was more clearly than ever as reluctant to travel "the full mile" as Gorbachev, and as hesitant to yield power as Smith. For the first two years, de Klerk had magnificently seized and held the political initiative and moral high ground, receiving the applause of the international community and a majority of South Africans. He had kept his major promises made in his speech of February 2, 1990, lifting the state of emergency, launching negotiations with the ANC, and scrapping all the basic legislative pillars of apartheid. Then, suddenly, his interest in reform had petered out as the reality of black power came closer; he became reactive to events rather than pro-active in shaping them, as he had been initially. Nor was there any follow-up to the reforms he had launched, and very often he allowed his ministers full rein to undermine the reforms' spirit, even their letter, through countermeasures. For example, hospitals were formally desegregated, but wards more often than not remained segregated, particularly outside the big cities. "There are certain reasons why people are grouped together or have been kept separately in hospitals. It can be because of pure medical reasons, religion or on cultural grounds," was Health Minister Rina Venter's disingenuous comment as she sought to clarify the government's 1990 announcement about the desegregation of white hospitals.

De Klerk's approach to reform seemed to be to do precisely what was required to obtain the lifting of American and European sanctions, but nothing more. The most obnoxious pieces of apartheid legislation were indeed repealed, but de Klerk never called upon Parliament to pass laws requiring reparations, integration, or penalties for continued racial separation. "Affirmative action" never became part of de Klerk's reformist thinking; in fact, he publicly attacked calls for such steps, whether applied to his own government or elsewhere in white society.

The consequences of what might be called his reformism without change were exactly what one might have expected—various forms of de facto apartheid continued unabated. Just as de Klerk was promoting the "privatization" of the economy, so he was allowing what often seemed to amount to no less than the "privatization of apartheid." Very little really changed for the vast majority of either whites or blacks, at least during the first three years of de Klerk's presidency. The various formerly segregated communities continued in their separate worlds, with no official encouragement to integrate. A few wealthy blacks moved into Johannesburg's northern white suburbs, and a slow trickle of senior black ANC officials, labor union leaders, intellectuals, and entrepreneurs spilled into the closer-in, middle-class white districts like hippie Hillbrow and yuppie Melrose. But the overwhelming majority of blacks continued to dwell in the same filthy, run-down, and poorly serviced all-black townships as before, while the white suburbs continued to be swept immaculately clean weekly by an army of orange-uniformed black street workers. Even the weeds growing through the cracks on the sidewalks in the northern suburb of Waverley were sprayed with pesticides to keep the sidewalks unencumbered for the few whites who used them. The first feeble attempts to move lower-class blacks closer to the white suburbs met fierce resistance. Transvaal provincial authorities drew up plans for building new townships around Johannesburg, and even began building several, but they were ever more distant from the city center and, of course, from the white suburbs. The old apartheid city and its architects, it seemed, were still alive and well.

So, too, were white prejudices. Liberals joined conservatives in putting up road barricades to stop blacks from settling close to their neighborhoods. These white protesters were dubbed Nimbies, from the acronym NIMBY, or Not In My Back Yard. The most famous case of a "Nimby rebellion" occurred in early 1992, when the provincial authorities tried to move a few thousand squatters living on the Zevenfontein farm, on the far northern fringes of Johannesburg, to a location adjacent first to one and then two other white suburbs. After stopping them with barricades and threats of violence at Bloubosrand, the whites of Diepsloot and Nietgedacht turned to the courts and used injunctions to halt any new settlements. In January 1993, nearly a year after the Zevenfontein squatters first made news, they were still squatting on the same farm grounds, awaiting resettlement.

White society seemed determined to show its disdain for the social crises of the black majority over housing, education, and welfare. The wholesale flight from reality was impressive. The big companies with a surfeit of capital on hand—and no interest in risky social investment—poured their handsome surpluses into endless new American-style shopping centers and office complexes in the seemingly ever-expanding white suburbs of Johannesburg or else into seaside resorts and game lodges. The most famous of these projects was the fancy waterfront development scheme in Cape Town, costing hundreds of millions of dollars, built in studied imitation of the Baltimore and San Francisco harbors and complete with an aquarium, a hotel, dockside restaurants, jazz clubs, beer halls, fast food joints, and seals playing in the water. The projects seemed to confirm Cape Town's reputation as the Land of the Lotus Eaters, the place more and more whites seemed to prefer after Durban's beaches became increasingly crowded with blacks.

The epitome of the fantasy land many wealthy whites were busy building for themselves as the day of black power drew nearer was doubtless the Lost City playland resort, with its grandiose Palace Hotel at the center. According to the promotion brochure, this was a $285 million "re-creation" of an exotic medieval palace that never really was, built by an ancient people (more Arab than African) who had never actually lived in an idyllic valley that may or may not have once existed in southern Africa. Legend had it, said the promoters, that the 350-room palace had been destroyed by an earthquake centuries ago. But they had decided to reconstruct the entire palace—with all 350 rooms—northwest of Pretoria in a deserted corner of the very real but fast-dying "kingdom" of Louis Mangope, president of the Bophuthatswana homeland that most certainly did exist. The grand visionary of this incredible Disneylandlike extravaganza was Sol Kerzner, the rags-to-riches casino king of South Africa. He had decided to reinvest some of the hundreds of millions of rands South Africans had willingly lost at his gambling tables into this final tribute to his own personal success and, seemingly, to the dying glory of Old South Africa. With the King's Suite going for $3,500 a night and a "standard twin" for $270 (a good monthly wage for an unskilled black worker), there was no need for white patrons to worry about rubbing shoulders with many blacks. Kerzner's dream project opened in early December 1992, claiming to be "the most extraordinary hotel in the world." Certainly, it was the most out of place for a country undergoing the kind of massive political and social upheaval taking place in the New South Africa.

De Klerk's government was on a different kind of fantasy flight in the final days of Old South Africa. Instead of making massive investments to solve the mammoth crises in housing, education, and welfare for blacks, it kept pouring billions of rands into various advanced military and technological projects—missiles to launch low-orbiting satellites for European or Asian clients; a super-modern, laser-based uranium enrichment plant; and sixty Swiss planes for the Air Force. Surprisingly, de Klerk's government largely escaped black criticism for its lavish spending on the development of a military and space industry. It was just not discussed by the ANC or any of the other black political parties, who seemed totally unaware of or indifferent to the government's massive investments in these projects. Yet the government easily diverted into its "special defence account" over ten billion rand between early 1990 and early 1993, literally while the country was burning. That amount of money could have built thousands of schools, houses, and clinics, and could have provided tens of thousands of jobs in housing and township rehabilitation schemes, had the government chosen to switch its priorities.

The massive Afrikaner-dominated administration did not change much in character or goals, either. The senior civil service remained a mostly closed reserve for Afrikaners, or at least whites. Of the 2,885 highest-ranking positions in the central and provincial administration, just fourteen were occupied by blacks in early 1992. De Klerk seemed totally uninterested in preparing the civil service for a new era of white-black cooperation. There was no substantive reform of the civil service whatsoever, not even a purge of the worst cold warriors and apartheid practitioners of the P. W. Botha era. Notorious ministers like Magnus Malan and Adriaan Vlok were rotated into lesser cabinet posts only when the political heat became too intense for de Klerk to stand it any longer. Those ministers who left—Barend du Plessis, Gerrit Viljoen, Stoffel van der Merwe—did so out of sheer exhaustion, ill-health, or personal choice. The high command of the South African Defence Force and South African Police also remained largely unchanged, until the multiple scandals of November 1992 finally obliged de Klerk to purge twenty-three military officers, mostly from the intelligence service.

The general pattern, however, was clear: De Klerk sought through inaction to keep intact as much of the Afrikaner power establishment as possible and to maintain it under the same old Afrikaner management. Yet it was this unreformed establishment that was supposed to implement the sweeping changes he had initiated. Little wonder, then, that nothing equivalent to the shattering process of de-Stalinization that occurred under Gorbachev in the Soviet Union ever took place under de Klerk in South Africa. In the end, de Klerk proved not so prepared to break "fully and finally" with the old apartheid system as he claimed, not when it came to taking steps that might weaken the Afrikaners' hold on the sinews of the government and the security apparatus. After three years of reformism, he still had a long way to go before accepting the implications of his own reforms, something he had accused Gorbachev of failing to do.

De Klerk's ambivalence toward reform was nowhere better illustrated than in his handling of the land issue. He scrapped, as promised, the Lands Acts of 1913 and 1936 that had reserved 87 percent of the land for the white population, but he took no steps to return any confiscated properties to their former African owners. Here was one area where de Klerk could have exercised some affirmative action and shown his commitment to social justice by at least making a token gesture and starting the redistribution of some state-owned lands. Instead, the government set up a toothless Advisory Commission on Land Allocation to hear disputes and make only recommendations to the president on black claims to former tribal or ancestral lands. Similarly, de Klerk took no action to reincorporate the ten black homelands, even though he had raised the need for their reincorporation into a unitary South African state as far back as his speech on February 2, 1990. Worse yet, his government actually acted to consolidate the homelands, turning over during 1992 more than one million hectares of land to four of these artificial, ethnically based statelets. Not surprisingly, given the government's political alliances, 660,000 hectares went to Chief Buthelezi's KwaZulu. At times, it seemed apartheid practices as applied to the land had just been "privatized," because underhanded business dealings between white bureaucrats and their farmer friends continued undisturbed. Similarly, various central and provincial bodies continued to buy and sell pieces of state land to white farmers throughout 1991 and 1992, oblivious to the crying needs of millions of landless and homeless blacks.

De Klerk's restrained reaction to the multiple scandals that rocked his administration in 1991 and 1992 was equally disturbing and revealing of his notably cautious attitude toward reform. He showed no more interest in setting better standards for clean government than had any of his predecessors, even though he ostensibly had every interest in doing so before the ANC took over the government. During the single month of November 1992, the government was rocked not only by the severely damaging revelations of the Goldstone Commission about the military's continuing sponsorship of various secret operations to discredit the ANC, but also by scandals related to extensive corruption or misrule in the Lebowa, KwaNdebele, and Ciskei homelands. Two of the three reports on the homelands involved massive waste, mismanagement, or embezzlement of billions of rands in government funds in Lebowa and KwaNdebele during the mid and late 1980s. Gerrit Viljoen and Stoffel van der Merwe, two of de Klerk's principal strategists during the first three years of the negotiations, were implicated, but no action was taken against them. Both men did, however, quit politics altogether.

With November's revelations, it was becoming progressively harder to believe that de Klerk was "out of the loop" about the undertakings of his senior generals and ministers, particularly when it came to something as sensitive as his own negotiations with the ANC. David Steward, his cabinet director, attempted to deflect the ensuing local and international criticism by portraying de Klerk as a leader walking a delicate political tightrope. He could not tear apart his own security services with sweeping purges and reforms without undermining the South African Defence Force, his main power base. De Klerk had no intention of making Gorbachev's mistake of allowing his military to become disaffected to the point of attempting a coup against him. Steward readily acknowledged, however, that de Klerk had to exercise a more forceful leadership or else face being tarred with the blame for the unsavory activities of his own military.

More evidence of de Klerk's dual-track strategy toward the ANC came from the former National Party general secretary, van der Merwe. A week after his November 9, 1992, announcement of his retirement from politics, he admitted in an interview that the party was deliberately pursuing such a strategy: The first track was aimed at achieving a negotiated settlement and necessarily required the government seeking the cooperation of the ANC; the second track involved preparing for the forthcoming elections for a constituent assembly and Parliament, in which the National Party and the ANC would just as necessarily be serious rivals. The analogy he drew was of various rugby, soccer, cricket, and baseball teams getting together to decide which game they were all going to play and what rules they would abide by. Initially, there had to be cooperation among them to establish both "the game and its rules." But once this was accomplished, each "team" would certainly play its hardest to win that game. The National Party, van der Merwe said, was not only negotiating "the game" to be played but was preparing to win the contest.

Despite all the polls showing the ANC with a commanding lead, van der Merwe was emphatic: It was not pie-in-the-sky thinking to believe that the National Party could achieve electoral victory. His calculations were the following: The NP would get 65 percent of the Coloured vote, 75 percent of the Indian, and probably 85 percent of the white. Finally, there was the all-important question of the black vote. Van der Merwe calculated that the NP could already count on at least 10 percent of it, but he judged that this could be increased to as much as 40 percent. His party, he said, had carried out a lot of "thorough-going scientific studies" in the black community, showing the potential for winning such a large minority of the black vote. It all depended on how effective the National Party would be with its electoral campaign, but campaigning was one thing it knew how to do.

Van der Merwe's figures and optimistic projections were based largely on the research of a University of California professor, Andrew S. Reynolds, who had spent the 1992 academic year at the University of Cape Town scrutinizing the electoral numbers and mulling over possible voting patterns among whites, blacks, Coloured, and Indians. He had produced a paper entitled "A Shock in the Making: The National Party (and their Allies) Potential to Win a General Election Held under Universal Franchise in South Africa." Reynolds's conclusion was that "the party which designed and operated apartheid" could well end up forming the first democratically elected government in South Africa, in coalition with Chief Buthelezi's Inkatha Freedom Party.

The key to his prediction was the assumption that while there were 14.4 million blacks of voting age in the country, only 10.8 million of them were likely to become eligible voters because many would be unable to prove their age or citizenship and thus would be disenfranchised. This would reduce the black weight on the electoral rolls from 68.5 to 62 percent, while increasing the white percentage from 18.8 to 23 percent. If the National Party could get 80 percent of the Indian vote, 65 percent of the Coloured, and 10 percent of the black, then the first free, all-inclusive election in South Africa would produce the following results: the ANC, 40.6 percent; the National Party, 30.2 percent; Inkatha, 11.4 percent; and the white right-wing parties, 6.5 percent. In other words, if the distribution of these votes among parliamentary districts was favorable, the National Party, together with Inkatha and the white right-wing parties, could form a majority coalition government. Never mind endless public opinion polls showing the ANC winning a clear majority of the votes, anywhere from 55 to 65 percent. And so it was that yet another American university professor— Arend Lijphart being the first with his power-sharing scheme—had become the basis for an Afrikaner fantasy to stay in power. There was hope after all for white power after the black vote.

De Klerk and his National Party began campaigning for a victory almost from the day Mandela walked out of prison. They wanted to build a centrist "Christian Democratic alliance" of moderate multi-racial forces, drawing its support from blacks living in the homelands, in rural areas, and on white farms, where the Nats were convinced the majority was, in its heart of hearts, very conservative and highly suspicious of the ANC. Their prime targets were traditional chiefs and church leaders who they believed still held control of large constituencies and could deliver them in blocks to the NP.

De Klerk made his first personal appeal to the "silent black majority" (as the Nats like to think of it) at the dedication in early May 1991 of a huge new cathedral belonging to the International Pentecostal Church in Zuurbekom, outside Soweto. He gave what amounted to a political sermon to the 20,000 assembled worshippers, urging them not to be swayed by groups seized with a "lust for power," which, he said, were causing all the violence. He also went in April 1992 to Moira, near Pietermaritzburg in the northern Transvaal, to attend the annual Easter Mass of the Zion Christian Church and address a crowd of over 500,000 people. His message was the same: Beware of those who "want power and are prepared to do anything to get it."

Another core constituency of this would-be Christian Democratic alliance were the three million Coloureds who spoke Afrikaans as their mother tongue and were the racial "stepchildren" of the Afrikaners—the result of over 300 years of miscegenation. Like the Afrikaners, the Coloureds are extremely conservative people who are mostly members of the Dutch Reformed Church. Many among them viewed the ANC as black, godless, and communist, and looked forward to its coming to power with as much fear and trepidation as white Conservatives. The vast majority of the nearly one million South African Indians held similar views. So Nats like van der Merwe were convinced that these various groups put to-gether—traditional and homeland chiefs, church leaders, Colour-eds, and Indians—could deliver enough votes to make Reynolds's prediction come true. "I do believe that it is possible, I don't say probable, for the NP to get an overall majority," van der Merwe said.

Van der Merwe's thinking helped to clarify de Klerk's attitude toward the ANC, which he viewed at once as ally and enemy, peace partner and electoral rival. If the National Party actually harbored the grand illusion that it could win an overall majority, alone or in coalition, then a campaign to discredit the ANC would obviously serve to promote such an electoral strategy. General Meiring's campaign against Umkhonto, as well as Military Intelligence's se-cret Project Echoes and *Newslink* paper for anti-ANC propaganda, seemed to be pieces of one overall political strategy. There was, as we have seen, other supporting evidence that the National Party was going for an electoral victory as well: for example, the govern-ment's decision to turn over more than one million hectares of land to curry favor with homeland leaders who were potential allies and de Klerk's wooing of the "silent majority."

Van der Merwe also shed light on another fundamental aspect of the National Party's electoral thinking—that is, that time was on its side. The political violence may have tainted the government's image in the eyes of blacks, but it had discolored the ANC's image even more, he argued. There had been a lot of disillusionment among its moderate supporters, particularly within white liberal circles. Many had fallen by the wayside either because of the politi-cal violence, the ANC's strong Communist Party connection, or its general disorganization and indifference to them. The ANC thus would not go to the polls covered in glory and wrapped in the banner of the conquering victors as Robert Mugabe's Zimbabwe African National Union (ZANU) had been able to do in his coun-try's 1980 independence elections. "From that perspective, time is not on the side of the ANC," he said. Indeed, it was slowly wearing down ANC militancy and discrediting its radical wing. As van der Merwe saw the general trend, ANC policies were undergoing a constant one-way transformation, and it was "from more extreme to more moderate."

National Party strategists found support for their thesis of growing ANC moderation reflected in two key documents that appeared
in late 1992. The first was the "strategic perspective" policy statement that Joe Slovo had been instrumental in selling to the National Executive Committee in September and October. Over the
vociferous objections of the radicals and revolutionaries, the document was adopted on November 18, clearing the way for the ANC
leadership to make a right-hand turn in the negotiations by rejecting the "revolutionary seizure of power" in favor of sharing power
with de Klerk's National Party. In earlier days, such a document
would have been branded as defeatism and counterrevolutionary
propaganda. Mandela had himself bitterly denounced power-sharing in the past as a devious scheme to make the majority powerless,
but he, too, had come around. "If this process continues long
enough," van der Merwe commented only half jokingly, "then
maybe one can look forward to a reasonable type of government."

The other document offering hope to the National Party about
the ANC's new "realism," as they liked to call it, was the "Mont
Fleur Scenarios" for the economic future of the New South Africa.
Though not an official ANC policy position, the scenarios had the
endorsement of its economics department and many of its senior
leaders, who met at Mont Fleur near Stellenbosch in September
1991. The Mont Fleur team had sketched out four political-eco-
nomic scenarios, three bearing names of birds, and one called
Icarus after the mythological Greek figure. Each assumed a different outcome to the political negotiations and foresaw vastly different consequences.

The "ostrich" scenario assumed that negotiations broke down
and that the de Klerk government tried to go it alone in alliance
with its own moderate black allies. The likely outcome would be
enormous political instability, the virtual "Lebanonization" of
South Africa, and total economic disaster. The "lame duck" scenario hypothesized that the negotiations would lead to a protracted
transition period with a coalition government lasting until the year
2000. Such a government would prove unable to make lasting
decisions or deal with the country's problems, and would thus be
incapable of generating investor confidence. In the "Icarus" scenario ("fly now, crash later") a truly popularly elected democratic

government would come to power and would embark on a "social spending spree" to overcome the legacies of apartheid. The short-term result would be a Latin America–style degeneration of the economy into massive debt, inflation, and economic collapse, as had occurred in Nicaragua under the Sandinista government. Finally, there remained the "flamingo" scenario, characterized by a political settlement that resulted in a truly democratically elected government, this time one that followed a slow but sustained economic takeoff that brought to mind a flamingo taking flight.

ANC economists assured the International Monetary Fund and the World Bank that they intended to avoid the pitfalls of the Icarus scenario and were opting for the flamingo one. Whether there were enough realists within the ANC hierarchy to adopt such a strategy remained unclear, but there was no doubt that ANC leaders would be under tremendous political pressure to adopt the Icarus scenario. The real irony lay in the course of negotiations, where both the government and the ANC were heading toward agreement on a five-year transition government and power-sharing—the perfect ingredients, according to the Mont Fleur strategists, for a "lame duck" government.

Were the Afrikaners indulging in pure political fantasy with their dreams of both an electoral victory and ANC moderation? Wasn't de Klerk committing the same cardinal error as Smith in Rhodesia by constantly delaying a solution in the vain hope that the black nationalist opposition would fragment, fade, or weaken in its radicalism? Or was Zach de Beer, the Democratic Party's often insightful leader, correct in his "convergence" theory, namely that the ANC and National Party would eventually have to rule together over the moderate center because, as he saw it, in the end "there is no other way that South Africa can be governed"?

As de Klerk and Mandela neared the end of their agonizing quest for the great historic compromise between South Africa's whites and blacks, these two worn peacemakers faced a frightening dilemma: Neither of their parties could rule the country alone, yet the forecast for the success of a partnership was equally gloomy. The agreement in the making for power-sharing seemed a formula

fit only for institutionalizing conflict under the guise of a "govern-ment of national unity." How would these two enemy-partners ever reach agreement on a common program over such issues as affirmative action; restructuring and purging of the security forces; redistribution of white lands; nationalization of banks and mines; foreign alliances? Yet, if either the ANC or the National Party were excluded from government, enormous political turmoil seemed a certainty. Each had enough independent power to make South Africa ungovernable without the other. The two parties seemed doomed to remain chained together, at least until they had finished their long and painful march to the New South Africa. The bitter-sweet relationship that had developed between Mandela and de Klerk had come to infuse the entire ANC–National Party relation-ship as well.

What would happen to the ANC–Communist Party alliance if the ANC became a partner in government with the National Party also remained a big question. Would the SACP be willing to become part of such a compromising coalition or would it break away and oppose it from the streets? Communist leaders readily admitted that they had a socialist agenda separate from the ANC, but seemed of two minds about its implications. Did this mean the two old allies would eventually go their separate ways? Slovo, Hani, and other party leaders sidestepped the question, saying it all de-pended on whether the ANC adopted socialist policies once in power. This was unlikely to happen as long as the ANC and Na-tional Party remained partners. Yet the SACP realized it would do far better remaining within the ANC, since it would have much more influence on its policies and thinking that way; it might also have a chance of eventually coming to power. Jeremy Cronin had once written that the most applicable model for a possible Commu-nist takeover in South Africa was Castro's Cuban revolution; the Cuban Communist Party had fused with Castro's non-communist 26th of July Movement and had eventually converted it into a communist one. "The notion lurks on," Cronin said, that "the same thing could happen here. The ANC leads the national demo-cratic revolution but we lead the second stage, the socialist revolu-tion." If the Communists did retain this strategy, it meant that

South Africa was headed for a government under a three-way alliance of the National Party, the ANC, and the SACP—hardly a formula for political stability.

Not surprisingly, few were predicting a smooth transition into the New South Africa. Buthelezi, the Pan Africanists, and the diehard white supremacists were all gearing up for their own kinds of wars of attrition against the compromise settlement in the making. Militants in the Communist Party, the ANC, and labor unions were restless and fearful lest the ANC sacrifice their socialist goals to get a taste of power. Eugene Nyati, one of the country's few independently minded black risk analysts, predicted that a settlement reached by 1994 would last no more than three to four years. "Public disillusionment and the lack of improvement in the quality of life will galvanize resistance against it. Civil and labor unrest will resume and render the country ungovernable once again." Under the unrelenting pressure of its constituency, he argued, the ANC would inevitably turn left and would adopt the black power philosophy of the Pan Africanist Congress and Azanian People's Organization. The great danger facing Mandela, according to Nyati, was that of going down in history as another Abel Muzorewa, the black Methodist bishop-turned-politician who in 1979 was elected "prime minister" of the short-lived, transitional, white-dominated government in "Zimbabwe-Rhodesia."

A similarly pessimistic scenario was offered by Deon Geldenhays, a professor at Rands Afrikans University in Johannesburg. Using the pseudonym Tom Barnard, he wrote what purported to be a "popular history" of the New South Africa in the making, a book entitled *South Africa: 1994–2004*. It became the rage of the white northern suburbs during the 1991 holiday season, as nervous citizens pondered whether to flee the country. Geldenhays, like Nyati, predicted the rapid breakdown of any government–ANC settlement. He described in 182 pages how a new "federal republic of South Africa" would shortly lead to civil war and the breakup of the country, with whites creating their own separate nation-state.

Even Willem de Klerk, the president's brother, could foresee no better than "cloudy weather" ahead for the country because it had such a shaky democratic tradition, and violence and revolution were still "too close to the surface." The Communists, meanwhile, feared South Africa would become another Chile and Mandela another Allende, overthrown by a violent counterrevolution led by right-wing whites supported by the white-dominated army and security forces.

As the two principal players grew closer to deciding the rules of their political "game," Buthelezi, of course, became ever more paranoid, contrary, and spiteful. One step forward in relations between de Klerk and Mandela always resulted in one step backward in their relations with him. The KwaZulu chief rejected their September agreement the day after its signing, cut off his bilateral discussions with de Klerk, and warned that he would oppose any bilateral agreement reached between the ANC and the government. There would only be civil war without him, he warned. He published Inkatha's own plan for a largely autonomous KwaZulu-Natal state within a weak confederation. While the chief assured everyone he was not suggesting secession, even by mentioning the word the threat was there. De Klerk and Mandela refused, however, to be blackmailed or to allow their bilateral talks to be held hostage to Buthelezi's war drums beating from Ulundi. But both offered him separate bilateral discussions, hoping thereby to draw Buthelezi back into the peace process.

Despite the ever unpredictable "Buthelezi factor," the ANC and the de Klerk government were progressively closing the constitutional gap that had separated them. There was even a sense that their senior officials were becoming "thick as thieves" as they plotted a bilateral settlement they hoped they could sell to the rest of the parties excluded from their private negotiations. But they seemed determined to forge ahead, with or without the odd man out and the extreme nationalist Pan Africanists and Azanians; similarly, de Klerk was not about to alter course because of white right-wing opposition. The participation for the first time in CODESA of both the PAC and the Conservative Party when it finally reconvened in early April 1993 gave hope to both the ANC and the government that the white right wing and black militant threats could ultimately be managed, or at least contained.

The reason for their common determination to forge ahead come what might was simple: Together they would probably win 70 to 80 percent of the vote in the first elections, a solid majority upon which to base a transitional government, so long as their bilateral relationship remained in working order. But whether they would ever succeed in constructing a political system strong enough to contain the various fringe parties lining up against their agreements-in-the-making was not so clear. The only thing that seemed certain was that a lot of turbulence lay ahead for the two key parties, even in dealing with each other in a coalition government.

What lay ahead for de Klerk and Mandela was the most intriguing question that remained. Mandela, if he lived long enough, seemed destined to emerge as South Africa's first black president when elections were held in April 1994. Though he had often said he would never serve in a transitional government, and would only accept the presidency if he was popularly elected to that position, the proposed five-year period of transitional government made that a risky proposition. After all, Mandela turned seventy-five on July 18, 1993, and the pressure was mounting for him to preside over the first provisional government as *the* symbol of national reconciliation.

And what of de Klerk's future? There was much speculation in early 1993 as to whether he would ever be willing to serve under Mandela either as a minister or perhaps even prime minister. Could the leader of the old Afrikaner ruling elite submit himself to the leader of the new black power elite? De Klerk might initially agree to do so in the name of national reconciliation and political stability, but this would probably be a short-term arrangement. Too much animosity had built up between these two men after three years of mutual disenchantment for them to work together effectively in close quarters for very long. The saddest truth of South Africa's contemporary history was that the world-acclaimed peacemakers had grown apart, not closer, in their pursuit of a peaceful settlement. Just as revolutions tend to devour their children, so the South African peace process had ravaged its leaders.

Whether it was because of his inability to get along with de Klerk any longer, or his failing energy, Mandela had progressively ceded to Cyril Ramaphosa the role of point man he had initially played in the ANC's dealings with the white government. Since their public falling out at CODESA I in December 1991, Mandela rarely met privately with de Klerk to discuss how to overcome the latest obstacle to negotiations or resolve the latest crisis over the violence. (They met secretly near Johannesburg for the first time in six months on March 22, 1993, and held several other subsequent meetings to break the deadlock over a date for elections.) Phone calls between the two were equally rare. Instead, Ramaphosa developed his own private line to the government, and he and a small group around him took over the responsibility for devising the ANC's negotiations strategy. Ramaphosa struck up his own special relationship with Roelof Meyer, the best and the brightest of de Klerk's scandal-ridden cabinet and the man who had taken over from Gerrit Viljoen as constitutional affairs minister in mid-1992.

The Meyer-Ramaphosa partnership seemed in many ways a fulfillment of what de Klerk and Mandela had doubtless once hoped to establish between themselves. This new political friendship, a by-product of the very political turmoil that had destroyed the de Klerk-Mandela one, seemed to consolidate itself on increasingly more solid ground as time passed. Perhaps it was because Meyer and Ramaphosa managed to keep their relationship low key and untainted by the political posturing that both de Klerk and Mandela had felt obliged to engage in as spokesmen for their respective political causes and constituencies.

Ramaphosa and Meyer were even said to have met secretly in September 1992 for a tête-à-tête "fishing" expedition on a private estate in the wilderness of the eastern Transvaal, the kind of off-the-record intimacy that de Klerk and Mandela had never succeeded in enjoying. Earlier, the two younger men had led the way in reestablishing the contacts cut off between the government and the ANC after the Biopatong massacre in June 1992. Starting as early as August 21, they had begun holding a series of unannounced meetings in which they discussed ways to renew bilateral discussions over the stalemated negotiations. Even the Bisho massacre didn't interrupt these meetings; in fact, it gave renewed urgency to their mission of finding a way back to the peace table. Clearly Ramaphosa and Meyer were taking over the burden of building bridges between their respective parties and communities.

◆   ◆   ◆

Strange images often haunt a reporter's mind long after leaving a country, images that do not necessarily depict the whole truth but, nonetheless, leave a powerful lasting impression of enormous symbolic importance. One of those for me was of South Africa's three principal leaders coming to live in physical isolation far apart from each other, like Alpine climbers perched atop different peaks in the same mountain chain. De Klerk, Mandela, and Buthelezi had each climbed different peaks, even though they shared the same majestic mountain, South Africa. In the process, they had not only grown out of touch with each other but, sadly, had become far removed from their respective peoples, who were fighting endlessly among themselves down in the valleys.

The main symbol of de Klerk's isolation was Union Buildings, the massive presidential complex surrounded by well-kept gardens and sprawling in solitary splendor across a hilltop just east of Pretoria's center. It has two rampartlike walls running in front of it, built as if to sustain a long siege and keep the angry street mobs from ever getting to the central amphitheater, let alone the government offices inside. Hardly a sound from the city squatting just below reaches the complex, and certainly not de Klerk's offices, located behind thick walls on the front side of the west wing. There is a sense of being on an Olympian height which wants or allows few visitors. Foreign tourists, and some white South Africans, do come to enjoy the magnificent panoramic view and wander around the grounds, but I hardly ever saw any blacks there aside from official homeland delegations on their way to see the state president or one of his ministers. In any case, no one is welcome inside except on official business or by special invitation; even reporters sometimes had to wait outside under the raised colonnade running above the empty amphitheater to be let in for press conferences.

The view from de Klerk's office is out over the city's jacaranda-covered streets toward another massive but this time compact, square-shaped granite mass that rises from the crest of another hilltop southwest of the city. This is the Voortrekker Monument, the imposing memorial to the stubbornness of the Afrikaners in their Great Trek from Cape Town into the interior, and to their mission of bringing "white civilization" to the "heathen Africans."

De Klerk must have often asked himself what finally would be posterity's judgment of his lonely role in the Afrikaner trek through history.

Mandela, isolated for twenty-seven years in prison, found himself in freedom once again cut off from his people—and again against his will. After his release, he had first gone to live in his old four-room home on Vilakazi Street in Soweto's Orlando West district; it was surrounded by identical tiny houses and a lively mixed lower- and middle-class neighborhood whose denizens constantly came to see him. Only a wire fence separated his house from his neighbors. Before many months had gone by, however, Winnie prevailed upon him to move to what the local media had dubbed Winnie's Folly, a grandiose 700,000-rand brick mansion with fifteen rooms and a swimming pool, protected by a 12-foot-high brick wall. She had built the house with proceeds from her book *My Soul Went with Him* and from foreign, mainly American, donations. It stood on a hillside, nicknamed Beverly Hills, in the same district. It was completed in 1987, but Winnie had never actually lived in it before Nelson's release, and it had even been badly vandalized in late 1989 while it stood vacant. Restored and refurbished, Mandela lived in Winnie's Folly for about two years, removing himself from the immediate street life of Soweto. But at least he had been surrounded within that confine by his extended family, and we often met him there for press conferences with one or another grandchild perched on his lap.

Then, for security and marital reasons, he had moved in early 1992 into a typical white upper-class home in Houghton, one of the plushest northern suburbs. There he again lived alone behind 12-foot walls, but this time he was surrounded by wealthy whites. The only blacks he could possibly talk to or meet in the streets were their servants; the only sounds he might hear were those of guard dogs barking to keep black strangers away from the properties of his white neighbors. The Mandela family had by then split up into three different residences around Johannesburg. Winnie had kept her "Folly" in Soweto, and Zindzi, his much-beloved daughter, had chosen to escape the domineering personalities of both her parents and had moved into her own home in Bezeidenhout Valley, a white suburb on the eastern side of Johannesburg. When I interviewed

Nelson in late July 1992 at his Houghton home, he struck me as an incredibly lonely figure. None of his children or sixteen grandchildren were living with him. Winnie had kept all the African artifacts that had made their Soweto home a museum. Instead, his Houghton residence was decorated and furnished in indistinct European style. Only servants could be heard bustling around a house that otherwise echoed of silence and muffled telephone conversations.

I realized how much he missed his people, and how guilty he felt about living in Houghton, after he visited the Phola Park squatter camp one Sunday in May 1992. He came directly from there to address the media at the end of an important ANC policy conference; he had been so moved by the squalor and hardship of the camp that at first that was all he had wanted to talk about. He even berated the white press for ignoring the plight of the residents. Of course, most of the reporters he was addressing had visited Phola Park often and knew precisely how terrible conditions were in the camp. But Mandela's reaction served to highlight how far removed he felt he had become from his own people and their daily sufferings.

Buthelezi was probably the most remote of all three leaders from the daily realities of South Africa. He lived in Ulundi, deep in the majestic but isolated mountains of northeastern KwaZulu. The tiny town, a two to three hour drive from Durban, sits in a vast bowl with a vista of towering mountains all around. It is the site of the nineteenth-century Zulu capital and of the last great battle and defeat of the Zulu people at the hands of the British army in 1879, which marked the collapse of the empire Buthelezi's ancestors had so proudly built. Full of history, Ulundi is nonetheless little more today than a crossroads with a few stores, a gasoline station, a Holiday Inn, and the chief's sprawling palace grounds where the KwaZulu parliament sits. Cows can often be seen grazing on the lawn just outside, as if they are there to underline the pastoral setting of KwaZulu's capital.

Ulundi is always extremely peaceful because only KwaZulu bureaucrats and Inkatha officials and members live there. Living there meant that Buthelezi could never have a sense of the daily strife and suffering his followers were experiencing throughout much of Natal, let alone in faraway Johannesburg, in their struggle with the ANC for his personal greater political glory. Yet it was from this Olympian height that the chief regularly threw down his verbal thunderbolts on the ANC and delivered his sharp-tongued tirades against all his enemies. If the remoteness of Ulundi offered him total protection from the ANC crowds so anxious to kill him, it also guaranteed his isolation from the real world of his own Zulu people so deeply divided in their loyalties between him and the ANC.

The isolated settings in which these three leaders found themselves was for me the painful reminder of what was happening to all of South Africa. Instead of coming together or even reaching out toward each other, the racial and political "communities" were turning inward for self-protection and were seeking to isolate themselves from their fellow South Africans. There were walls of intolerance, walls of fear, and walls of despair everywhere. Whites were building ever-higher walls around their homes or putting new ones up around their suburbs to keep out neighboring black squatters and itinerant criminals. Inkatha was turning hostels into fortresses behind which its members could barricade themselves and keep out the ANC. ANC supporters were busy building invisible walls to demarcate their township turf from those of their rivals and drive out anyone they suspected of being against them. What South Africa seemed to need desperately were social and political bridge builders; instead, all it had given birth to at the dawning of its new era were wall builders.

I couldn't help feeling that somehow de Klerk and Mandela had in the end missed their historic opportunity to become the first great bridge builders of the New South Africa. Instead of showing the way for national reconciliation by forging an exemplary cooperative relationship, they had set a disappointing example of black-white distrust and mutual recriminations. In the end, the only thing that seemed to hold them together was their keen sense of *realpolitik* and their common commitment to a peaceful settlement through compromise. They were, indeed, like two escaping convicts chained together and hating each other, but realizing full well that they needed one another to make good their run to freedom. One could only hope that Ramaphosa and Meyer, younger and more flexible, would succeed in taking over what their mentors had begun: the mission of national reconciliation and racial cooperation. It was time to pass the baton to a new generation of peacemakers and bridge builders.

CHRONOLOGY

This chronology lists the major events relating to the negotiations toward a New South Africa that took place during the period covered in this book.

February 2, 1989   State President P. W. Botha, recovering from a stroke two weeks earlier, decides to step aside as leader of the National Party, though he remains state president. At a party caucus later that day, F. W. de Klerk, minister of home affairs, national affairs and national education, is elected National Party leader.

July 5, 1989   Botha meets the imprisoned African National Congress leader Nelson Mandela, the first time any South African president has seen him since 1962.

August 14, 1989   Botha is forced to resign as state president in a cabinet revolt against his leadership. De Klerk becomes acting president.

September 14, 1989   De Klerk is elected president for a five-year term.

December 13, 1989   De Klerk holds his first meeting with Mandela.

February 2, 1990   De Klerk's presidential address before Parliament at which he announces both his intent to implement major reforms and the impending release of Nelson Mandela.

February 11, 1990   Mandela is released from prison, having been incarcerated since his arrest on August 5, 1962, and sentenced, along with other "Rivonia trialists," to life imprisonment on June 12, 1964.

March 26, 1990   Massacre in Sebokeng township, near Johannesburg (eleven killed, over four hundred wounded by police fire) causes the postponement of the first ANC–government "talks about talks."

273

March 28, 1990 Inkatha attack on ANC strongholds around Pieter-maritzburg (Natal Midlands region); the worst single day of fighting since 1987 (over the next week, eighty killed and hundreds wounded). Chief Buthelezi denies fomenting violence. Harry Gwala, a regional ANC leader, a couple of days later scuttles a meeting Mandela had hoped to have with Buthelezi to talk about the violence.

May 2–4, 1990 First official ANC–government talks finally take place at Groote Schuur in Cape Town. The document that comes out of this meeting is called the Groote Schuur Minute.

July 2, 1990 ANC mobilizes a one-day national strike against Chief Buthelezi and his KwaZulu homeland; the strike has little visible effect.

July 22, 1990 At an Inkatha rally in Sebokeng township, the first major clash in Johannesburg region between ANC and Inkatha since Mandela's release (more than thirty killed); police failed to heed a warning about potential violence from the ANC; de Klerk and Mandela on July 24 have an angry exchange over the police failure to act.

August 6, 1990 ANC and government delegates meet again, this time in Pretoria. The Pretoria Minute is the document that comes out of this meeting (in which ANC agrees to "suspend" armed struggle).

August 31, 1990 Government revises "Zulu code" to allow the carrying of "dangerous weapons" to political rallies if person has "bona fide intentions" for traditional Zulu usage (Inkatha is the chief beneficiary of this change); the decree takes effect September 30.

November 15–19, 1990 Massive Inkatha attack on ANC strong-hold, the Zonkizizwe squatter camp outside Johannesburg, which ends in the Inkatha takeover of the camp; during last months of the year ANC–Inkatha violence continues to escalate.

December 14–16, 1990 ANC consultative conference is held, at which negotiations and other issues are discussed (this was in lieu of a national conference, postponed until July 1991).

January 29, 1991 Mandela-Buthelezi summit takes place; the peace agreement signed there is quickly soaked in blood.

February 4, 1991 Winnie Mandela's trial begins in Rand Supreme Court in Johannesburg; she is charged with kidnapping and accessory to assault in case involving murder of "Stompie" Moketsi Seipei in last days of 1988 (the body is found on January 6, 1989). The trial continues for fourteen weeks.

February 12, 1991   The D. F. Malan Accord between ANC and government signed at Cape Town airport (accord is named for a post–World War II prime minister).

March 8–10, 1991   Inkatha moves into Alexandra township outside Johannesburg; forty-five are dead in three days of fighting; Inkatha seizes control of Madala Hostel, where two to three thousand migrant workers live.

March 17, 1991   The Inkatha rally held in Alexandra to celebrate its foothold there comes close to a pitched battle between ANC and Inkatha supporters; six die that day.

March 24, 1991   Police open fire on ANC demonstrators in Daveyton, east of Johannesburg, killing at least twelve.

April 3, 1991   Mandela addresses U.S. Congress members and their aides at a symposium organized by the Aspen Institute and held at Mount Nelson Hotel in Cape Town; he delivers a tirade against de Klerk about the continuing violence (however, this was closed to the press so it was not publicized); de Klerk addresses the same group the following day, seemingly unaware of how angry Mandela is at him (their falling out doesn't become public until November 1991).

April 4, 1991   Mandela announces to ANC National Executive Committee meeting that he had been wrong to call de Klerk a "man of integrity."

April 5, 1991   In the form of an open letter, ANC delivers an "ultimatum" to de Klerk (it contains seven demands), saying talks about talks would be over unless he did something to curb the violence. ANC gives the government until May 9 to meet its demands.

May 13, 1991   Judge Michael J. Stegmann hands down the verdict in Winnie Mandela's case and sentences her the following day to five years on kidnapping charges and one year on accessory to assault (the sentence is reduced on June 2, 1993; Winnie doesn't have to go to jail).

July 2–7, 1991   First ANC national conference held within South Africa for more than thirty years. Nelson Mandela is elected president, Cyril Ramaphosa secretary-general; the sixty-six-member National Executive Committee is also elected. Later in the month, a twenty-six-member National Working Committee is chosen from the ranks of NEC to run ANC on a day-to-day basis.

July 19, 1991   Inkathagate scandal breaks (the government had been helping fund Inkatha, including money for rallies held in November 1989 and March 1990).

September 4, 1991 National Party federal congress in Bloemfontein and a conference in Cape Town at which the government's terms for settlement are outlined.

September 14, 1991 National peace conference (among fifty business, church, civic, and political groups) is held at Carlton Hotel in Johannesburg; the first face-to-face meeting of Mandela, de Klerk, and Buthelezi; the conference is basically a disaster. National Peace Accord is signed (but will have little effect).

September and October 1991 Mandela and de Klerk, despite public differences, hold numerous private meetings to try to overcome their differences.

November 28–29, 1991 Sixty delegates from twenty parties hold preparatory talks at the Holiday Inn near Johannesburg's Jan Smuts International Airport. They agree on the ground rules for multi-party talks, though Pan Africanist Congress walks out on the second day. Parties agree that Convention for a Democratic South Africa (CODESA) will convene on December 20 at the World Trade Center, also near Jan Smuts Airport (this after twenty-two months of prenegotiations and talks about talks).

December 5–8, 1991 The South African Communist Party holds its Eighth National Congress and elects Chris Hani as its general secretary to replace Joe Slovo, who becomes national chairman.

December 20–21, 1991 CODESA opens with eighteen delegations plus the government (Chief Buthelezi refuses to attend but sends an Inkatha delegation; PAC had dropped out of the negotiating process); at the close of this first session de Klerk delivers a broadside against ANC, causing Mandela to explode. CODESA I breaks up with no one knowing what lies ahead.

February 19, 1992 National Party suffers a stunning defeat in the by-election held in Potchefstroom. The next day de Klerk schedules a nationwide referendum on his policies for March 17, saying he will resign if the referendum is defeated.

March 7–28, 1992 Inkatha celebrates the anniversary of its takeover in Alexandra by launching another push to grab more territory, creating the zone nicknamed Beirut; 11 dead, 341 injured in fighting.

March 17, 1992 De Klerk's referendum passes; it is approved by 68.6 percent of the voters (all white).

April 13, 1992 Mandela announces his separation from his wife, Winnie; they had been married since June 1958.

May 7, 1992 Scandal about government corruption in Department of Development Aid becomes public when the report of Judge Pickard's investigation is released.

May 8, 1992 Scandal about government involvement in 1985 killings of four ANC activists in Cradock breaks.

May 15–16, 1992 CODESA holds its second plenary session, again at World Trade Center, after four-month hiatus (ANC and government officials had been working behind the scenes); the previous day, Mandela and de Klerk have their first tête-à-tête since the eve of CODESA I. ANC and government are still far apart on the terms of settlement; CODESA II ends in a constitutional and political haze.

June 17, 1992 Boipatong massacre; forty-six people are killed by an Inkatha raiding party; ANC, outraged by the performance of police, puts the already stalemated talks on ice.

June–August 1992 "Rolling mass action" campaign is organized by SACP, culminating in the August 3–4 national strike.

September 7, 1992 ANC–SACP march on Bisho, capital of Ciskei homeland, ends in a massacre by Ciskei troops and police—29 dead and 200 injured; a serious miscalculation on the part of the ANC leadership.

September 26, 1992 Mandela-de Klerk summit results in an agreement to get the peace process back on track; the document that comes out of this meeting is called the Record of Understanding; ANC National Executive Committee formally approves the resumption of talks a few days later; Buthelezi is infuriated by the bilateral agreement.

Last week of October 1992 ANC National Working Committee discusses an internal policy document called "Strategic Perspective," which sparks debate within the ANC alliance over what negotiations will achieve. In late 1992, SACP seems to be rethinking its strategy, tactics, and past mistakes of judgment. Joe Slovo is principal advocate for reformism.

November 16, 1992 Judge Richard Goldstone, who had been investigating security force misconduct since February, announces that his commission has just conducted an unprecedented raid on a secret Military Intelligence operations center, seat of the "dirty tricks" department. Two days later de Klerk announces that he will conduct his own investigation; a month later he announces the early suspension or retirement of twenty-three officers, but not some of the most notorious ones.

November 18, 1992 The ANC National Working Committee adopts the "Strategic Perspective" document, clearing the way for it to accept a compromise on power-sharing with the National Party.

Early December 1992 ANC and government begin series of bilateral talks, which produce the rough outlines of a potential settlement.

February 12, 1993 ANC and government announce agreement in principle on a five-year transition during which a multi-party cabinet, government, and Parliament would share power on the basis of the outcome of the general election to be held probably in early 1994.

March 5–6, 1993 CODESA process resumes after ten-month break with a preparatory meeting to organize a new session.

March 22, 1993 De Klerk and Mandela meet secretly to try to break the deadlock over the negotiations; they also have several subsequent meetings.

April 1–2, 1993 CODESA holds its third plenary session, with twenty-five parties (plus the South African government) participating. For the first time, CODESA includes representatives from the white Conservative Party and the black militant Pan Africanist Congress.

April 10, 1993 Assassination of Chris Hani.

April 24, 1993 Oliver Tambo, president of the ANC from 1967 to 1991, dies of a stroke at age seventy-five.

June 3, 1993 Target date of April 27, 1994, is set for nationwide elections; negotiations continue.

INDEX

Adams, Erica, 57
Advisory Commission on Land
  Allocation, 256
African Communist, 223, 224, 226
African National Congress (ANC):
  anti-apartheid movement influenced
    by, 120–21
  armed struggle by, 20, 28, 29,
    30–31, 36–39, 94, 95, 103, 106,
    108–10, 112, 121, 123, 124–34,
    178–81
  ban lifted on, 13, 20, 25, 75, 79,
    80, 81, 88, 101, 123, 225
  banning of, 39
  in CODESA talks, 210–12, 215,
    216–17, 223–28, 233, 245–46
  consultative conference held by
    (1990), 110–11
  decision-making in, 156–58,
    160–61
  de Klerk's Parliament speech and,
    79, 80
  dual leadership and membership in,
    91, 95–96
  economic policy of, 121, 160, 263
  electoral victory for, 257–62
  exiled leaders of, 27, 108, 110, 123
  factions in, 22, 85–97
  founding of, 35
  Freedom Charter of, 42–43, 85, 86
  grassroots level of, 36, 41, 112
  headquarters of, 70
  Inkatha vs., 90–91, 96–97, 116,
    117–22, 123, 124–34, 164, 165,
    168, 221, 225–26, 230, 236–39,
    243–44, 271
  leadership of, 29, 39–41, 87, 88–89,
    90, 91, 112, 156–58, 160, 163

  Mandela's influence in, 9, 21–22,
    35–41, 48–49, 85–86, 89, 90,
    95–96, 97, 111–12, 156–61,
    249–50
  Mandela's loyalty to, 20, 160–61
  membership of, 111–12, 204
  militancy of, 217–23, 249
  moderates in, 249–50, 260–62
  national conference of (1949),
    35–36
  national conference of (1991),
    133–34, 155, 156–57, 162
  National Executive Committee
    (NEC) of, 39–40, 41, 88–89, 90,
    91, 92, 95, 100, 107, 110, 111,
    133, 138, 147, 153, 157, 158,
    179, 219, 220, 245, 249
  nationalism advocated by, 83,
    85–86
  National Reception Committee of,
    14–15, 17
  National Working Committee
    (NWC) of, 158
  negotiations with, 9, 26, 28, 30–31,
    101, 102, 104–13, 133–34,
    157–58, 210–12, 216–17, 223–28,
    245–46
  NP alliance with, 126, 163, 171–72,
    262–63, 264
  NP compared with, 98, 99, 100,
    120, 200, 257–62
  as political party, 88, 108, 119–20,
    180
  realists in, 261–62
  regional leaders of, 41, 90–91,
    96–97, 129, 155, 161
  reorganization of, 156–58
  Revolutionary Council of, 94

279

ABOUT THE AUTHOR

DAVID OTTAWAY is a journalist who has covered African affairs for more than thirty years, writing extensively on the numerous independence struggles, civil wars, coups d'état, revolutions, and droughts as the continent came of age. A foreign and national security correspondent for the *Washington Post* since 1971, he has served most of that time abroad. With his wife, Marina Ottaway, he is co-author of books on Algeria's independence and socialist revolution starting in 1962, the overthrow of Emperor Haile Selassie in Ethiopia in 1974, and the rise and fall of communism across Africa.

After five years in Washington, Ottaway returned to South Africa, a country he had often visited in the mid-1970s, in January 1990, just in time to witness the release of Nelson Mandela and the setting of the sun on white minority rule. Reporting from there over the next two and a half years, he spent many hours with both Nelson Mandela and F. W. de Klerk at press conferences and rallies, on trips, and in private conversations and interviews, returning late in 1992 to complete his research for this book. In January 1993 he took up his current assignment for the *Washington Post* as a correspondent in Eastern Europe, where he spends much of his time in the former Yugoslavia.